DOWN THE YEARS

DOWN THE YEARS

BY

THE RT. HON.
SIR AUSTEN CHAMBERLAIN
K.G., P.C., M.P.

CASSELL AND COMPANY LIMITED
LONDON, TORONTO, MELBOURNE
AND SYDNEY

First Edition . . . September 1935
Second Edition . . . . October 1935
Third Edition . . . . October 1935
Fourth Edition . . . . October 1935

PRINTED IN GREAT BRITAIN BY THE EDINBURGH PRESS, EDINBURGH AND LONDON
10.1035

PREFACE

As GOOD wine needs no bush, so a readable book should require no preface, but Publisher's law has decided otherwise and like a good citizen—may I say of the world of letters?—I obey the law.

If I had ever kept a diary, or if my memory were less faulty, I ought certainly to be able to write an interesting book of memoirs, for my life has been passed among interesting people, and I have assisted at great events. As it is, the pages which follow are no more than random recollections of men and events, among which I have moved, based upon an occasional memorandum made at the time, or on letters written to relations, and more especially to my father when he and I were separated. To these I have added slight sketches of some of the men with whom I have worked. If these pages have any merit, they owe it in the former case to the fact that they were written in the midst of, or immediately after the events chronicled and are uncoloured by subsequent results or later judgments and, in the latter case, to the fact that they are written with the sympathy and understanding which are bred of admiration for the man's qualities, and esteem for the man himself. They are not history, but perhaps I may claim that they are sidelights on history and, as such, may have some little permanent value as well as their immediate interest for those who knew the men or can recall the events.

Some of these have already appeared in the *Daily Telegraph* or *Sunday Times* in England, *The Figaro* and *Journal* in

France, *The Christian Science Monitor* in America, and *Co-operation Press-Service for International Understanding* on the Continent.

I have added two or three essays, written for my own amusement in " Idle Hours." The essay on " How great Speeches are prepared," appeared many years ago in the *Empire Review*, where my letters from Berlin also first saw the light, though without much of what is now included. " My Cottage Garden " was written for *The Countryman*. It is endeared to me not only by the memories it evokes, but by a singular act of kindness from a fellow-member of the House of Commons who rejects my politics but shares my love of flowers. On reading the article when it first appeared, he wrote that he could not bear to think of me without a garden and should send me flowers from time to time on condition only that I did not write to thank him. Nearly every week during each succeeding Session these gifts have been renewed. Truly the House of Commons is a place of much kindness.

To the Editors of these Papers and Reviews my thanks are due for the permission to re-publish the articles.

CONTENTS

PART I

MEN AND MEMORIES

7

CONTENTS

LIST OF ILLUSTRATIONS

PART I
MEN AND MEMORIES

I

A STUDENT IN PARIS

I TOOK my degree at Cambridge in the summer of 1885 and in the following September began a nine months' residence in France. The Aumaitre family with which I was to stay in Paris were at the moment taking their holiday at Dinard-St. Enogat, where I joined them in plain but comfortable lodgings over a baker's shop at the farthest end of what was then scarcely more than the village of St. Enogat. My room looked straight on to the open country and just below us lay the little bay of St. Enogat, from which we could look across the larger bay of Dinard to St. Malo and a semi-circle of rocky islets. I was at once enchanted by the place and thought I had never seen any-thing more lovely than the red rocks, golden sands and vivid blues and greens of the sea. The family consisted of Monsieur Aumaitre, a Répétiteur-en-Droit who coached pupils for the law examinations, his wife and three children, two boys and a girl whose ages ranged from fourteen to eleven, and Madame Aumaitre's widowed mother, as is so often the case in French households. They were a delightful family, and the children's constant chatter was a great aid to me in my first efforts to speak the French language. With them or other members of the family, I bathed, roamed the countryside and made excursions to places of interest in the neighbourhood, such as the Mont St. Michel and the charming and then unspoiled old town of Dinan. Many of the houses dated from the sixteenth century or earlier and the occupations of their inhabitants seemed as ancient. There were old crones at their spinning-wheels, an old man working at a hand-loom and a group of men at a forge with a dog to work the bellows—like a prisoner on the treadmill, always climbing and never advancing. It was all very new and fascinating to me and, to add to my delight, when we moved to Paris at the end of the month, the elder boy and I broke the journey at Chartres, where I saw for the first time the grandest of all the French cathedrals and the splendour of its marvellous stained glass.

Hardly any of the people to whom I had letters of introduction had yet returned to Paris, nor had the École Libre des Sciences Politiques opened its winter session; so I spent my days walking the streets and visiting the museums and many of my evenings at the theatre. There is no better school in which to learn a spoken language, and no more delightful method. And what incomparable actors they were. Sarah Bernhardt had already left the Théâtre Français and was playing at the Porte St. Martin—not, it was thought, without some loss to her art, but Coquelin was still faithful to the House of Molière. I think he was at his best in *Tartuffe* and *Les Précieuses Ridicules*; but whatever he did, his acting was perfect and Coquelin cadet was only second to himself in these or similar rôles. Coquelin's son had not then begun to act, but though Coquelin declared in later years that his son was a greater actor than himself, this appreciation was inspired by his paternal pride rather than his critical faculty.

Then there was Mounet-Sully in classical tragedy, and for comedy Got, who played magnificently the parts of old men, Delaunay who must, I think, have been already well past the age of fifty but still played the *jeune premier* with incomparable grace and vivacity to the *ingénue* of

Mademoiselle Reichemberg, at whose age at the time it would have been an impertinence to guess, but behind the footlights she was still the perfect representative of the parts which she had taken for so long. I can still see them as I saw them then, playing together in Alfred de Musset's *Proverbes*—"*On ne badine pas avec l'amour*" and "*Il faut qu'une porte soit ouverte ou fermée.*" Nor can I forget the charm and perfect acting of Marie Brohan, who now took such rôles as that of the Duchess in "*Le monde où l'on s'ennuie*" and was the perfect great lady, or Jeanne Samary who played the soubrettes—her lovely rippling laughter was itself sufficient for an evening's entertainment—and Madame Bartet, whom I met again long years afterwards in London. All these one might see at the Français. There were others like Jeanne Grannier and Rèjane not unworthy to rank with them at less historic houses, and Madame Sorel, unless my memory is at fault, was winning her first success at a theatre on the Boulevards.

Meanwhile I was taking a daily lesson from M. Aumaitre in French law and administration and presently, when the École des Sciences Politiques reopened its doors, my mornings and some part of my afternoons were spent there. The School had been founded some ten years earlier by Émile Boutmy, who was still its Director. He and those associated with him attributed a part of France's misfortunes in 1871 to the rigid control exercised over education by the governments of the Second Empire, and they resolved to create a school for the study of history, politics, law and administration where the truth could be told fearlessly, uncontrolled by the wishes or necessities of the Government of the day. It was therefore a private venture; it accepted no subsidy and admitted no interference from the State. It was in this sense that it was The Free

School and not as we speak of Free Education in England. So successful had it been that its diploma was already recognized by the State and most aspirants to a diplomatic career, as well as many others, pursued their studies there. I was the only Englishman among its pupils at the time, but the School already had a European reputation and apart from the French friends whom I made, I got to know a certain number of foreigners, especially from the Balkan States.

As my stay in Paris was limited, I could not take the full course, but, on the advice of M. Boutmy who, though no great lover of the English, received and treated me with great kindness, I attended lectures by some of the most distinguished teachers of the day. Albert Sorel, author of *L'Europe et la Révolution Française*, delivered a course of lectures on the Diplomatic History of Europe from 1832. In the History Tripos at Cambridge my studies had ended with the Peace of Amiens, so this was new ground for me. The wide sweep of his survey, the clarity of his style, the vigour and conviction of his delivery enchanted me, and then, as when I had listened to Sir John Seely on " The Expansion of England," I found history rescued from the Dry-as-Dusts and related to the living problems of to-day. What, for example, could be more penetrating and suggestive than such a phrase as this : " On the day when the Turkish question is settled, Europe will be confronted with a new problem—that of the future of the Austro-Hungarian Empire."

Next came Anatole Leroy-Beaulieu, himself a distinguished publicist, and brother of Paul Beaulieu, the well-known economist. He lectured brilliantly on the political history of Europe from 1870, simplifying it perhaps a little too much in his desire to present it as a coherent

whole, but never allowing the trees to obscure the wood.
I still recall my discomfiture when I was presented to him
by our hostess at an evening party. I bowed ceremoniously;
he bowed still lower but said nothing. I waited anxiously
but still he said nothing; then overcome by confusion and
unable to bear the silence, I took my courage in both hands
and plunged. "Monsieur," I said, "it is a very great
pleasure as well as a privilege for me to be presented to
you, for I have the honour to follow your course of lectures
at the École des Sciences Politiques." I confess I thought
I had acquitted myself creditably for a shy Englishman,
struggling with the difficulties of a language which I had
as yet very imperfectly mastered. What then was my
consternation when Leroy-Beaulieu, sweeping a magnificent
gesture with his crush-hat and bowing this time from the
hips, replied, "Then, Monsieur, I have need of all your
indulgence!" It was useless to attempt to vie with French
politeness; I retired abashed.

Léon Say, Senator and ex-Minister of Finance, was
equally polite, though more restrained. He lectured on
"Democracy and Finance" and one lecture was devoted
to my father's Unauthorized Programme, of which he
was a severe critic. After the lecture he called me up,
expressed his hope that what he had felt bound to say had
not given offence to me and excused himself by a graceful
tribute to the outstanding importance of my father's ideas,
which it was impossible to ignore in any survey such as
he had undertaken.

There was another course on the principal types of
constitution, mainly conducted by Jules Dietz, who was
afterwards for so many years editor of the *Débats*, but to
which Boutmy and Ribot contributed. "Do you know
Monsieur Clemenceau?" I was asked by my hostess,

Madame Clémentel, one evening during the peace negotiations in 1919. "Oh, yes," I replied, "I have known him and Monsieur Ribot for thirty-five years." "It is not possible," she exclaimed. "You must have been a child at that time." "Nay, Madame, to prove it, I will tell you what each of them did for me; Monsieur Ribot lectured me on the French Constitution and Monsieur Clemenceau introduced me to the *première danseuse* of the Opera!"

I had in fact been first introduced to Clemenceau, whilst still at Cambridge, by Admiral Maxse, and for greater security carried with me a letter of introduction from my father, who, in his Radical days, found a natural affinity between himself and the French Radical, and dreamed, as Morley has recorded, of a practical co-operation between them in the service of European democracy. I visited Clemenceau at the office of *La Justice*, which was then his organ, dined with him both at his apartment and in restaurants, met many of his political friends of the moment and heard much political talk. I noted in my letters home that he, too, was advocating a graduated income-tax and succession tax, state insurance against inability to work or illness and free education. My sympathies were drawn to him by his congenial view of English Radicalism and his desire for a good understanding with England, but nearly all my other French friends looked upon him with undisguised horror, and warned me against the dangers of his political company.

He had at that time just helped to overthrow the government of Jules Ferry, who was beginning in Tonkin the new French colonial empire of Indo-China. Clemenceau, the Republican of 1870, grudged the diversion of any atom of France's strength to distant spheres whilst Alsace-Lorraine

lay unredeemed. I can still picture the scene in the Chamber
when, stung to interruption by Clemenceau's fierce invective,
Ferry interrupted him :

" And the honour of France, Monsieur ? "

" The honour of France! I will show you how you
have smirched it," retorted Clemenceau, and the invective
continued more fiercely than ever till, roused to fury, the
whole Left of the Chamber sprung to their feet, shook their
fists at Ferry and shouted to him, " Down on your knees,
traitor! Down on your knees! "

Clemenceau, indeed, at that time was the *enfant terrible*
of French politics, the destroyer of Ministries. No one then
dreamed that he would live to be unanimously acclaimed
as having " *bien merité de la Patrie.*"

It was by Clemenceau and in the lobbies of the Chamber
that I was introduced to Blowitz, the Paris correspondent
of *The Times*. " Monsieur de Blowitz," said Gambetta,
" has all the vices. He is Slav, Jew, Baron and decorated ";
but he was a power in his time, courted by governments
and Ministers from Bismarck downwards, and he remains
legendary to this day. He, in turn, introduced me to Jules
Ferry, but of my interview with him I have to confess that
I remember nothing but my amazement at his long Dundreary
whiskers.

Ribot and his wife, an American lady, were among the
earliest and kindest of my Paris friends. He was in every
way a perfect contrast to Clemenceau. If Clemenceau
resembled an English Radical, Ribot was the Goschen of
French politics, a moderate, like him, with a mind more
critical than constructive and a tendency to rest content
when he had made a great speech, as if he had already
accomplished a great act. In face and figure they were
equally contrasted. Clemenceau, when I first knew him,

was not unlike in appearance to the Clemenceau whose portrait became familiar to everyone during the war, but he was slight, wiry, talkative and as lively as quick-silver. Ribot was tall, reserved in manner, gentle of speech and moderate in the expression of his views, with a fine head that recalled a portrait of a nobleman by Van Dyck or Rubens. The walls of the Minister's Cabinet at the Quai d'Orsay are decorated with Gobelin tapestries re-producing scenes from the great series of pictures painted by Rubens to celebrate the marriage of Henri IV and Marie de Medici. One of them represents Jupiter carrying Marie to the arms of Henri. Briand, between whom and Ribot not much sympathy existed, told me in later days how on the fall of some government in which he had held the portfolio of Foreign Affairs, he was suc-ceeded by Ribot. The outgoing Minister, as is customary, introduced his successor to the principal officers of the Department and then prepared to take his leave. With his hand already on the door, Briand turned back : " Just a word of advice, my friend, if you permit it. Get rid of that tapestry ! "

" What ! Remove that tapestry ? But it is magnificent."

" Yes, but you know what they call it in the Bureaux ? No ? Ribot carrying off a naked woman." And with that Briand closed the door behind him. " But I didn't have the last word," he added in relating the tale. " Before I could cross the antechamber, the door opened again and Ribot put his head out. " My dear friend, a thought has just occurred to me which may have some interest for you. It has just struck me that it is ten years since I was last Minister of Foreign Affairs. It has taken me all that time to get back."

At the Ribots, I met mainly moderate Republicans,

members of the Academy and men of letters. At another house—that of M. Rothan, a diplomat of distinction who had been French Minister at Frankfort under the Second Empire, I met at dinner or at evening parties in his fine picture gallery most of those who then wrote for the *Revue des Deux Mondes*, to which he himself contributed reminiscences of his diplomatic career. The modest house of the Darmsteters, Arsène and James, themselves wells of learning, in the Place de Vaugirard, was the meeting place of men of letters and of professors from the Sorbonne. Here I met Renan. Madame Gaston-Paris opened to me her famous salon in the rue du Bac, where on Sunday afternoons I met a host of literary celebrities, amongst others Taine, whom I described as a little, rather dry-looking man who brightened up wonderfully as he talked. The talk was mostly of literary subjects. My letters record an afternoon when the conversation turned first on George Sand and her quarrel with Alfred de Musset and, later, on Victor Hugo. Taine defended George Sand against all attacks, spoke of her wonderful generosity and kindness and said that she was the only communist he had ever known who lived up to her principle that the people had as much right to what she earned as she had herself. Then the talk passed to the Romantic School and the forthcoming publication of the first posthumous volume of the works of Victor Hugo, who had died a few months earlier. " They must make haste," said Taine, " or they will find no readers. The men of thirty don't read him now." He singled out *Les Châtiments* as of all Hugo's work the most likely to endure. The letter concludes with the wish that I could get hold of a copy of Sorel's parodies of his poems—" so full of wit and such fine verse at the same time." I wonder whether they have ever been published. I certainly have never met with them and suppose I must have heard some of them recited in Madame Gaston-Paris' salon.

Another early friend was Cherbuliez, a publicist of distinction, a frequent contributor to the *Revue des Deux Mondes* and the author of several very readable novels, of which the most striking was, I think, *Ladislas Bolski*, a study of a Polish conspirator who betrayed his companions. Cherbuliez was by birth a Genevese who lived and wrote in Paris and, as Henry James did in England during the Great War, naturalized himself in his adopted country as a mark of sympathy with France during the war of 1870. He lived with his wife and daughter close to the Luxembourg. I wrote home in December :

"Last week I was as busy as ever amusing myself. In particular I dined with Monsieur Cherbuliez who sent messages to Father. The party comprised amongst others Jules Simon, and a lady whose name I cannot remember, but who has written *La Jeunesse de Mme. d'Épinay*.

"The conversation was not of a serious character, but these two were very amusing. Jules Simon occupied all dinner-time in telling anecdotes of Victor Cousin, not altogether to his credit. Everyone else listened deferentially and certainly the stories were well told. After dinner the nameless lady (she was in fact Mdlle. Herpin) had her turn and related a series of amusing mishaps which had occurred to her, especially an interview with a M. Scherer, the representative of an Insurance Office, who called on her just when she was expecting M. Edmond Scherer, the eminent critic and whom in her excitement she mistook for the latter. This story and another recounting her interview with ' an expert in disagreeable noises ' who called upon her in connection with an action she was threatening against a neighbour were very wittily told and amused us much. We all agreed that they would make into splendid farces."

It is amusing to find recorded my first impression and impudent comment on another Frenchman, who was afterwards so well known and well liked among us and rendered such great service to this country as well as to his own. My letter continued:

"Monsieur Cambon, Governor-General of Tunis, with not much to say for himself, though got up with great care and very good to look at, and Monsieur Rothan were also there."

The Mdlle. Herpin here mentioned was a handsome white-haired lady of equal charm and wit, who, under the *nom de plume* of Lucien Perey, had just published *La Jeunesse de Mme. d'Épinay* in collaboration with her cousin Gaston Maugras. For a time they continued to work together, but later dissolved their partnership and continued their delightful series of eighteenth-century studies separately. She occupied a small but charming apartment in which she had made herself an eighteenth-century salon so that, as she said, she might be in a proper frame of mind for these studies, and here she gave delightful little dinner parties of six or eight people every Thursday and received a few friends afterwards. I was bidden to dine the following week, and afterwards invited to come on any Thursday evening after dinner. On this occasion the Rothans and Cherbuliez, Gaston Maugras and myself were the guests, and as we sat in the little salon after dinner the talk turned on Mme. d'Épinay and her circle. Mdlle. Herpin and Maugras were passionate partisans of that charming if not impeccable lady and sworn foes of all her enemies. On a little table in the centre of the room, among other bibelots, were minute busts of Voltaire and Rousseau, which Mdlle. Herpin had just acquired. While she was denouncing Rousseau's infamy, Maugras picked up his bust and prepared to hang the villain with a strand of wool drawn from the hostess's work-basket. At the critical moment the wool broke and I can still hear Maugras's cry of disappointment: "*Ah, le coquin! A-t-il de la chance?*" (What luck the beggar has!) I think it was Cherbuliez who took up Rousseau's defence, but I thought Maugras's answer conclusive: "No, if Rousseau were right, too many honest folk would be in the wrong."

There were other salons that I frequented. Mme. Menard-Dorian had a fine hotel, full of objects of art from China. This was a salon of the Left, where I met Clemenceau at a ball and Alphonse Daudet, creator of the immortal Tartarin; Mme Schlumberger of an Alsatian family had a lovely hotel *entre cour et jardin* in the Faubourg St. Honoré. She was a Protestant, but lived much in Catholic circles and perished finally in the disastrous fire at the Charity Bazaar [1] which threw all the Faubourg into mourning. She had a son then working in the Foreign Office and a nephew who afterwards became a Member of the Institute. My first meeting with them was at Versailles, where Mme Schlumberger was spending the autumn months. After luncheon they took me over the Château. The elder of the two had taken part in the war of 1870; I have never forgotten the bitterness with which, as we entered the Hall of Mirrors, he suddenly hissed into my ear: "And it was here that that scoundrel the King of Prussia was crowned German Emperor." His talk gave me some idea of the horrors of war and the bitterness it leaves behind in the minds of the vanquished. He himself had just finished his medical studies and was taking a holiday in Italy when war had broken out, but on the news of the first reverses he had returned at once to Paris and volunteered his services. His first

[1] 1897.

experience had been a hasty summons in the middle of the
night to some small station near which he was in bivouac.
Two troop-trains had collided. Many of the men, closely
packed and weary, had fallen asleep as they sat with their
heads resting on their rifles for support and when the collision
happened scores of them had been impaled.

I owed much during my Paris visit to the kindness of
Madame Schlumberger and her son, who was nearer my
own age. Years later, I tried to repay a little of my debt
when he and his charming wife came to London during the
festivities attendant on King Edward's coronation. I was
then Financial Secretary of the Treasury, and I invited them
to my room which overlooked the Horse Guards Parade, to
witness the review of the military contingents which
represented the armed forces of all His Majesty's dominions
over seas. The first day's parade was confined to the
contingents coming from what we should now call The
Dominions; he was delighted with the pageant, but it
was on the second day devoted to the contingents of India,
the Crown Colonies and the Protectorates that he became
really enthusiastic. The spectacle of these men of so many
different races, creeds and civilizations, each with one white
officer and all united in their loyalty to the King-Emperor,
profoundly impressed him. " Now," he said, " I understand your English pride. You have a *right* to be proud ! "

The names and faces of many others besides those I
have mentioned, to whom I was not less indebted for their
first cordial welcome and constantly renewed hospitality,
recur to my mind as I recall those happy months.

I lived, in fact, wholly among French people—the only
exception being certain American ladies, like Mme Ribot,
who had married French husbands. In whatever circle I
found myself I met nothing but kindness; those to whom

I had taken letters of introduction passed me on to their friends and so my circle of acquaintance widened. The Darmsteters, for instance, took me to call on Ernest Renan, then an immensely fat old man who sat half-buried in a great arm-chair and poured out for my benefit a stream of platitudes couched in the most mellifluous French. Another day I was taken to Pasteur's laboratory and presented to that great Frenchman, but my memories of him are dim, for I regret to say I nearly fainted and was obliged to hurry out into the fresh air. At the Ribots I met Paul Bourget, whom, I am sorry to find, I described as the writer of clever but detestable novels and disappointing in conversation. He was, I think, then and later a good deal of a poseur.

T. B. Potter, then Chairman of the Cobden Club, on a visit to Paris, introduced me to Wilson, President Grèvy's scapegrace son-in-law, and by him in turn I was taken to lunch with the President himself, who had just entered on his second term of office and was shortly to be forced into resignation by the scandals in which his son-in-law involved him.

Of that meeting I have no recollection, but I still recall the scenes at an evening reception at the Elysée, a veritable "bear-garden," as I wrote at the time, where a certain famous beauty of the day was mobbed in a corner of one of the reception-rooms by a crowd of the curious anxious to get a glimpse of her, and an angry crowd of hungry guests besieged the entrance to the supper-room, already crowded to suffocation, and groaned loudly when the doors were closed against them. It was not a distinguished company which was being entertained on that particular evening.

At other times I was taken to the studios of some of the artists of the day. Indeed I saw a little of all worlds except the Faubourg of which I think I caught glimpses only at

Mme. Schlumberger's. Those were the days, in home politics, of the fall of Mr. Gladstone's second Government, of the interim Government of Lord Salisbury (mockingly called by my father "the Government of caretakers") until the redistribution of seats could be effected and elections held on the new franchise; of my father's Unauthorized Programme,[1] and of the general election which placed the balance of power between the English parties in the hands of Parnell, and provoked Mr. Gladstone's final conversion to Home Rule. I suppose my father's name would have been about as popular in the Faubourg as that of Clemenceau himself. Indeed, my father's views created something like consternation even in the moderate Republican circles in which I mostly moved, and excited as much alarm as interest. Only from Clemenceau and, curiously enough, at the opposite extreme of French politics, from the Comte de Mun, did I receive any sympathy for them. Somehow the Count read a note which I had written for the Annales of the École des Sciences Politiques on the once famous "Three Acres and a Cow." He wrote expressing his complete agreement and asked me to call to discuss it more fully with him. He was a devout Catholic, a great orator and at that time still one of the leading figures on the Extreme Right of the Chamber. "His redeeming trait," I wrote, " is a leaning to socialism." It became more than a leaning later. I think it was he who took me one evening to a kind of French Rowton House, but with a definitely evangelizing character. The memory is interesting to me because it was on that occasion that I met Anatole France for the first and last time.

Most of the elder men I knew would have been classed

---

[1] 1885, advocating free education, small holdings, graduated taxation and local government.

at home as Whigs and it was with moderate liberal opinion in England that they sympathized, but if they disliked the growth of Radicalism and condemned the tendencies of its domestic policy, they were united in their distrust of Lord Salisbury, whom they thought to be little better than an instrument of Bismarck. "All the party," I wrote after a dinner at the Rothans, "were anxious for Liberal successes in England and dreaded very much the foreign policy of Lord Salisbury. They feel him to be the friend of Germany, and this feeling overcomes in the French Conservatives their sympathy with his domestic policy." Rothan himself crowed "over the check which Bismarck would receive by Salisbury's downfall" and Clemenceau declared a Liberal Government in England to be the necessary counterpoise to Bismarck's Germany.

What a varied and interesting society it was among whom I spent these months; how much was taught me; what new horizons it opened out to my eager eyes; above all, what kindness was showered upon me by all these friends and by others whose names I have not mentioned here. No wonder that, in spite of the exciting changes which were taking place in English politics and of my desire to be with my father at a time of so much anxiety and difficulty for him, I prolonged my stay till the middle of May and left at last with real regret that so happy an interlude was over. I am sure that my words at parting can but faintly have expressed the gratitude that was in my heart.

II

BERLIN IN 1887—THE CLOSE OF AN EPOCH

It was in February 1887 that I started for Berlin as a young man of twenty-three, intent on learning the German language and seeing what I could of German politics and German ways of life. Except for the hot summer months, which were divided between a pleasant stay in the little town of Friederichsroda in Thuringia and a visit to my family at home, I spent the whole year there, returning to England only at the end of the same month in the following year. I have never been back, though my plans for a visit with my wife in 1914 were all made. She had her tickets for the Bayreuth festival; I was to join her as soon as the parliamentary session ended and together we were to ramble through South Germany, finishing up with a week in Berlin. But that visit was never to be made. The war broke out, travel became impossible and there was other work to be done. I never saw the Berlin of William II, nor have I yet seen the Berlin of the Republic. I suppose that I should hardly recognize in it the city that I once knew, so changed must it be, not only in outward aspect but in inward character.

The Berlin of 1887 was, I suppose, not greatly changed in outward appearance or manner of life from what it was while still only the capital of Prussia. It had recovered from the wave of speculation which followed the war of 1870, and from the financial crash which that speculation brought in its train. It had resumed its old simple ways and bore, to the eye of a foreigner accustomed to London and Paris, a slightly provincial air. What is called "society" was narrowly confined almost to the noble families and officers of the army; big business had not made its appearance; *la haute finance* was growing in wealth and importance but was not, I think, as yet recognized at Court except in the person of Bleichroder, the Berlin correspondent of the London house of Rothschild, who owed his position there to the gratitude of Bismarck for the help which he had rendered in fixing, at a higher figure than other authorities thought possible, the indemnity to be paid by France for the war. He was admitted to these exalted circles and I was told that when he and his daughter were invited to Court Balls, it was necessary to command officers to dance with the lady who would otherwise have found no partners. Classes did not mix and only in the circle of the Crown Prince and his English wife did art and letters find recognition. Political divisions were equally sharp. "Do you ever see Dr. Bamberger?" I once asked the British Ambassador. "No," he replied, "for in this country it is useless to know the Opposition since they never become the Government, and besides it is *mal vu* in high quarters." If a foreign representative wanted to find favour in Bismarck's eyes he must not frequent the company of his opponents.

I carried with me a letter of introduction to the Ambassador, Sir Edward Malet, who had married a daughter of the Duke of Bedford of the day. Sir Edward was a remarkable man who had made his reputation as Consul-General in Egypt in the days of Arabi's rebellion, where it was said that, however dangerous the crisis, he was always cool, and however unexpected the summons of foreign representatives to the Palace, he was always the first to appear, and whatever the hour of the day or night at which the summons reached him was always immaculately dressed. He was, in fact, a very able diplomatist who stood deservedly high in the estimation of Bismarck and his fellow ambassadors. It was no light task to fill worthily the position just vacated by Lord Ampthill.

Sir Edward and Lady Ermyntrude received me with much kindness, as indeed did all the members of his staff from Mr. (afterwards Sir Charles) Scott, who was then Councillor of the Embassy and later went as Ambassador to Russia, downwards. It was there that I began my happy friendship with Rennell Rodd (now Lord Rennell of Rodd), then at the beginning of his distinguished career and already clearly marked out for higher things. There, too, I renewed my friendship with my old schoolfellow, Reggie Lister, whose premature death while serving as Minister at Tangiers closed a brilliant career which would surely have led to one of the highest posts in the service. I wonder whether Lord Rennell remembers our parties to the theatres and the suppers afterwards at a small but celebrated oyster bar, where we ate cold partridges and drank Greek wine; or a Sunday at Potsdam with the Scotts, where they had taken a villa by the lake, and we three bathed from a boat instead of from a bathing-shed, and with less clothing than was expected, and were surprised by a boating party of the royal family and the commotion which followed. Mrs. Scott was able to disclaim having seen anybody bathing, but the road in front of her villa was picketed by the police for a fortnight. Simple pleasures, but relished at the time and dear in retrospect. Nor can I forget on the same occasion the delightful reply of her youngest daughter, then I think a child of three or four years old. She had been sitting on my lap for so long that Mrs. Scott feared that I might be tired of her company. " Now I think you might leave Mr. Chamberlain alone. You never want to sit so long on *my* lap. " No," said my charming playfellow, " womens bores me ; mens never does ! "

But to return to Berlin itself. I arrived at a singularly interesting moment, and the year which I spent there was in fact the closing year of an epoch. The three great men who had created the new German Empire still survived, dominating the scene of their triumphs, the last of a race of giants beside whom all other men looked small, all other combinations petty.

The old Emperor's venerable figure, bowed by age but still tall and soldierly, might be seen at the Palace window any morning at the changing of the Guard, and there was always a small crowd of Berliners or visitors from other parts of Germany and abroad waiting to catch a glimpse of the man who by his age and his achievements had become almost legendary in his lifetime. I was there on his ninetieth birthday and stood for hours in the great crowd before the Palace entrance to watch the brilliant succession of German Princes and foreign representatives who came to present their own or their Sovereigns' greetings. It was the year of Queen Victoria's first jubilee, and the homage paid to her was scarcely greater than the respect shown to the aged Emperor.

In winter, when the lake in the Thiergarten was frozen over and we all flocked there to skate, one might see Moltke, taking his daily walk in the park, and the skaters would break off from their figures and cut across the ice from point to point to meet and salute him. But for his uniform, that slight figure, those handsome features, that fine and intelligent face, above all that noble forehead, would have made one guess that he was some great philosopher—a professor perhaps of metaphysics or of the more abstruse mathematical studies—a student at least, wrapt in high thought and undisturbed by the common cares of man. Great student, indeed, he was, but his study was the art of war. Europe was his chessboard and his pawns were armies.

Lastly, there was Bismarck, the Iron Chancellor, the greatest of them all, a veritable colossus in stature as in achievement, tight-buttoned in his general's uniform, still watching from the palace of the Chancellor over the Empire which he had forged by blood and iron. My father had met Count Herbert Bismarck in London and they had become friends. I carried with me a letter of introduction to the Count, which I duly delivered about a month after my arrival. A few days passed and then I received a note from Count Herbert saying that " Prince Bismarck having heard a great deal about your father, and knowing that he is one of your foremost statesmen," had charged him to ask me to dinner. I was to come next day—at six o'clock, I think—" in jacket " which I thought it best to interpret as a frock-coat.

I went, flushed with pride and curiosity, but very shy. As I entered the salon the Prince rose to greet me with a beautiful old-world courtesy, offering me an apology for the absence of the Princess, who was confined to her room by indisposition, as if I had been a guest of consequence, and presenting me to the other guests. As I wrote at the time:

"It was almost a family party—Bismarck, Count Herbert, B.'s daughter and her husband, his secretaries and his doctor, who appears to look sharp after him. I took his daughter in to dinner, and sat between her and the great man, or one of the great man's dogs I should say, whom he kept one on each side of him and stuffed with everything. Bismarck was jolly, talked no politics, either German or foreign, but told stories of his student days, and regretted the degeneracy of the present age. He was particularly shocked at the idea of 'varsity men drinking *coffee*, but complained that the students here were as bad, and so on. Nothing serious but amusing enough. Hamann is in the seventh heaven; my dining with Bismarck casts a reflected glory on his house."

That, alas! is the only record I seem to have made of this memorable evening, but the letter recalls some of the talk that passed at dinner. We were half-way through dinner and I was becoming anxious as I was plied first with one wine and then another, till a formidable row of glasses faced me. I was little accustomed to wine in those days and fearful lest these Bismarckian potations should prove too much for me. Suddenly Herbert Bismarck called out from the other end of the table: "But, of course, you like dry champagne, Mr. Chamberlain." I hastily replied that I had all I could desire, but the Prince checked me, "Don't refuse dry champagne when Herbert offers it," he said, "or you will make an enemy of him for life. He is always seeking an excuse for getting it up." And then Schwenniger, the physician who had discovered how to treat Bismarck's troubles and been rewarded by the professorship of Medicine at Berlin University, to the great indignation of the Faculty, asked, "What do the undergraduates drink at Cambridge?" I confessed with shame that we were a weak generation; wine parties were rare, we mostly asked our friends to come round to coffee. "It's just the same here," exclaimed the Prince. The young men don't know how to drink nowadays." And then he added with a twinkle in his eye, "I can't complain of Herbert and his friends, but the young men of to-day can't drink. When I was a young man, we used to fight and we used to drink—why, we were drunk for weeks together. But the young men of to-day—ah, they'll never be the men we were!"[1]

Nearly forty years later his grandson lunched with me in London. Remembering the stock from which he sprang, I was fearful lest my small cellar should fail to satisfy his wants. Anxiously I consulted my butler and at last said in despair: "Well, you had better get up a bottle of everything there is." To my astonishment, after a single glass of wine, the Prince asked for water. "Prince," I exclaimed, "you a Bismarck and asking for water! What would your father and grandfather have said?" He answered in the Chancellor's own words: "Ah! we shall never be the men they were!" Thus was I revenged.

But to return to the evening with the Chancellor. When we rose from table and returned to the salon, he settled himself on a *chaise longue*, bidding me sit by his side and excusing himself as if I were somebody to whom some explanation were due. "I am like the boa-constrictor; I have only one meal a day and he (pointing to the physician) makes me rest afterwards." A rack of long German pipes stood by his side, and his servant handed him one already charged and lighted it. I remember he made some laughing allusion to the pipe and then talked pleasantly to me, but I feared lest I might outstay my welcome and soon took my leave.

A little later I wrote to my sister:

" All the Secretaries, etc., of the Embassy here are madly jealous of me for having dined with Bismarck. Such a thing

---

[1] Sir Charles Dilke used to declare later that Bismarck had said to him: " A nice boy, that young Chamberlain. Pity that he's such a poor drinker."

has never been known ; not one of them has ever exchanged so much as a good day with him, and even the ambassadors only dine with him once a year on the Emperor's birthday, and hardly ever, if ever, see him on business. So you see how favoured I was, and may imagine how proud it has made me."

After nearly half a century it remains one of the most interesting memories of my life and what stands out most in retrospect is the stately but very gracious courtesy of the greatest figure in Europe to the young man who was his guest.

Another picture of him is given in a letter I wrote a month later :

2/4/87.

" Yesterday morning I spent in the Prussian House of Commons, and was lucky enough to hear some very interesting speeches. The ' House ' is an oblong room, with the President's seat and the tribune in the middle of one of the long sides, whilst the corresponding place on the opposite side is filled by the Ministers' box, partitioned off from the seats of the deputies, and up to which, but *not* inside of it, extends the President's authority, as Bismarck once told him when called to order, thereby producing, as you may imagine, a ' scene.' The House was yesterday discussing a new Government Bill for repealing more of the May Laws against Catholics, another step towards Canossa on Bismarck's part in spite of his ' Never,' spoken ten years or more ago.

" The debate was opened by Dr. Gneist on behalf of the National Liberals. He spoke against the Bill, and I believe his words were words of great wisdom, but like some other professors, who are very distinguished in their way, he is a bad speaker and a bore in the House. Whilst he was speaking, the door from the Ministers' private room into their box slowly opened and Bismarck appeared, dressed in his dark-blue general's uniform with orange collar. All his colleagues got up to greet him and there was what the reporters call a sensation in the galleries.

"Dr. Windthorst, a clever short-sighted little old man, but a very sharp debater, followed with a short speech and read a written declaration on behalf of his section, the Centre or Catholic party. At a first glance he was something like Thiers, whilst the speaker who followed him bore the same sort of resemblance to Gambetta—the stout body, the head stuck upon the shoulders without any neck to speak of, and the rather long black hair brushed away from his forehead. This was Richter, leader of the Freisinnige or Liberal Party, which has come off badly at recent elections. He spoke for about three-quarters of an hour, fiercely attacking Bismarck, assailing him with argument and abuse and laughter.

"Meanwhile, the Chancellor, having run through his notes (written in a large hand on foolscap), was fidgeting uneasily. He is said to be very sensitive to attack, and, though he says sharp things of others, cannot bear them himself. He kept moving in his chair and writing nervously with a great carpenter's pencil. At last Richter finished, and he got up. His speeches read well, but the words do not flow easily as delivered. He always uses the right word, but sometimes it takes him a long time to find it. And his sentences are broken by a short disagreeable cough, which is probably more painful to his hearers than to him. His gestures, too, or rather, I should say his movements (for he uses no gestures) are awkward; he sways from one foot to the other, his hands are always fidgeting, now with his pocket-handkerchief, now with his moustache, and every now and then he gives a sort of jerk that is suggestive of his coat being a bad fit and 'catching' him under the arm.

"But everybody listens with intense interest, for his speeches are full of matter, illustrations from history or contemporary facts in other countries, and sound argument lit up by jokes at the expense of his opponents, apt quotations —more often from Shakespeare than any other writer—or now and again an amusing story. Finally, as the last touch to the speech there comes—if the situation is critical and a majority for the Government uncertain, as is the case in these Church laws—a threat of resignation. 'His honour is engaged. The Pope will never believe that the Bill would not have been carried, if he had really done his best.' So he begs they will spare him the humiliation of this position. Besides *he* says the bill is good and necessary. If they have not confidence in him, he will ask the King to relieve him of his office, which the King, by the by, will *not* do. But the majority is secured, the end is attained in spite of the jeers of the opposition who remember to have heard all this before.

" There is a very faithful account of a more than usually interesting sitting of the Landtag, and I hope it won't have bored you. To make the picture complete I need only add that Bismarck sustains himself during his oratorical exertions by drinking copiously strong brandy and water— a tumbler to every quarter of an hour I counted. None of your nasty water for him."

The correspondent of *The Times* assured me a little later that he had actually seen Bismarck's empty tumbler replaced with a full one seventeen times in the course of a speech in explanation of a new army bill, which had lasted, if I remember rightly, a little over two hours.

I met or dined with Herbert Bismarck, then Secretary of State for Foreign Affairs, on several occasions. One such dinner is recorded in a letter of October 7th, 1887:

" I dined last night at Herbert Bismarck's. Mr. and Mrs. Scott, Graf Bismarck-Bohlen, a Graf Holstein and two people from the Foreign Office, whose names I must find out. It was a very pleasant party. H. B. was in great spirits, talked about father with great admiration, and said I must bring him over here. H. B. said, if only father would come, he would do everything possible to amuse him. In return he promised again to come down to Highbury on one of his visits to England. Father's cigars have left an indelible impression on his mind. He keeps very good ones himself."

It seems strange to find myself writing " a Graf Holstein." I was evidently unaware what a strange and powerful personality was in front of me. Had I realized the part he had already played, still more the part he was destined to play in the future, I should have studied him more closely, for he was none other than the Baron Holstein who had been Bismarck's spy on Arnim, under whom he served in the Paris Embassy, and his tool in bringing about Arnim's fall. He was or appeared at that time to be a great friend of Herbert Bismarck, but it has since been said that he never forgave Prince Bismarck the dirty work he had done for him and he deserted father and son in their fall. For years he was the most powerful figure in the German Foreign Office and did, perhaps, more than any other man to prevent an Anglo-German understanding in the years before the Anglo-French *entente* gave France the only ally whom Germany might have won.

Bismarck had no exaggerated respect for either the Prussian Landtag or the German Reichstag, but on one occasion at least he paid a tribute to the British Parliament. "I rather envy you English statesmen the excitement of the House of Commons," he said to Goschen in the early 'eighties. "You have the pleasure of being able to call a man a damned infernal scoundrel. Now I can't do that in diplomacy." He had perhaps not measured exactly the forms of English parliamentary speech, but with his usual acumen he had seized its substance.

It was on the same occasion that he entertained Goschen and the British Ambassador, Lord Odo Russell, later the first Lord Ampthill, at dinner. A dish of lampreys was served. "Do you know what we call those?" asked Bismarck.

"We call them 'nine-eyes' (Neun-Augen). I once ate eighty-one 'eyes' at a sitting."

"But had you no cause afterwards to regret your prowess?" asked Lord Odo.

"Ah," said Bismarck, "I have often regretted what I have eaten but never what I have drunk."

"What?" exclaimed Lord Odo, "have you never been the worse for your potations?"

"I did not say that I had never been the worse for them," Bismarck retorted, "I said that I had never regretted them."

Goschen in later days when I was the junior member of his Board of Admiralty, loved to tell such stories and told them extraordinarily well. This one recalls that gallant sportsman, Henry Chaplin,[1] equally unspoiled by good or evil fortune. "Is it very bad, old man?" asked a friend who found him in the throes of a torturing attack of gout. "It's hell," replied Chaplin, "but thank heaven I have earned every twinge of it."

After the sitting of the Landtag described in the fore-going letter, I saw no more of Bismarck either in public or private. I envied Sir William Richmond who came to Berlin to paint the Ambassador and Lady Ermyntrude Malet. Bismarck had a tender spot in his heart for Sir Edward, whose father he had known and liked and whose appoint-ment to Berlin he had welcomed. Sir Edward persuaded Bismarck to sit to Richmond for his portrait and in wel-coming the artist to Friederichsruh, his country home, Bismarck had greeted him as Malet's friend and had added: "There are few things I would not do if Sir Edward asked me." Richmond stayed a week at Friederichsruh and the Prince chatted freely with him at sittings and during meals. Richmond delighted the Chancellery of the Embassy, who

---

[1] President, Local Government Board, 1895–1900.

had made me, so to speak, a member of their mess, with his stories of the great man. I would have given much to see the Prince thus among his tenants, foresters and retainers. Here he was surrounded by all the formative influences that had determined his outlook on life and given to his genius its particular bent. Great men sometimes give the clearest picture of themselves not in their work but in their recreation. Is any picture of Bismarck complete which does not include that sentence from the *Reminiscences*, which he compiled after his fall, in which he wrote : " I cannot deny that my confidence in the character of my successor (*i.e.* Caprivi appointed Chancellor on Bismarck's dismissal) suffered a shock when I heard that he had cut down the ancient trees in front of his—formerly my—residence. . . . I would pardon Herr von Caprivi many differences rather than the ruthless destruction of ancient trees? " Or again another sentence of reminiscence in some letter to his sister or his wife which I read, I suppose, forty years ago in some published correspondence that I have never in later years been able to trace. I quote it therefore from memory and cannot vouch for the actual words, but of the general sense I am certain. It must, I think, have been written whilst patriotic Prussians still smarted under the humiliation of Olmutz and probably when Bismarck was the Prussian representative in the Bund at Frankfort. It ran as far as I can remember thus : " It was about this time that I reached that confidence in myself out of which a real belief in God's guidance of the world springs." Prodigious ! as Dominie Sampson would have said, but the strength of Bismarck's Germany lay in this conviction that God willed the triumph of Prussia and the union of Germany.

The year 1887 was marked by strained relations between Russia and Germany and the air was filled with rumours of war. In March I wrote home that I had seen Moltke out walking alone, saluted with every respect by all who saw him, "And glad," I continued, "they all are to see him out, for if he has time to take a walk, they say, all the preparations for war must be complete, and they may go home with their minds at rest. At rest, however, they are not, for the rumours of a war with Russia in the near future are very disquieting. I was talking to a late member of the Chamber the other day who told me that he thought the best informed people were convinced that it could not be avoided, and if once Russia began, France would certainly follow suit, though she would not lead off alone." My informant was George von Bunsen, son of the old Prussian Ambassador to the Court of St. James's and uncle of Sir Maurice, who was British Ambassador at Vienna when the Great War broke upon the world. I carried with me a letter of introduction to him from my Rugby House-master and to his kindness I owed many happy hours and not a little information about Germany and the Germans of that day.

Bunsen himself was a man steeped in the traditions of the liberal movement of '48. He was a member of the Freisinnige Partei and as such had held for a time a seat in the Reichstag. He and his friends had supported the policy of the Iron Chancellor, reconciled to much that they disliked by his success where the men of '48 had failed, in uniting all the German peoples in the new German Empire; but he belonged to what we should call the Manchester School of politics, broke with Bismarck when he adopted protection and lost his seat. He was a man of wide culture, liberal views and great charm—in short of those very qualities which endeared the late Sir Maurice de Bunsen to all who knew him.

He amused me on this occasion with stories of Moltke, one of which has a bearing on the passage just quoted from my letter. On the day on which war was declared in 1870 a friend met Moltke taking a similar solitary walk. "What news is there?" he asked the Field-marshal. "Potatoes are up three pfennigs," said Moltke, who was an agriculturist as well as Chief of the General Staff. "How can you think of such trifles at such a moment?" exclaimed his friend. "I should have thought you must be overwhelmed with work." "Ah! my work was done yesterday," replied the Field-marshal; "I shall not be wanted now for ten days." It was, I think, just a fortnight later that the opening battle of the war was fought at Spicheren. Other stories followed to indicate the care with which all the preparations for war had been made and the exact knowledge which the Germans had acquired of all that it behoved the invader of France to know. Though most of them have escaped my memory, they made an impression on my youthful mind to which such ideas were unfamiliar, and the impression deepened as I listened to the talk of the students at the university or the young officers whom I met at dinners and dances.

But the real revelation came from Treitschke, whose lectures on Prussian history at the university I regularly attended. I recorded my impression of his teaching and its effect in a letter dated October 31st, 1887:

"Treitschke," I wrote, "has opened to me a new side of the German character—a narrow-minded, proud, intolerant Prussian *chauvinism*. And the worst of it is that he is forming a school. If you continuously preach to the youth of a country that they stand on a higher step of the creation to all other nations, they are only too ready to believe it, and the lecturer who descends to this will be popular and draw big audiences. But it's very dangerous. I fear my generation of Germans, and those a little younger will be far more high-handed and will presume far more on the victories of '66 and '70 than those who won them. There is a school growing up here as bad as the French military school, and if they come to the front, why, *gare aux autres*. They are likely to find a friend in Prince William, who is said to be thirsting for warlike distinction and is the idol of the military party and the youth. . . ."

Again on January 11th next year I wrote:

" V. Treitschke has recommenced his lectures with a field-day against ' faithless Albion,' and, to use his own words, ' cursed the blue from heaven ' over her having got the better of Prussia towards the close of the seventeenth century."

What luckless English Princess had then married some Prince of the House of Hohenzollern, I do not now remember, but I still recall the fierce invective which he hurled against the poor lady's memory. It was, in fact, but a thinly disguised attack upon the Crown Princess Frederick, and as such it was understood and applauded by his class. It was not a comfortable class-room for an Englishman.

Already the Crown Prince's illness was casting its shadow over the future. I had written on November 18th:

" People here are very much saddened by the Crown Prince's illness, which seems quite hopeless. The Liberals, especially, are quite overwhelmed. He was their last hope. As Dr. Bamberger, one of their leaders, said to me the other day, it is the only blow which remained to be struck at them. And now they must look forward to Prince William's accession, a high-tory Prussian officer, caring for nothing but soldiering and anxious above all to win his spurs. Again, as Dr. Bamberger said, ' We must pray that Bismarck may be spared.' Fancy this from a member of the party on whom the Chancellor has so trampled. What irony of fate! But he feels that Bismarck can keep Prince William in order, and perhaps no one else could."

Bismarck himself was reported to have said a little later that for three months the young Emperor would cling to his coat-tails, for another three the old Chancellor would run after him, checking him with difficulty, and that then he would break loose and insist on going his own way.

In November the Emperor Alexander III paid a visit to Berlin and the atmosphere cleared for a moment. "Peace has suddenly broken out," exclaimed some wit, but the clouds gathered again. The arsenals were working overtime; another half-million men were added to the Army and people talked of war between Russia and Austria as almost a certainty and then Germany and Italy would be drawn in. One day in early February Bamberger asked me: "What do they think in your Embassy of the present state of affairs?" I answered that I believed they considered it serious. "And what do you yourself think?" he asked me; to which I replied that I now believed a war near, though till lately I had not joined in the scare, alluding to the scare of a French war last Spring. "Oh, no," he said, "that was all humbug (using the English word) *Aber ich sehe jetzt sehr schwarz.*" [1] He added he thought war with Russia a certainty; as regards France one of three things might happen. It might at once join sides with Russia, or it might wait to see how things went and only take part against Germany if Germany suffered defeat at the beginning; or, on the outbreak of war with Russia, Germany might at once attack France, preferring to anticipate her action rather than to leave her to choose her own time.

[1] "But the outlook now seems to me to be very black."

45

He believed that the last course would probably be the one pursued."

The same evening I reported Bamberger's gloomy views to Sir Edward Malet, the British Ambassador. Sir Edward did not share his fears; there was nothing for the Powers to fight about and the publication of the Austro-German alliance ought to have a quieting effect. I asked what we should do if war came and added that I supposed that we should hold aloof.

" In that case," said Sir Edward, " it's quite certain what the other Powers will do. There will be a short war, quickly patched up, and then they will all turn on us. None of them love us for our *beaux yeux*. If we won't take our part in helping to make or maintain peace, the others will make peace at our expense. They have told me as much here." And then he repeated: " We are the Eldorado of all these Powers; they all would like to plunder us."

This was in the first week of February 1888. I left Berlin at the end of that month. On March 9th the old Emperor died. In June the Emperor Frederick followed him to the grave. Before two more years had passed the old Pilot was dropped and the Emperor William II had fairly begun his disastrous reign.

The old order had passed. Let me close my memories of it by a story told to me by George von Bunsen about the Emperor William I and King Victor Emmanuel which is, I think, honourable to both Sovereigns and characteristic of the men and the times in which they lived.

It is a well-known fact that on the outbreak of the war of 1870 the French Government expected help from both Austria and Italy, and that Grammont led the French Chamber to believe that they had promised it. Victor Emmanuel, not unmindful of the help received from

Napoleon III in the establishment of the kingdom of Italy, desired to go to the assistance of France, but was prevented by the resistance of popular opinion, which made such action impossible as long as French troops occupied Rome and prevented the transfer of the capital of the new kingdom to that city.

Two or three years after the war Victor Emmanuel made his first State visit to Berlin and was met by the Emperor William at the station and conducted by him to the Palace. When the formal presentations at the Palace were completed and the King had been conducted to the rooms which he was to occupy, the Emperor turned to his Staff and said: "I have always admired His Majesty the King of Italy; now I must add that I love him."

One of the Staff asked the Emperor if he would tell them what had happened to make him speak so warmly of the King, and the Emperor William replied:

" At the station and for some little time afterwards there was so much noise and cheering that it was impossible to say anything, but at the moment when it became possible to converse, His Majesty turned to me and said:

" Sire, the late Emperor Napoleon was my oldest friend. I was under infinite obligations to him and, when war unhappily broke out between Your Majesty and him, I did my utmost to go to his assistance, and only desisted when my ministers convinced me that it would cost me my crown. Now that the Emperor is dead, those obligations no longer exist and I hope that Your Majesty will find me as faithful a friend as it was my wish to be to Napoleon III."

Surely a saying not unworthy of *Il Re Galantuomo*.

III

GERMANY AGAIN

1. A Conversation with the German Ambassador in 1908

I was at Cambridge in the last days of May 1908 and happened to meet Sir Charles Waldstein [1] and Count Metternich, then German Ambassador to the Court of St. James's, who was passing the week-end with him at King's College. Waldstein asked me to breakfast with him next morning. I was unwilling to desert my wife who had accompanied me, but, Waldstein taking me on one side, pressed his invitation, saying that it was given at the express desire of Metternich, who very much wanted a quiet talk with me. I accordingly yielded. The conversation, even now after the lapse of so many years, seems not without interest. I transcribe the account of it which I sent to my father on my return to London:

"Now I must go back to Waldstein's breakfast and Metternich's conversation. After breakfast, at which we discussed Balzac and Anatole France, socialism, humanitarianism, jingoism and patriotism, Waldstein left to write letters and Metternich began:

M. "You are coming back to power soon—when? Two years? Two and a half years?"

A. "Yes, we are coming back; but I can fix no date. I hope not too soon."

---

[1] Slade Professor at Cambridge, later known as Sir Charles Walston.

48

M. " And it will be on Tariff Reform? It seems to me that that will be the big question? "

A. " Oh undoubtedly! "

M. " Well, if your duties are moderate I cannot find that my countrymen think they will do them great harm. They are not much alarmed about them. They think that they will still be able to trade with you unless you put on very high prohibitive duties, and they do not view your proposals with any jealousy. Of course if you put on such high duties throughout the Empire as to forbid foreigners to trade with the Empire at all, I don't think other nations would stand that. There would be a combination of other Powers against you, for the Empire is too large a portion of the world for us to be content to be excluded altogether from its trade."

A. " Well, of course our proposals are for very moderate duties—more moderate for instance than the German. . . ."

M (interrupting). " Oh! but remember ours are the lowest of any industrial country."

A. " Except Belgium, but . . ."

M. " Yes, except Belgium. If it were not for our desire to maintain an agricultural population and not to become wholly dependent on foreign food, I doubt if we should maintain anything but revenue duties. I don't think our manufacturers much care about them now, but we cannot afford to let our agriculture go."

A. " Exactly, and if you wish to protect agriculture you must give a *quid pro quo* to the industrial classes. You are quite right. I don't blame you. You don't do it to annoy us. You have to look after your own interests. So must we look after ours. I only say that our duties are likely to be lower than yours and they will not exclude trade with you, though they may cause some temporary inconvenience

D 49

and may somewhat alter the character of the trade that is to be done. Your duties have not decreased your foreign trade. They have increased it. You buy more than ever from abroad. So shall we."

M. "Well, but if that is so and we have no need to be enemies, why are you always treating us as an enemy? I confess I am not very sanguine about the situation. Why, for instance, are you so hostile to the Baghdad Railway? What are the trade reasons? What are the strategical reasons which make you so hostile to it? We seek to do trade there, but not to exclude you and others. We do not seek any special trade privileges; and as to strategy, can anyone suppose that we are going to send an army corps down the line to the Persian Gulf? I do not know how they are to get to the line. They would have to go across half Europe and no one explains how. But if they do go and get to the Persian Gulf, what are they to do? Why, there they remain!"

A. "Yes, and a very unpleasant place to remain in too! To tell the truth I do not know that I am a very good person to point out the strategical dangers, as I have never myself seen very clearly wherein they consist. No doubt such a movement would force us to keep extra ships in Indian waters and put us to extra cost; but I admit that I do not see that it would greatly threaten India. But of course if the break-up of the Turkish Empire were to come, I expect that Germany would then claim Asia Minor as her share, basing her claim on the interests she had established there by the railway, etc.; and that would be a very different thing."

M. "Oh! but even if the Turk were driven out of Europe, he would be very strong in Asia Minor. That is his home; that is where all his strength comes from even now. Europe is his weakness. Asia Minor is his strength. That is a very fanciful danger. But now about trade."

A. " Well, as to trade, what Englishmen fear is that without excluding other trade *eo nomine*, all your influence would be used to favour German trade at the expense of British trade. And your influence would be immense and most powerful for this purpose. In any proposals you have made hitherto for French and English co-operation, you will admit that you have always maintained a predominant influence for yourselves. You control absolutely the Anatolian railway and its port. Well, we think that under those circumstances German goods and German traders would fare better than British. Now if you want to meet us, would your Government agree to link up the Smyrna-Aidin line with the new system? That is an English line, it is true, as the Anatolian is German, and it comes to Smyrna, a port where we have no such predominant position as Germany in Anatolia but where England is well represented. Put Smyrna in a position to share on equal terms the trade of the Baghdad Railway and you give us an alternative debouché. That might do something to influence British opinion."

M. " Well, I cannot answer that question, for I do not know what my Government would say."

A. " Well, there is another point. At present you are constructing the railway from the north only. Our people fear that as you get to the Tigris and Euphrates, you will tap and divert the trade which at present goes south to the Gulf. This would not happen if the railway were built simultaneously from both ends. Of course we should expect the same kind of predominating interest at the Gulf that you have at the Anatolian end. I only name these

51

as points for consideration if you really desire English co-operation and wish to remove English distrust. I do not pretend that the moment is very opportune for this kind of discussion and co-operation between the two countries."

Metternich then left the question of the Baghdad Railway and reverted to the general situation, again emphasizing the fact that he had come to view it "very seriously." He spoke very slowly and deliberately, choosing his words carefully and evidently intending me to understand that the position was grave. Of course in his story the German wolf was blameless; the English lamb was troubling the waters. The movement of English opinion was becoming more menacing. The English Press—notably the *National Review*—fanned the flame. "A few years ago it was generally thought in well-informed circles in Germany that England intended to attack Germany. I was the only person, having *voix au chapitre*, who did not take this view. Happily I was right then, but now—well, I am not sure. I do not conceal my opinion that the situation is becoming very grave."

A. "Of course I accept from you the statement that Germans really believed that we were going to attack them. But *you* know England, and you *must* know that no English Government could, if it wished, begin a war unprovoked, merely because it had become convinced that a conflict was inevitable sooner or later and thought the particular moment more favourable to us than a delay. With our politics and people you know that we cannot pursue such a policy as Bismarck's."

M. "But Bismarck did not hate England. He had no wish to quarrel with you."

A. "Oh no! I did not suggest that. What I meant. . . ."

M. " But then why is there this persistent hostility to us? Why is there this constant distrust, this effort to isolate us? Look, for instance, at the President's visit.[1] Nothing could be more natural in itself, but at once your Press begins to talk about a new triple alliance and turns the friendly visit of the French President into a demonstration against Germany. France does not want to be your ally. Your army cannot help her. She has everything to lose and nothing to gain by an alliance and she does not intend to be dragged into a quarrel with Germany by you. She does not wish to be made use of by you. And Russia! Russia is poor and weak. She can do nothing and she does not want to be your ally. Why are you trying to isolate us? Why do you not cultivate an understanding with us? "

A. " Well, Count, before the *Entente* with France was established, before our negotiations with her began, Germany was given her chance. Why did she not take it? You know to what I am alluding—my Father's speech.[2] Of course I know *The Times* d——d it next day and it did not look very easy. But my Father has been d——d by *The Times* more than once and has got over it. He has never been afraid of unpopularity. He was prepared to go on, but the next word rested with Prince Bülow. Why didn't he speak it? Why did he go to the opposite extreme and pour scorn on the idea? You know our proverb: 'He who will not when he may,' can't always be sure of having the opportunity repeated."

M. (throwing up his hands and shaking his head sadly). "Ah! yes, I know. But the times were not propitious. England used to be unpopular in Germany. Germans

[1] M. Faillières' visit to England in the same month.
[2] At Leicester, Nov. 30, 1899, advocating alliance between Great Britain, Germany and the U.S.A.

thought Englishmen cold and haughty. They held aloof so much, and then came our great struggles and England was coldly neutral and we did not like that. Germans thought that England was seeking . . ."

Here M. stumbled and hesitated a good deal about his words. I distinguished "profit" and "risk," but he seemed unable to frame his sentence to his own satisfaction, and so I pleasantly suggested:

A. "You thought England wanted to share the apples without taking any of the risks of robbing the orchard?"

M. "Ye-es. Well, then came the Boer War and all the rest of the world rightly or wrongly sympathized with the smaller Power—perhaps in France more violently than elsewhere—but the feeling was universal. Passions were roused, hot words were spoken, feeling ran high. But the time passed, feelings cooled down and we began to respect you. We saw, as we say in Germany, that the muscles were not swallowed up in fat—*die musceln waren nicht in fett unter-gegangen.* We began to respect and sympathize with you. Look now, all this friendship to France is very artificial. I believe that Englishmen are really more in sympathy with Germans than French. . . ."

A. (interrupting). Oh! do not make a mistake about the *Entente*. It is not artificial. It is very genuine and very widespread and popular."

M. "Just at the moment, yes; but it is not deep rooted."

A. "Well, we are talking frankly—that is the interest of the conversation, and I will continue frankly. Ever since I have known English politics—say since the early 'eighties—there has been a real desire among the masses of our people for a good understanding with France, partly no doubt because they wished to see an end put

to the secular rivalry and distrust between these two great
nations facing each other across twenty miles of sea; partly
because they thought there was a closer communion of
ideas between these two great liberal nations than between
ourselves and any other."

M. "Oh! but . . ."

A. "Mind, I don't say that the community of ideas is
as great as they think. To that extent the basis of the
Entente may perhaps be artificial—imaginative rather than
real; but the feeling is there; and there is nothing artificial
about the universal satisfaction felt and expressed at our
intimate relations with France."

M. "I believe it is all a false idea. I believe that there
is really much more sympathy between us than between
you and the French. We do not want to quarrel with
you. Why should we? There is trade rivalry, no doubt;
but I always find that it is precisely those who are engaged
in trade who most dislike the idea of war, however much
they fret at the trade competition. And for what else
should we fight? For conquest? We do not want conquest—territory. Emigration from Germany has almost
ceased. We want markets, but we want to keep our
people at home. They do not want to emigrate. And what
could we conquer? Canada? If the British Empire breaks
up, Canada goes to the United States, if to anyone. India?
India goes to Russia or to anarchy. Australia? No German
is so mad as to dream of conquering Australia. South
Africa? Your war has shown that no nation can conquer
South Africa if it is united. You could not do it yourself.
What remains? A few outlying islands! Great nations
do not go to war for such a cause. No one in Germany
desires it."

A. "I agree. I do not believe that your people desire

55

war with us in the abstract—or the Emperor. I don't believe that he desires war at all in his time. What I dread is the growing feeling in your country that a war is inevitable and . . ."

M. " Ah ! but that is what your Press is teaching here."

A. " That and the effect of your teaching in Germany on opinion in this country. It is not that either nation desires war in itself, but that all the youth of Germany is being taught that the war must come and that they must prepare for the inevitable conflict."

M. " But I do not know of any such teaching in Germany. I never hear of it."

A. " Well from the days of Treitschke downwards——"

M. " Now listen ! Mr. Chamberlain. Till I came to this country I never heard of Treitschke. He was nothing in Germany. He was a firebrand and he insulted everyone. But he had no influence."

A. " That is not my experience. Certainly he was a firebrand. I listened to his lectures and, as you say, he insulted everyone, but especially the Coburgs and the English. But he was a most popular firebrand. With every physical defect a public speaker could have, he was the most popular professor at the University of Berlin. His ' insults ' were received with loud applause at crowded classes. And that is not all. The same thing went on in the public schools. I know it from the stories brought home and the questions asked by the fourteen-year-old son of the man in whose family I boarded. Well, my experience is twenty years old. But my friends who know Germany to-day tell me that the same thing is going on throughout the whole educational system of Germany, from top to bottom. Do you wonder that I agree with you that the situation is grave or that we take note of what is passing? There lies the danger—in the growing belief, deliberately planted in the whole youth of Germany, that a conflict is inevitable. And when such a belief takes hold of the German mind, the whole Bismarckian policy is there to warn us of what may come. I do not criticize Bismarck's action with Austria in '66 or France in '70. I note it. A nation which has thus twice preached the doctrine of ' the inevitable conflict,' which has prepared for it with such patience and endurance, which has even gone to meet the heavy sacrifices which it entailed and has twice provoked the conflict with extraordinary skill at the most favourable moment to itself, whilst leaving to its opponent the odium of appearing at the time the aggressor— such a nation is indeed a formidable opponent when it begins to preach and prepare for a third ' inevitable war.' "

M. " But those are not similar cases. The war with Austria was necessary if Prussia was to have the hegemony in Germany. The war with France was necessary if North and South Germany were to be united. But there is no ' inevitable ' conflict here."

A. " I quite agree; but I dread the state of opinion in Germany—Oh! in both countries, if you will. That is where the danger lies."

We had now been discussing the subject for nearly an hour and a half and I rose to go. But Metternich begged me to wait a little and he again passed the whole situation in review—the survey lasting five or ten minutes, but not revealing anything fresh. He concluded: " I have sometimes been optimistic. I am not optimistic now."

" Nor I," I answered. " We can only wait and see. Let us hope the two Governments will be careful. For my part I think the less we hear of one another the better for the present."

And so we parted. We had talked, as I say, from ten-thirty till past twelve, and though from my summary it looks as if I had done half the talking, that was in fact not so. M. led the conversation and did most of the speaking. Of course my summary is not complete, nor have I always got the order quite right, but I think you will get from my report a good idea of the whole and in some cases the actual words.

There was a good deal more I should have liked to say had time allowed or M. given me the opportunity. But I let him talk on without interrupting him and followed the track he marked without insisting on following out my own thoughts if he interrupted with a new argument. It was in this way that I was prevented from really challenging him for instances and proof of the persistent hostility or aggressiveness of English policy. I wanted to take him to task about the German attitude to the *Entente*, at the Morocco conference and elsewhere, and generally to show him how and why the policy of Germany appeared to us unfriendly. However, perhaps I said enough! and any way the more interesting thing was to hear what he thought or wished to be thought to think!

I told A. J. B. of my conversation with Metternich a couple of days ago. To-day he said that Rothschild had been to him to report a similar conversation. I observed that this looked like the campaign of menacing talk which Germany organized in Paris just before Delcassé fell, " but we won't hound Grey out of office here ! "

2. A Conversation in 1911

I first met Sir Henry Angst during a visit to Switzerland with my father in 1897. He had married many years earlier an English lady, rather against the wishes of her parents, who would have preferred that she should choose an English husband. She had proudly replied that she would make him an Englishman and he as proudly boasted that she had been as good as her word. He was at that time plain Mr. Angst, and had already held the post of British Consul at Zurich for some years. He was later promoted Consul-General and his services were recognized by a Knighthood. He was one of the founders of the Landes Museum at Zurich, in which are preserved so many souvenirs of the old life of Switzerland. He loved his country and its history; and he loved and admired England second only, if second at all, to the land of his birth. Whenever he came to London, he visited my father in Prince's Gardens and his talk was always interesting and well-informed.

In 1911 my wife and I spent our summer holiday in Switzerland, travelling direct to Zurich and a couple of days later Sir Henry Angst carried us off to lunch at his country house at Regensberg in the hills above the town. It is (or was at that time, for it may well have changed since) a quaint little village with less than a hundred houses perched two thousand feet up on an outlying spur of a ridge of hills, some fifteen miles to the north of Zurich by road. Originally it was the castle of the Counts of Regensberg under the Austrian dominion and the central tower, or keep, which is still standing, dates from the thirteenth century. Round the castle gathered a few houses and the whole tiny space was still in Sir Henry's boyhood surrounded by its old walls and defended by four fortified gates. But a corrupt mayor, who subsequently absconded with much of the Commune's money, found it necessary to make work for the people in order to get their votes and so caused the larger part of the fortifications and three of the gates to be pulled down. Even now the view of the village as you approach it is most picturesque and the panorama from the village is magnificent—from the Black Forest and the mountains beyond the Lake of Constance in the north, round to the mountains at the head of the Lake of Zurich on the south. In old times the place was of some importance—the Governors of Zurich lived there—it had a fair, permission to exercise trades (not usually accorded to little hamlets of the kind) and the right of low justice. Angst's people had lived there for several generations. His mother's people were schoolmasters somewhere on the Lake for 250 years from father to son. That, he said, was an old, unchanging Switzerland which already belonged to the past.

Sir Henry dwelt lovingly on this older Switzerland and lamented its passing. Industrialism had crept in and was changing the character of the people in more ways than one. The country was very prosperous but it was losing its old spirit. He talked despondently about the future. Perhaps his pessimism was partly caused by the state of Lady Angst's health, for she was gravely ill at the time and died not very long after. He was very pro-English and very distrustful of German aims.

A letter home recorded the substance of our talk.

He said the Germans had it all their own way in the German-speaking Cantons. The newspapers were wholly dependent on them for news and comments on news, largely copying from the German papers so that their readers saw nothing but the German point of view. German money had been flowing into the country and had largely created its industrial development, but besides this legitimate use of German capital the " Reptile Press Fund " had also been used to influence opinion. The people were wholly German in sympathy. He doubted whether if a European war broke out they would make more than a show of resistance. German Switzerland would be swallowed up in the German Empire. A gloomy foreboding indeed, and happily as the result proved quite unfounded.

More interesting was his account of a recent conversation with Bebel, the German Socialist leader. Bebel's daughter was married and living in Zurich and Bebel often visited her. Sir Henry often met him on these occasions and had conceived a great respect for him. He described Bebel as a very fine old man, sober and level-headed, not a wild man at all.

On his last visit, my letter continued:

" Bebel had told him that the German Government was mortally afraid of the progress of the Socialist Party; they expected them to come back 100 strong at the next elections, ' and before that,' said Bebel, ' you mark my words, the Government will try to make some patriotic coup to stimulate the bourgeoisie and rally people to the flag so as to lessen the Socialist gains.' Hence Agadir and the resurrection of the Moroccan question.

" There are many Germans here—some in business and some in disgrace. Angst likes neither class, but he says they talk very freely here, more freely than at home, and their jealousy and bitterness against England is extreme. ' It's useless,' he said, ' to talk of disarmament and peace conferences to Germany. Germany is Prussia—South Germany does not count and has no influence and will have none till a great ruler arises in Bavaria, Saxony, or Wurtemburg, and combines the three in a common policy of resistance to Prussia—but at present Germany is Prussia and Prussia is the Junker. To propose disarmament to him is to rob him of his bread and butter. He has no career save in the army, or under Government. Trade and com-

merce are forbidden to him, and the monarchy is dependent
on him and cannot afford to offend him. How long will
he last? Well, till there is a revolution, or an unsuccessful
war. A revolution will be long in coming. Bebel says,
' We are many, but we can do nothing. There are whole
regiments where every man—Officers, N.C.O.'s and rank
and file—are all Socialists, but we are powerless. We
should be shot down and blown away with grape shot.
We can do nothing but march. But if there were a defeat
at the beginning of the war, there would be a revolt.
Whole regiments would rise.' "

My own comment on this conversation was given at the
end of the letter:

" I confess I doubt the last statement, but Angst feels as
so many of us do, that sooner or later Germany will make
war again and this time England will be the real enemy,
though France may be first struck at."

3. Increasing Tension in Europe

Nineteen hundred and eight, the date of my conversation
with Count Metternich, was the year of the annexation of
Bosnia-Herzegovina by Austria under Aehrenthal's leadership and of the revival of the Moroccan question in consequence of incidents at Casablanca arising out of the arrest
by the French authorities of certain German deserters from
the Foreign Legion whom the German Consul had taken
under his protection. Nothing but the weakness of Russia
caused by the disastrous Russo-Japanese war of a few years
previously had preserved peace in the former case, and
though the Casablanca incident was eventually settled by
a reference to the Hague Court, it had for months kept
European nerves on edge.

Nineteen hundred and eleven, the year of the second conversation recorded above was still more disturbed. On July 2nd the world had been startled by the announcement of the sudden despatch of the *Panther* to Agadir, and some three weeks later by the grave warning addressed to Germany by Mr. Lloyd George (then Chancellor of the Exchequer) at the Mansion House. Peace, he had said, was the greatest of British interests, but if Britain was to be treated where her interests were vitally affected as if she were of no account in the Cabinet of Nations, peace at that price would be an intolerable humiliation. Such words coming from the mouth of a Minister who was supposed to belong to the most pacific section of the Cabinet produced a profound impression, which was not lessened when it became known that the King had postponed his visit to Goodwood and that the Atlantic Fleet, which had been on the point of starting for a cruise in Norwegian waters, had been ordered to Portsmouth. A brief statement was made in Parliament on July 27th by the Prime Minister, who appealed to the House to postpone all further discussion. Balfour at once declared that the Opposition would observe the rule that no party differences should prevent national agreement where British interests abroad were at stake, though he added (for it was at the height of the Constitutional crisis and party feeling was running very high) that adherence to it had never been more difficult; and he reinforced the Chancellor's warning by saying that if anyone was counting on their acting differently, he had utterly mistaken the temper of the British people and the patriotism of the Opposition.

It would have been well for Germany if her rulers had remembered this declaration in August 1914 when it is supposed that they reckoned on the violence of the passions aroused by the Home Rule question to paralyse British action and to prevent us from entering the war to defend our own interests or to come to the assistance of France or Belgium.

It was not till towards the end of November that an agreement was reached between the French and German negotiators. Meanwhile the air was full of rumours, some true, some false, of military and naval preparations, and all Europe was kept in a state of strained and dangerous tension. When on the last days of that month the House of Commons was able to proceed to the discussion which it had been promised and the Government made a full statement on the events of the last few months, it was clear for all who had eyes to see and ears to hear how grave the situation had been and how perilously near the nations had stood to the brink of war.

Next year Lord Balfour of Burleigh and I had occasion to visit Petersburg on business. Sir George Buchanan had invited us to stay at the Embassy and it was certain that we should meet the principal Russian Ministers. Before leaving, therefore, I called on Sir A. Nicolson, later Lord Carnock and then holding the post of Permanent Under Secretary of State, at the Foreign Office, to ask if he could give me any guidance as to what it might be wise for me to say or, quite as important, to refrain from saying. He embarrassed me by replying that he would prefer to leave what I should say to my discretion. When, therefore, the Foreign Minister, Sazonov, engaged me in a conversation which must have lasted for nearly two hours, I turned rather anxiously, as soon as we were alone, to the British Ambassador, who had been a listener, to ask if I had been in any way indiscreet. He was good enough to assure me that on the contrary what I had said would be very helpful to him. I carried away from the conversation the impression that neither the Russian Foreign Minister nor the Ambassador had had any very clear impression of the aims and purpose of the British Government and that this uncertainty did not make for peace.

Like other people, I was becoming increasingly anxious as to the future. It seemed to me that the tension in Europe was becoming greater year by year; incident followed incident leaving the nerves of all the parties more strained and inflicting a wound on the pride, first of one nation and then of another, which was neither forgotten nor forgiven. First France had suffered the humiliation of having to dismiss her Foreign Minister at the bidding of Germany; then Russia, still smarting under her defeat by Japan [1] a few years before, had suffered a similar humiliation in the crisis which followed the annexation of Bosnia-Herzegovina, and this time the wound was not in the Far East in an adventure to which her people were indifferent, but in the Near East where Slav pride had always been most sensitive and national feeling was most easily and strongly moved. And now Germany, unsuccessful at Algeciras [2] and dissatisfied with the solution of the Casablanca incident,[3] felt herself equally humiliated by the results of the Agadir crisis.[4] No great nation could suffer patiently a second humiliation such as had now fallen to each of these in turn; any repetition of such an incident would leave the Government no choice but war, for the only alternative to war would be a revolution in which the Government itself would be overthrown.

I did not suspect the German Emperor of desiring war. In spite of his boastful and provocative speeches, I still thought that he in his own person offered the best guarantee

[1] The war of 1904-5.   [2] The Conference of 1906.
[3] 1908.   [4] See p. 63.

that Germany would keep the peace, and I should have been far more alarmed if power had fallen into the hands of the Crown Prince, whom, in my mind, I identified with the military party. What I feared was not that Germany would deliberately provoke war, but that her Government would blunder into it without knowing what they did, for German diplomacy since Bismarck seemed to me the clumsiest in all Europe. Bismarck's successors found it easier to copy his faults than to understand his merits. It was certain that sooner or later the attempt to seek Germany's security by setting all her neighbours by the ears must result in those neighbours perceiving that they only burned their fingers for another's profit and equally certain that sooner or later they would tire of being the dupes of such a policy and prefer to settle among themselves disputes the benefit of which inured only to the advantage of a rival. That was the seed of disaster which lay in Bismarck's post-1870 policy, but Bismarck enjoyed an immense prestige and played his cards with a master hand. The same could not be said of his successors. They failed where he excelled; they had no sense of those *imponderabilia* which Bismarck declared were, in the last resort, always decisive and to which he was himself so amazingly sensitive. No Government so miscalculated the effect of its words and actions on foreign nations as that of Germany under Bülow and his successors.

Peace seemed to me, therefore, to lie at the mercy of an accident which a clumsy hand might provoke at any moment. What would be our position if war broke out? The *Entente*, as I thought, had come to have all the obligations of a formal alliance without its advantages. We had been on the brink of war at the time of the Agadir crisis, yet the public mind was wholly unprepared for it.

If war came, we should be obliged to intervene; it was dangerous to conceal the real position from the country and to attempt to ride a democracy in blinkers. What we needed was something in the nature of a British Monroe doctrine. Many plain American citizens might be puzzled to give a clear definition of the Monroe doctrine, but every American knew that if a foreign nation attacked that doctrine it laid its hand on the very Ark of the Covenant and all Americans would be united to defend it. A formal Alliance, or so I thought, would involve us no more deeply than we already stood committed and would be a beacon to guide the steps of Parliament and the country and to secure a united nation if the struggle came.

But if it had these advantages at home I thought it would be not less useful abroad. It would help to steady the nerves of the French people, and it would give us an influence on French policy which no other method would afford. As it was, we might be dragged into a war fought on some issue which we thought wholly insufficient; but if our support was guaranteed to France on certain conditions, any French Government would make sure that those conditions were fulfilled in the eyes of the British Government before embarking on war.

Lastly, I believed that the knowledge that such an Alliance existed might exercise a sobering effect in Germany, and might prevent the German Government from blundering into a war with us without knowing what they were doing.

I felt so strongly the dangers of our existing situation that at last I sought out Sir Edward Grey and laid my fears and suggestions before him. It is not necessary to repeat his answer here, for he has himself set forth his reasons for not taking the course I urged in the curiously detached and objective account which he has given of his stewardship in the anxious and troubled years during which he presided at the Foreign Office.[1] The plain fact is that even if he had thought it the right policy, he could not have carried it, but it is tempting, though probably futile, to speculate on what might have been. Many continental writers have held that if such a treaty had been known to be in existence, there would have been no war. That was at one time my own view, but in the light of all that we now know, I can no longer sustain it. I now think that it might at most have postponed for a year or two the outbreak of the struggle. If this be true, perhaps it was better that the issue should be fought out then. In the end the invasion of Belgium did for us what I had thought a treaty of Alliance would do: it made our duty plain and brought us into the struggle a United Nation.

[1] See *Twenty-five Years*, by Viscount Grey of Fallodon.

IV

A GREAT SPEAKER
ARTHUR WELLESLEY PEEL

THE first Parliament in which I sat was the one elected in
1886 after the defeat of the first Home Rule Bill in which
the Conservatives and Liberal Unionists together had a
majority of one hundred over the combined forces of
English Home Rulers and Irish Nationalists; but it was
already moribund when I was returned unopposed at a
bye-election in East Worcestershire in 1892, and all thoughts
were already turned to the coming elections. I was
introduced by my father and uncle in the last days of
March. I remember that the strong feeling stirred in me
by the occasion made my hand tremble so violently that
I could scarcely sign my name on the Roll. It is a difficulty
which in my case has often recurred. Growing up in a
circle where political interests held a high place, and looking
forward from boyhood to becoming some day a member
of the House, I early imbibed and have always cherished a
profound respect for its august traditions, and entered it
with an earnest desire to win the good opinion of my
fellow-members. To this day I never rise to address it
without trepidation and that uncomfortable feeling in the
pit of the stomach which in our childhood we used to
call " bath-pain " because we associated it with the first
sudden plunge into cold water. I doubt whether anyone
has ever made a lasting success in the House of Commons
of whom this is not in some measure true, for no man

69

ever wins the respect of the House unless he himself respects it.

Parliament was dissolved only four months later and my first House of Commons has left only one abiding impression on my mind. It is of the greatness of Mr. Speaker Peel. The House has had many great Speakers, but I doubt whether in its long history it has ever had a greater than Arthur Wellesley Peel. Others have served it faithfully and many of them with great distinction, but Speaker Peel *dominated* it. In the opinion not only of one like myself who was still a young member when he retired, but of older men who had been present at his first election, he stood in a class by himself, over-topping his predecessors, never equalled even by the most successful and respected of his successors. He had a natural dignity and a formal but genuine courtesy which well became the occupant of the Chair, and, besides, a dramatic gift which in great moments raised him so far above his fellow-members that the whole House trembled at his rebuke. At such times his stature seemed to grow before our eyes, his deep resonant voice dominated the tumult and he appeared as the living embodiment of centuries of parliamentary tradition.

One such moment occurred in the closing days of the Parliament of 1892. A Select Committee of the House had been inquiring into the hours of work of Railway Servants, and among the witnesses who had given evidence before it was the stationmaster of some small station on the Cambrian Railway. He had subsequently been called before three of the Directors and the General Manager of the Company and dismissed, nominally for some irregularities in his accounts but really, as was obvious from the questions put to him by the Directors, on account of the evidence which he had given before the Select Committee.

Viscount Peel

*From the portrait by Hubert von Herkomer, in Balliol College, Oxford.
By kind permission of the Master and Fellows*

The Committee, of which Sir Michael Hicks Beach [1] was chairman, took evidence as to what had passed and made a special Report to the House on the case as a breach of Privilege. Of the three Directors involved one, Sir John Maclure, was an old and much-liked member of the House. A day was fixed for the discussion and an order was made by the House that the honourable member for Stratford should attend in his place and that his co-Directors and the General Manager should appear at the Bar. They were asked if they had anything to say and Sir John Maclure offered an apology with which the others associated themselves. They were then ordered to withdraw while their case was considered, and Hicks Beach moved: " That this House while recognizing that they had expressed their unqualified regret for having unintentionally infringed any of its Rules and Privileges is of opinion that they have committed a breach of Privilege . . . and that they be called in and admonished by Mr. Speaker."

This seemed a rather lame conclusion and there was a good deal of sympathy with the proposal made by T. P. O'Connor to add that the House would not consider that they had purged their contempt till they had reinstated the discharged man. Efforts were made privately to get them to do this, or at least to compensate him, but they remained obdurate. Hicks Beach's resolution was supported by Mr. Gladstone, but his advice was rejected by the great majority of his followers whose zeal for the injured man was perhaps stimulated by the value of the railway vote at the general election which was known to be imminent. A long, wrangling discussion followed and it was not till midnight that a division was taken and Hicks Beach's resolution carried.

[1] Afterwards Viscount St. Aldwyn.

Then the Directors were once more called in. Sir John Maclure evidently felt his position acutely, but the other three appeared at the Bar defiantly and almost jauntily. They had successfully resisted the desire of many members, not confined to one side of the House, that they should compensate the man, and now they were to have what schoolboys call a " pi-jaw " from the Speaker—that was all the House of Commons could do to them.

Mr. Speaker Peel spoke for less than ten minutes. " I would have you to know—each and all of you gentlemen— that though the Privileges of this House are not to be put into operation on any light or trivial occasion . . . yet a Privilege of this House is no unreal, shadowy or un-substantial thing; it is what the House clings to and what it is determined to maintain." And then after expatiating on the enormity of their particular offence, he declared, " The House in its judgment and, I should add, in its mercy has decided that I should admonish you," and he proceeded to administer the admonition.

The bald words of what he said, recorded in *Hansard*, convey no idea of the devastating effect of that short allocution. The men who had come to the Bar so defiantly a few minutes earlier wilted under his admonition; beads of perspiration stood out on their foreheads and, when he dismissed them, they crept away like whipped hounds, while the rest of us shook ourselves like dogs coming out of the water and thanked heaven we had not been in the position of poor Maclure.

Peel was not less impressive, though in a different manner, when after his re-election to the Chair in the new Parliament he presented himself before the Lords to receive the royal confirmation of the Commons' choice. The contrast between the dignified humility with which in the time-honoured forms he " submitted himself to Her Majesty's gracious commands " and, when they had been signified, prayed " that if any error should be committed, it may be imputed to me alone and not to Her Majesty's faithful Commons," bowing each time deeply as he spoke, and the lofty tone in which, drawing himself to his full height, he then claimed the Commons' privileges—" freedom of speech, freedom from arrest and freedom of access at all times to Her Majesty " seemed to epitomize history. Every movement, every gesture was intensely dramatic. In truth he was a great actor on an historic stage and he succeeded, as other great actors have done, because he did not merely play a part, but for the time being was that part.

Indeed, so high was his sense of the position to which he had been called while he occupied the Chair, that he thought no occasion too trifling, no pains too great to preserve its dignity. Returning from an Easter recess, I once expressed my hope that he had had a pleasant holiday. He replied that it had not been particularly enjoyable. The fact was, he explained, that as Speaker he could do so little for his constituents at Leamington that when they had asked him to open the new golf course which had been provided as an additional attraction for visitors to the Spa, he had felt bound to accede to their request, though he was no golfer. He had therefore felt obliged to spend the whole of his holiday taking lessons from a professional in order that he might drive the first ball in a manner not unbecoming to the holder of his office and the House of which he was the representative.

Peel owed his original nomination to the Chair to Mr. Gladstone, in whose Government he had been a Junior Whip; but not even Mr. Gladstone could successfully dispute his authority when he had once entered the Chair. "During the struggle which occupied the greater part of the session of 1887," the *Annual Register* recorded when he retired in 1895 after eleven years' service, "Mr. Peel's tact and dignity saved a situation which might easily have plunged the House of Commons into a serious crisis. The attitude of Mr. Gladstone and his colleagues throughout the discussions in Committee on the Irish Crimes Bill of 1887 might have ended in wrecking the authority of the Chair had it been occupied by a less firm or a less wise Speaker." "Without the support of the House," he had said on his re-election in 1892, "a Speaker can do nothing; with that support *there is little he cannot do.*"

He had proved the truth of his own words. His retirement following so closely on the final withdrawal of Mr. Gladstone from political life marked the close of a parliamentary age.

V

MR. GLADSTONE'S LAST PARLIAMENT

I AM often asked how the House of Commons in recent years compares with the House as I first knew it, more than forty years ago. It is not easy to give a satisfactory answer. Each House of Commons differs from its predecessor and has some special characteristics of its own, though the deep-rooted traditions of the Assembly persist, in spite of even the most violent changes in its composition, and its power of assimilation overcomes in time even the most refractory material. I am inclined to say that in some respects the present House is superior and that the average of ability and knowledge is greater. Certainly the questions which its members are called upon to decide are more intricate and call for more exacting study, but its debates excite less interest among its members and have less influence on the country than in earlier days. More than one factor has combined to produce this result; some are external to the House and beyond its control; others lie in the character of the debates themselves. If the general level of competence is higher, there are fewer outstanding figures. Members take less pains about the form of their speeches and parliamentary oratory is almost a lost art. Above all, the debates have lost that dramatic quality to which they formerly owed so much of their interest, and a vicious habit of reading " speeches " has crept in, largely owing to the fault of the two Front Benches, with the consequence that debates have ceased to be debates and degenerated into the lifeless delivery of written essays. Hartington once yawned in the middle of one of his own speeches. To-day the speaker is often the only member in the House who is not yawning as the steady drone goes on.

Of all the Parliaments in which I have sat—and I am now, I think, in my thirteenth—that of 1892-95 was by far the most exciting. Passion was at fever heat from the very first, parties were very evenly divided, the Government majority was small and the Opposition was determined to use its rights to the uttermost and to give no quarter. When the House met for business in January 1893, the debate on the Address was only concluded by the unusual expedient of a Saturday sitting; that on the introduction (now a purely formal stage) of the Home Rule Bill took five days, and the debate on the Second Reading lasted no fewer than twelve. The later proceedings were in proportion, and the Session itself lasted till within a day or two of the Easter of the following year. " Time," said Lord Randolph Churchill, " is the life-blood of a Government," and the Opposition had decided to bleed the Government to death.

I was appointed junior Whip of our small Liberal Unionist Party, with Harry Anstruther as my chief. The first question that arose was where we were to sit. In the last Parliament our leaders had sat on the front Opposition bench, much to their own discomfort and to the annoyance of the Gladstonian leaders at whom their speeches were constantly directed. My father, who had succeeded Hartington in the leadership on the latter's accession to the peerage a few months earlier, arranged with Harcourt that we should take our places below the gangway on the Opposition side if the Irish would move across the House, but, though they intended to support the Government, they declared that to sit among its supporters would be too compromising and that they must retain their old seats. The Liberal Unionists were, therefore, obliged to seek seats on the Government side, but it was rumoured that the less responsible Gladstonian Liberals meant to refuse the usual courtesy to our leaders and if possible to leave them and us without seats at all. Several members of our Party, therefore, assembled on the first morning, at what was then thought the extraordinarily early hour of six, and effectively occupied the greater part of the third and fourth benches below the gangway on the Government side with our hats—so effectively in fact, that the report spread that I had come down to the House in a four-wheel cab filled with band-boxes, and I was so pictured in caricature! The Government were thus exposed to a crossfire of criticism—from Liberal and Radical Unionists behind them and from the Conservatives in front. It added much to the liveliness of the debates, perhaps also to their bitterness, but it had from our point of view the disadvantage that the leaders of the two wings could not consult in any sudden emergency. It was a lesson in parliamentary art to see how, in spite of this difficulty, Balfour and my father played into one another's hands.

Exactly ten years earlier Mr. Gladstone, complimenting my father on the skill with which he had piloted a complicated Bankruptcy Bill through all its stages, had declared that for himself he might still be of some use in set debate but that he could never conduct a great measure through Committee again. Now, in his eighty-third year, he was triumphantly to refute this self-depreciation. He expounded the provisions of the Home Rule Bill in a speech lasting two and a half hours with scarcely a sign of fatigue; he defended it on second reading at almost equal length and throughout the Committee and Report stages he was always in the forefront of the battle and ever the most skilful of dialecticians. He had at command every resource of the orator except wit. He was occasionally grimly humorous, but if he raised a laugh it was seldom a kindly one. He was pleading and minatory by turns; at one moment he cajoled his hearers, at another he overwhelmed them, and whatever his purpose, he had at his service every resource which art can place at the disposal of native genius. The tones of his voice were rich and varied, his figure full-chested and erect, his gestures free and copious, and nature had given him a magnificent head and "an eye like Mars to threaten or command." "Mr. Gladstone," my father said to me at this time, "is the only man I am afraid to have follow me," and this confession was made when, in the opinion of so experienced a judge as Speaker Peel, my father was "the best speaker in the house with one exception, and the best debater without exception."

It is, I suppose, impossible for anyone now reading his speeches to recapture or even to understand the effect which they produced upon his audiences at the time. Divorced from the personality of the orator and from the moral fervour which he exhaled, those long and involved sentences defy the arts of the printer and exhaust the patience of the student. Yet as they rolled from his lips, each phrase and sub-phrase, each condition and proviso fell easily into place and his followers not only felt that they were listening to the pure milk of the word, but were convinced that they understood him.

Disraeli's speeches live not only by the brilliance of his phrases and the power of his invective, but also by those flashes of insight into the heart of a problem which are as illuminating for us in our difficulties to-day as they were at the time when they were spoken. In Gladstone's case there are no such depths of thought and no such prophetic vision. It might be said of him as Landor makes Romilly say of Pitt—he, " who could speak fluently three hours together, . . . came about us like the tide along the Lancashire sands, always shallow, but always just high enough to drown us ! " He excelled above all in persuading each man that he had heard what he wanted to hear and had received the assurance which he sought. " If Mr. Gladstone had only taken as much trouble that his hearers should understand exactly what it was that he meant, as he took trouble afterwards to show that his meaning had been grossly misunderstood, all might have been well. As it was, he seemed to be completely satisfied if he could only show that two propositions, thought by plain men to be directly contradictory, were all the time capable on close construction of being presented in perfect harmony." So wrote his biographer in a phrase which delighted Balfour as much for what it left unexpressed as for what it said.

Goschen used to relate an experience which illustrates this trait. As President of the old Poor Law Board in Gladstone's first administration, he had introduced a local Government Bill which had shared the fate of so many ambitious projects and been sacrificed in the " massacre of the innocents " at the end of the session. Goschen had been deeply chagrined and had even offered his resignation, but was persuaded to withdraw it on being promised, as he thought, the first place for his Bill in the next session. When the draft of the Queen's speech was submitted to the Cabinet, he found to his dismay that four or five other important measures were given precedence. He sought out the Prime Minister and reproached him. " You can't do this ; you not only promised me first place for my Bill, but you stated in the House that it would have the first place." Mr. Gladstone demanded to be shown when he had said that. Goschen produced *Hansard* and pointed triumphantly to the words in which Mr. Gladstone had declared that the Bill would be " in the forefront " of the legislative programme of the coming session. " Yes," said Mr. Gladstone, emphasizing his words with outstretched forefinger, " but don't you see that the forefront is *a line, not a point*!"

Mr. Gladstone had once rather shocked his devotees by describing himself as " an old parliamentary hand." Never did he make a finer display of his parliamentary skill than in this final stage of his public career. In the long and intricate committee discussions on the Home Rule Bill he never missed a point, and it was in vain that ingenious snares were laid to entrap him.

I remember one such incident. Sir Henry James had framed a too ingenious amendment on the supremacy of the Imperial Parliament. If Mr. Gladstone accepted it, the Parnellites would revolt; if he refused it the hollowness of his pretence that that supremacy was maintained would become apparent. The amendment was called at dinner-time. My father, who had been dining every night in the House, believed himself safe for a couple of hours and went off to his Club, telling me that he did not wish to be disturbed. But in less than an hour Akers-Douglas, the Chief Whip, despatched me in a hansom cab to bring him back. Mr. Gladstone had neither refused nor accepted the amendment. He professed his agreement with Sir Henry's purpose, but doubted whether his words were apt to achieve it. He suggested a slight alteration which he thought would better express Sir Henry's meaning. James found himself caught in his own snare. If he accepted

80

Mr. Gladstone's carefully worded formula there would be no Irish revolt, and he would have admitted that the supreme authority of the Imperial Parliament was now adequately safeguarded. Mr. Gladstone would have scored a triumph. James struggled, but from being the angler he had become the fish and was being slowly but surely brought to the bank. My father hurried back, watched the sport for a few moments and then, following Gladstone's lead, countered with a further amendment just to make the meaning quite plain. And so the merry game went on till the House rose at midnight.

A similar instance of Gladstone's quickness of apprehension occurred in the select committee on the Grants for the Prince of Wales' children. My father had made some proposal which Morley at once vehemently denounced. "Morley is all wrong," said my father to Harcourt, next whom he was seated. "I was trying to help you out of a difficulty." "That's what Mr. G. has just said to me," replied Harcourt.

The duel between my father and Gladstone was constantly renewed. It was indeed a battle of Titans. Each could admire the other's skill; each regarded the other as his most dangerous adversary. We may apply to them the words which F. S. Oliver wrote of Alexander Hamilton: "They never dealt in trivial annoyance. If they wounded, it was not because they desired to hurt, but because their intention was to destroy." "He is the only man except my father whom I always addressed as ' Sir,' " so said my father to me in later years.

But if some measure of restraint was kept in the duels between Gladstone and my father, it was a fight with the gloves off between my father and the Irish. Colonel Saunderson, the witty leader of the Ulster Orangemen, might announce in his richest brogue that " County Cark, Sir, is remarkable for the production of two very marketable commodities—butter and Home-Rule members," and the Nationalists would join in the general laughter and Tim Healy would be content to reply that he would not attempt to " paint the Orange lily." Such a jibe from the member for West Birmingham would not have been so easily forgiven. Tim Healy, not yet mellowed by age and disillusionment, T. P. O'Connor, " the genial ruffian," as a fellow-member described him at the time, Dillon, always a sour spirit, more moved, as it seemed, by hatred of England than love of his own country—these and many lesser men thirsted for his blood. No quarter was asked or given on either side.

Three incidents among many, stand out in my memory. On one occasion my father quoted a violent incitement to outrage from one of Dillon's speeches. Dillon challenged its accuracy and for that once my father had not provided himself with the reference. " I will send the honourable gentleman the reference," he said. " I will reply when the Right Honourable gentleman can produce it," retorted Dillon, and the Liberal and Irish ranks cheered delightedly, believing that this time they had their enemy at their mercy. Some days later in another debate my father recalled the incident. He had sent the reference to Dillon. It was contained in the report of his speech in the *Freeman's Journal*. Dillon had promised to reply: he had not done so. My father now read it again and challenged him directly. Dillon rose in a hushed and expectant House. He now admitted the correctness of the report, but said that the words were spoken in circumstances which might excuse them. He had gone to that meeting fresh from witnessing the massacre at Mitchelstown, where he had seen a peaceful meeting broken up and blood shed by the police. It was not very generous of the member for Birmingham to taunt him with a few rash words—and so forth, amidst the sympathetic murmurs of Liberal Home Rulers. "Austen," whispered my father, "get me the date of Mitchelstown. I know he's lying."

I hurried to the library and searched in feverish haste, for at any moment Dillon might sit down. Presently a member found me still searching vainly. "Don't worry," he said, "T. W. Russell has given your father the date." So I returned to the House. A moment afterwards Dillon resumed his seat and my father rose again. He recalled how Gladstone had bidden his followers "Remember Mitchelstown." Dillon had learned the lesson; he had "remembered Mitchelstown," but he had remembered it before it had happened! His speech had preceded the riot at Mitchelstown by nine months. The House rang with cheers; Dillon's face, always pale, went white; for once the Irish were silenced. "I ought to have sat down at once. I was a fool to add another word," my father said to me afterwards. When he did finish, the debate ended; members trooped into the lobbies for the division, still buzzing with excitement. As we moved to the Bar, Gerald Balfour asked me : "Have you ever seen a man caught cheating at cards have his hand pinned to the table with a knife?"

"No," said I. "Have you?"

"No, but now I know what he looks like."

In the second incident Healy played the principal part with a very different result. The House was in Committee on Morley's Evicted Tenants Bill. "We have heard a great deal of absentee landlords," said my father, "but this is a bill to create absentee tenants—men who left Ireland years ago or their descendants who have never seen Ireland."

Healy rose to reply. He began badly. "Talk about absentee tenants," he exclaimed, "what about absentee landlords. When did a Duke of Devonshire last visit his Irish estates?" "At Easter," interjected Russell. "And before that, how long was it since he had seen them?" "Not since you killed his brother," shouted Russell. It was true. When Lord Frederick Cavendish was murdered in the Phœnix Park the old Duke had extracted a promise from Hartington that he would forgo his annual visit to Lismore. He had lost one son in Ireland; he did not wish to lose another.

Most men, met with such knock-out blows at the opening of a speech, would have stumbled through a few sentences, and sat down in confusion. Not so Healy. He shook himself like a spaniel coming out of the water. In a few moments he was somehow back at the siege of Limerick, describing it with a burning passion that silenced the cheers and counter cheers, and held the House breathless. It was as if the events he was narrating had happened yesterday, and he had come hotfoot from the scene. As he resumed his seat, Balfour rose and, pointing at Morley an accusing finger, exclaimed, "And now, at last, perhaps the Right Honourable gentleman begins to have some glimmering of the depth of the passions he has stirred." Healy had turned disaster into triumph and won a success that perhaps no other man could have secured.

In the third episode my father was again the central figure. It was the incident which led to the fight on the floor of the House. It was the night when the Guillotine, then first applied to any Bill, was to end the Committee stage. My father and Balfour had agreed that to mark the novel character of this violent suppression of free speech the debate should be so arranged that an important amendment should be under discussion as the clock pointed to the hour, and a front bench man be speaking to it. Balfour took the first night. As the Speaker rose to put the question and Balfour was forced to break off and resume his seat, there were angry cries of "shame" and "gag, gag," but nothing worse, though the House was excited and members felt that a parliamentary *coup d'état* had been accomplished.

On the last night it was my father's turn to be the victim of the Guillotine. The matter under discussion was a set of new clauses entirely altering the financial provisions of the Bill as it passed its second reading. My father criticized the new clauses and then recalled how Mr. Gladstone had in like manner boxed the compass on the hotly contested question of the retention of the Irish members at Westminster. In his first Home Rule Bill he had decreed their total exclusion: in the present Bill he had at first proposed that they should be retained for Imperial affairs, but excluded when purely English matters were under discussion. This new plan found favour in no quarter and was riddled with hostile criticism. At the last moment and after much secret lobbying, Mr. G. abandoned it and proposed that the Irish members should be retained for all purposes, but in diminished numbers. What happened is well described by Mr. Garvin :

"July 27th was to be the last of forty-seven sittings in Committee. At ten o'clock the beheading-machine was to begin its final exercises. At a quarter to ten Chamberlain rose from his coign of advantage on the third bench below the gangway. His accents had his peculiarly ominous intonation—the underswell of anger made more contagious by sardonic modulations of voice. Real and pent-up were the passions of that night. Though the Guillotine was about to descend on masses of undiscussed clauses the dense tiers of Unionist benches believed to a man that the country was with them. This view Chamberlain meant to drive home with blistering mockery. His opponents felt that his sentences sprayed vitriol.

" We may follow him as far as he got. He gibed—that the Government by the guillotine procedure had reduced to a discreditable farce the forms of the Mother of Parliaments. He jeered—that the Ministerialists regarded their Bill as perfect and unimprovable.

" At this, Roby, an excellent Gladstonian, was misled to throw in the banal phrase, ' under the circumstances.' It was notoriously unsafe to interrupt Chamberlain. No one approached him in seizing upon an interjection to improvise a satire. Quick as a flash he caught up the word and sported with it :

" They think that—' under the circumstances ' the proposals cannot be improved. Yes, but they thought the last scheme was perfect and could not be improved. They think every scheme as it successively proceeds from the fertile brain of the Prime Minister is perfect and cannot be improved—' under the circumstances.' That has been their attitude with regard to the whole, notwithstanding the fact that the measure has been changed again and again in the course of the last few weeks. . . .

" I say this Bill has been changed in its most vital features and yet it has always been found perfect by the honourable members behind the Treasury Bench.

" The Prime Minister calls ' black ' and they say ' it is good '; the Prime Minister calls ' white ' and they say ' it is better.' It is always the voice of a god. Never since the time of Herod . . .

" It is admitted that his tone and air, as he watched the

clock so as to be sure of putting in as much as possible in a quarter of an hour, were quizzical, not savage; but at the last word—'Herod'—a furious cry broke, not for the first time that summer, from the Irish camp—'Judas!' One more audible sentence, and only one, Chamberlain got in—'Never since the time of Herod has there been such slavish adulation.' Whether he tried to add another syllable never can be known. Typhoon swooped on the House."

A member moved that the words be taken down. The Chairman did not hear the motion or hoped to escape trouble by ignoring it. The hands of the clock pointed to ten. He put the question but his words were unheeded and inaudible amidst the din. Again the member moved, this time seated and with his hat on, that the words of the honourable member for the Scotland division be taken down. Three-quarters of the House remained seated; those who had passed into the division lobbies returned. Logan, the Liberal member for the Harborough division, was seen gesticulating in the middle of the floor and was assailed with shouts of "order! order!" from those nearest to him. "I'll put myself in order," he cried, and forthwith flung himself on the front Opposition bench, falling rather than sitting on the top of Carson. Hayes-Fisher, sitting immediately behind, seized him by the scruff of his neck and propelled him on to the floor. Logan was a big man of the build of the late Colonel John Ward. He fell

> "As falls on Mount Avernus
> A thunder-smitten oak."

One of the Irish, rushing to his support, tripped and fell, knocking off Colonel Saunderson's hat and hitting him a severe blow on the back of his head in his fall. The fight had begun. As Mr. Garvin says, it was more a scuffle than a fight and most of the members involved in it were trying to part the combatants. But it looked worse than it was to the strangers watching this unprecedented violence. "The dread rebuke of hissing from the Gallery helped to recall the House to its senses." Far more potent was the news that the Chairman had done at last what he ought to have done at first—sent for the Speaker. The House awaited his coming in uneasy consciousness of its guilt. He asked the Chairman to tell him what had occurred; the Chairman's account was disputed; the Speaker called angrily on Mr. Gladstone and Balfour to give him the facts. He required and received an apology from T. P. O'Connor. I shall never forget the spectacle of Mr. Gladstone sitting with bowed head and face half hidden by his hands as we once again moved into the division lobbies.

The incident was at an end, but two stories are worth recalling. Mr. Speaker Peel had been unwell. When his doctor called early the next morning, without having opened his daily paper, he found his patient's condition much improved. "I am glad to find you so much better this morning," he said. "That new tonic has given you a fillip." Only later did he discover that it was not his tonic but the row in the House which had restored the Speaker's nerves.

The other story came from Lord Darling, then Mr. Darling, Q.C., the member for Deptford, with whom I was comparing accounts of what we had seen and heard. "Did you hear the hissing in the gallery?" I asked him. "Yes," he said. "It's rather curious. I had two con- stituents up there. I went up afterwards and asked them what they thought of it all. They happened to be two prize-fighters. "We was fair disgusted," they said. "When we saw that fellow let out right and left and no one went down, we was that disgusted that we hissed, we did." Such was the true explanation of the public indignation which loomed so large in the Press next day and finds its echo in Mr. Garvin's pages.

The Parliament maintained its reputation for dramatic surprises to the last. After Mr. Gladstone's retirement in the spring of 1894, the process variously known as "ploughing the sands" or "filling up the cup," continued with diminishing government majorities and little credit to Ministers. The Opposition moved several Votes of Censure, but these only served to rally the divided ranks of the Government's supporters, for no Liberal could afford to absent himself on a day which in advance was marked as critical. The Government, however, were taking Supply on every Friday, then a full parliamentary day. At last my father told me that he had proposed to Balfour that the Unionists should make a special effort to secure the presence of all their supporters, unless they had provided themselves with a "live pair," on these Supply days. "I told him," my father said to me, "that if we could keep our men for a month of Fridays, I would undertake that we should beat the Government. He has agreed and will speak to Akers-Douglas. So now it's up to you and Harry Anstruther to see that our men attend."

The first Friday came.

Campbell-Bannerman, who had with difficulty secured the resignation by the Duke of Cambridge of the post of Commander-in-Chief which he had so long held, was expecting congratulations rather than censure; but Brodrick (now Lord Midleton) had given notice that he would call attention to the shortage of small-arm ammunition and move a reduction of the vote. The debate proceeded in a comparatively thin House. It was obvious that many of the Liberals were absent. Anstruther and I had succeeded in whipping up all our small party, but the Conservative Whips, with their much larger numbers, had been less successful. Akers-Douglas thought that they had nearly as many absentees as the Government, and I reported to my father during the Division that we had failed.

When, however, the clerk at the table received the numbers from the tellers, he handed the paper with the figures to Akers-Douglas, a sure sign that the Opposition had the majority. The tellers, who were already taking their accustomed places at the table with the Opposition on the Speaker's right and the Government Whips on his left, changed places and a roar of cheering went up from our benches. But the result was so unexpected by Akers-Douglas, that he, generally the coolest and most phlegmatic of men, lost his head. He glanced at the figures, misunderstood them and handed the paper to Tom Ellis, the Government Whip. The tellers again changed places.

The Unionists sat in dismayed silence, whilst the Liberals and Nationalists cheered themselves hoarse. Even as they did so, Ellis, after looking again at the paper, returned it to Douglas, and the tellers changed places once again. By this time everyone was in a state of breathless excitement, and when Douglas read out the figures :

for the reduction . . . 132

against 125

showing a majority of seven against the Government, our pent-up emotions burst forth in a roar of cheering, with difficulty suppressed as the Speaker repeated the figures from the Chair.

The Government, whose majority a few days earlier had dropped to the same figure, when Sir William Harcourt had boldly declared that they would continue as long as they had a majority of one, was too weak to resist even so slight a blow. The Parliament was at an end: ten years of Unionist administration were shortly to begin.

VI

WHEN WAR CAME

THE Great War has been followed by the opening of the archives of all the principal Governments and the publication of their secrets as well as by a mass of biographical material unexampled in any other epoch.

A recent contribution to these revelations is contained in Lord Newton's *Life of Lord Lansdowne*.[1] But Lord Newton has felt it necessary to compress his story within the limits of a single volume, and dismisses the events of the early days of August 1914, in a couple of pages. Lord Newton calls attention to the inadequacy of the late Lord Oxford's reference in his *Memoirs* to the action of the Unionist leaders, and comments on the discrepancy between Lord Lansdowne's note of his conversation with Lord Haldane as to the despatch of the Expeditionary Force and Lord Haldane's subsequent account of his attitude.

But Lord Newton himself has fallen into an error on a matter of historical importance. He writes:

" The acute period of the crisis arrived (as had often been predicted) during a week-end when the various political chiefs were scattered in the country, but, thanks to the energy of the present Lord Lloyd, of General Sir Henry Wilson, and Mr. Maxse, the Unionist leaders were brought hurriedly back to London and at a little meeting late on the Sunday night at Lansdowne House, which was of infinitely greater importance than other gatherings at the same place which have made much more noise in the

[1] Macmillan & Co. Ltd.

world, it was decided to offer full support to the Government in the event of war. It was rightly considered that it would be inadvisable to mark as ' Private ' the historic note to the Prime Minister, which was taken by Lord Lansdowne's car to Downing Street on the Monday morning."

There is here confusion between two meetings—one held at Lansdowne House late on the evening of Saturday, August 1st, and another held at Bonar Law's residence early on the following morning, and the delivery of the famous letter to Mr. Asquith is post-dated twenty-four hours at a moment when every hour counted.

In these circumstances it can now do no injury to anyone, and may be useful to the student, that I should publish the record of events which I made at the time. I do not pretend that it is in itself complete—doubtless, much took place of which I was unaware, and some portions of it do not profess to be more than a record of the reports which reached us; but as far as it relates to facts which were within my own knowledge, it is a contemporary record dictated as to the first part on either the Monday or Tuesday, and continued from day to day. The Memorandum deals with the action of the leaders of Opposition from Saturday, August 1st to Wednesday, August 5th. I copy it textually except where otherwise indicated.

MEMORANDUM

Friday, July 31st, 1914.

I went to Westgate on Friday, July 31st, to join the children, in the confident belief from all that I had heard, publicly or privately, that the Government had made up their minds to support France and Russia in the present troubles.

Saturday, August 1st.

On Saturday, about three o'clock, I received a telegram from Amery saying that owing to serious developments he was coming down to see me and would arrive about five. Owing to a breakdown of his train he only reached Westgate a little before eight. In consequence of what he told me I returned by the next train at 9.37, reaching London about one o'clock a.m. We were met on the platform by George Lloyd, and proceeded to my house. Briefly what they had to tell me was as follows :

George Lloyd had been in communication with Monsieur Cambon.[1] From him he learned that the Government were not supporting France, and were taking no steps in that direction. Monsieur Cambon spoke of the situation as most critical and with great bitterness of the inaction of the British Government. He said : " It is true that you are under no written obligation and there is not a scrap of paper. But there is more. All our plans have been arranged in common. Our General Staffs have consulted. You have seen all our schemes and preparations. Look at our fleet ! Our whole fleet is in the Mediterranean in consequence of our arrangements with you, and our coasts are open to the enemy. *Vous nous avez livré.*" Cambon went on to say that if France and Russia were victorious in this contest, while we stood aside, they would never forgive us. He did not suggest that France would ever join against us, but she would look on at our ruin without a movement of sympathy. Whilst, if France and Russia were beaten, " Well, your condition will be even worse." Then, with a bitter cry, he exclaimed, " Honour ! Does England know what honour is ? "

[1] The French Ambassador.

George Lloyd continued that he had fetched Bonar Law back to town from Wargrave, where he had been staying with Goulding. He had come to the station straight from a meeting at Lansdowne House at which Lansdowne, Bonar Law and Balfour were present. General Henry Wilson had gone with him. The last-named was in despair. Mobilization orders ought already to have been issued, but he could not get any permission to take the most preliminary steps. Wilson and Lloyd had been distressed by their conversation with the leaders at Lansdowne House. Lloyd said Balfour, of course, understands the position, but Bonar Law does not know what it means, and Lansdowne does not seem to understand. I at once said that Lansdowne would obviously appreciate its full meaning—he must have misunderstood him. In any case they had parted without taking any steps, and George Lloyd put it to me that I was the only person who could persuade them to move.

It was now past two o'clock. We parted to go to bed.

Sunday, August 2nd.

Next morning, as a result of telephone communications with Law and Lansdowne, I was at Lansdowne House at 9.15, a quarter of an hour in advance of the time I had fixed, and Lansdowne was not yet down. While waiting for him I hastily wrote a draft letter for despatch by the Unionist leaders to the Prime Minister. The draft (A) was as follows :

" We feel it our duty to declare that, in our opinion, any hesitation in now supporting France and Russia, our intimate friends (with one of whom at least we have for years past concerted naval and military measures affecting gravely her own military and naval dispositions at this moment), would be fatal to the future security of the

United Kingdom; and we offer His Majesty's Government the assurance of the united support of the Opposition in all measures required by England's intervention in the war."

Lansdowne came down at 9.30. I found him as much alive as I was to the perils of the situation, and convinced, like myself, that for England to hang back now was for her to incur indelible disgrace and lasting danger and insecurity. I at once put my proposal (A) before him. He told me that at the close of their meeting last night the Unionist leaders had offered to see Asquith if he desired. They had no answer as yet, and he was reluctant to take any further steps. I argued the matter further with him, urging that it was not a time to wait for the Government, but that he and Law should go down to Downing Street and demand to see the Prime Minister and make him a declaration to the effect of my written statement.

Lansdowne then went to get his breakfast, and while he was at breakfast I drafted (B) as a basis of a further communication to be made verbally to the Prime Minister by the Unionist leaders if in an interview they found that the Government had irrevocably decided not at once to intervene. This was founded on a suggestion made by Henry Wilson to George Lloyd.

B.

" If the Government are found to have definitely decided against the immediate declaration of war, urge (1) that mobilization be at once ordered; and (2) that the Government require from Germany within twenty-four hours a categorical undertaking to respect *in all contingencies* the neutrality of Belgium (or the Low Countries)."

By ten o'clock Lansdowne and I were at Bonar Law's. I repeated my proposal to him, and found him agreed as to the proper policy for this country to pursue, but reluctant, like Lansdowne, to take any further steps unless Asquith invited them to see him. It appeared that on Saturday F. E. Smith [1] had been in communication with Winston Churchill. From him it was learned that the Cabinet was divided, but how much divided could not be exactly stated. Winston and Grey were certainly for fulfilling our national obligations. Asquith was thought also to be in favour, but large numbers of the Cabinet, and probably the majority, were against any action. Winston had invited Bonar Law and F. E. Smith to dine with him and Grey on Sunday night, but Bonar Law had thought that it was undesirable for him to accept this invitation lest he should appear to be intriguing with a section of the Cabinet behind the Prime Minister's back.

I continued to urge my proposal that the leaders should either go down and demand an audience of Asquith or should send him a letter. The Cabinet was to meet at eleven. The matter was urgent. If the communication was made privately to the Prime Minister it could give no excuse to anyone to complain. If the Cabinet were agreed to take the right steps it could be no embarrassment to them, and if there were differences among them it might be proper for those who were ready to act to know the attitude of the Opposition; and here I mentioned that Cambon had told George Lloyd that Grey was pleading the attitude of the Opposition as an excuse for inaction.

It then appeared that Balfour had met Nicolson [2] at

---

[1] Afterwards Lord Birkenhead.

[2] Sir Arthur Nicolson (afterwards Lord Carnock), Permanent Under-Secretary of State at the Foreign Office.

dinner on Wednesday night; that Nicolson had spoken as if it were a matter of course that we should join in at once with France and Russia, and that thereupon Balfour had very characteristically put the other side of the case, though in fact entirely agreeing with Nicolson: that Nicolson had apparently misunderstood Balfour and reported to Grey Balfour's objections as if they expressed his real mind: that Balfour had become aware of this (on Saturday, I think) and had at once sought an interview with Grey, and, failing to obtain that, had sent a message to Grey's private secretary to explain that he was entirely misunderstood. It also appeared from a telephone message while we were talking that Bob Cecil,[1] having found that Hugh Cecil had written to Winston urging our complete neutrality, had himself written expressing the opposite view and warning Winston that Hugh spoke for no one but himself. Lansdowne and Law seemed to conclude from this that there was no need to do more. I drew the opposite inference, and urged that these were additional reasons for the course which I proposed.

It then appeared that on Saturday Winston had been asked whether there was anything the Opposition could do, and had at that time replied in the negative, and Law put it to me that it would be unwise to do as I proposed if Winston did not wish it. I maintained my opinion; and Law then said that he would try to get into touch with Winston through F. E. Smith on the telephone.

I am not quite clear what exactly followed, as there were two or three interruptions, and I left the room to take a telephone message, but rather suddenly, to my surprise, Law said, " I am not sure that after all Austen is not right. I think we ought to write to the Prime Minister "; and

[1] Lord Robert Cecil.

we there and then agreed on a draft which ran, I think, almost verbally, as follows : [1]

"DEAR MR. ASQUITH,

"Lord Lansdowne and I feel it our duty to inform you that, in our opinion, as well as that of all the colleagues whom we have been able to consult, any hesitation in now supporting France and Russia would be fatal to the honour and to the future security of the United Kingdom, and we offer H.M. Government the assurance of the united support of the Opposition in all measures required by England's intervention in the war."

This was despatched by special messenger to Mr. Asquith, and must have reached him before eleven.

Returning to Egerton Place, I rang up Lloyd and found that he and Amery were together at his house, where I joined them. Lloyd handed to me paper C, information just received by him from the French Embassy.

C.

"Goschen asked Jagow yesterday whether Germany would guarantee not to violate Belgian neutrality. He answered 'No.'

"German Minister in spite of negotiations in Paris at the same time was 'demenaging' his house preparatory to leaving.

"While Russia and Austria negotiating directly to find satisfactory basis for Serbian difficulty, Germany declares war on Russia. This looks as if it was Germany who was insisting on the war.

"*Private*.—Grey tells Cambon we probably shall not allow an attack on French coasts; but no assurances as to our attitude if Germany tried to prevent Algerian troops from coming over to France—8000 men will have to come from Algiers."

[1] I have printed the actual text. The version in my memorandum is not exact.

D.

" From George Lloyd at 5.10 that German troops had already crossed the frontier without a declaration of war.

" At 5.45 from Amery :

" ' I have had a message from Wilson that Asquith has allowed him to hold up all the trains that were to have taken Territorials out to camp, except some forty trains which have gone already ; having these trains held in readiness means a most important saving of time if mobilization is decided on, and Wilson construes Asquith's consent as a favourable sign as far as it goes.' "

At 9.30 p.m. I joined Lansdowne and Victor Cavendish at Brook's. Having sent a message to Law at the Carlton that we were there he came round with Carson and joined us. Winston had sought and obtained an interview with Balfour in the course of the day, and had talked to him freely about the position. John Burns had resigned, but was holding his resignation over at the Prime Minister's request. The Cabinet were very much divided, and probably a majority of them would go if any action were taken. Meanwhile Winston, acting on his own authority, had mobilized the fleet. As far back as Wednesday all the ships at Portsmouth had proceeded up Channel during the night and had passed through the Channel—" twenty-five miles of ships " was Winston's phrase—without a word having got into the papers on the subject.

At four p.m. Grey had communicated to Cambon that the British Government would not allow the German fleet to act against the French coasts or French shipping in the Channel.

Bonar Law brought with him a communication from Asquith. It was most unsatisfactory. It stated that we were under no obligations to France. He rather inconsistently admitted immediately afterwards that the disposition of the French fleet made it impossible for us to allow the German fleet to attack them in the Channel. It referred us to Mr. Gladstone's declaration, *Hansard 203, 1887,* for the Government's view of the obligations of the Treaty of Guarantee of Belgium. It admitted that it was a British interest not to see France crushed. But the whole document appeared extremely wavering and looked as if the Government were searching for excuses to do nothing. I wrote to Lansdowne that night as follows:

> "9, EGERTON PLACE, S.W.,
> "*August* 2, 1914,
> "11.0 p.m.

"MY DEAR LANSDOWNE,

"With reference to No. 1 of Asquith's memo. to Law ('England is under no obligations express or implied to France'), there recurs to my mind a passage in the account George Lloyd gave to me last night of Cambon's conversation.

"C. said: 'There is no written agreement of any sort or kind. There isn't a scrap of paper. But there is more. Every thing, every act of the last few years gave us the assurance of your support, etc., etc.' And then came a bitter cry: 'Et l'honneur? Est ce que l'Angleterre comprend ce que c'est que l'honneur?'—or some similar words.

"Compare what you said to-night, 'An entente is stronger than an alliance, because it is not defined.'

> "Yrs. ever,
>
> "AUSTEN CHAMBERLAIN."

"P.S.—Amery has just been in (11.45), having been at *The Times* and *Morning Post* offices. Both Gwynne and Geoffrey Robinson believe that the Cabinet is stiffening and that the evening meeting was more satisfactory. Harcourt is said to be leading the peace-at-any-price party. Henry Wilson got leave this afternoon or evening to call in all outlying detachments to their regiments. This was refused earlier. Artillery and baggage were moving in Victoria Street as Amery passed through.

" A small crowd was cheering outside the French Embassy as I came home.

" I suggest that you should ask Asquith whether it is true that Germany has refused to pledge itself to observe the neutrality of Belgium.

" I believe German troops are in Luxembourg, but this I think is not new though contrary to the Treaty of 1867 (May 31) article 2 to which we are one of the guarantors."

It was agreed, this time on Law's suggestion, that Lansdowne and he should seek an interview with Asquith, and a message was at once sent to him that night or next morning before the Cabinet. He fixed 10.30 in the morning of Monday, the 3rd.

Monday, August 3rd.

I went to Lansdowne House by appointment at eleven a.m. Arthur Balfour, Lansdowne and Law also present. We were joined a little later by Victor Cavendish and by Salisbury and Bob Cecil, and still later by Walter Long.

Lansdowne and Law had found Asquith very tired and obviously anxious to get rid of them as soon as possible. They had urged upon Asquith that it was inevitable that we should be drawn into the struggle sooner or later, and had pressed him to take part in it with honour and in time instead of waiting till it was too late and we were dishonoured.

It appeared clear that Asquith's memorandum last night

did not represent his real state of mind. He apparently was with Grey and Winston Churchill, but was mainly occupied in trying to preserve as large a portion of his Cabinet as possible.

We heard that Harcourt, Morley, Samuel, Beauchamp, Mackinnon Wood and others were likely to go. Lloyd George's attitude seemed doubtful.

It is noticeable that the *Daily Chronicle* has gone completely round this morning.

Asquith mentioned that Belgium had been offered an *entente* by Germany if she would allow the passage of German troops and had been given till seven o'clock this morning to decide. They asked him, " Is that not a reason for acting at once? " He replied that the Government did not yet know whether the statement was true, but in any case they were agreed that neither on military nor on political grounds ought the Expeditionary Force to be sent at once. When this was reported, Balfour very pertinently asked *when* they had arrived at that decision. It is wholly inconsistent with what we know of their plans at the time of Agadir.

A note from Winston Churchill, handed to Balfour while we were together, explained that Grey had made his announcement about the fleet to the French Ambassador only, and that it had not been communicated to the German Ambassador, who would learn it only from the declaration made this afternoon in the House of Commons. I held up my hands in horror at this slipshod way of conducting affairs, saying : " Suppose the German fleet comes out not knowing of our intentions—is the British Admiral to fire a shot across its bows and order it to go back? "

It appeared the German fleet was already out and its exact whereabouts not known.

I said that Leverton Harris had telephoned to me that Girouard had just been to see him, saying that affairs at the War Office were in some confusion owing to the fact that the Prime Minister had no time for his departmental duties as Secretary of State, and suggesting that Kitchener, who left London at 11.30 this morning, might well be kept and used at the War Office. This idea was taken up, and Balfour sent an immediate note to Winston, then at the Cabinet, asking if it had occurred to the Prime Minister that Kitchener might be more useful in organization at the War Office at this moment than in Egypt. If the Prime Minister approved the idea there would be time to stop Kitchener at Dover.[1]

Tuesday, August 4th.

Milner telephoned me at ten o'clock this morning to ask me if I could join him. I found that he had learned from General Henry Wilson that whilst the Government had at last given the order to mobilize, they had given it in an incomplete form. The full order would be " mobilize and embark." The order actually given was " mobilize." The result of this, according to Wilson, would be that the railway arrangements would be disorganized and that the eventual despatch of an Expeditionary Force would be delayed a further four days. Milner was very anxious that the Opposition should put fresh pressure on the Government. It was not clear what we could do, but he and I proceeded to Lansdowne House, where we discussed the matter with Lansdowne. I left Milner there, joined by Lovat, who had just come from Bonar Law's, and I myself went on to Balfour's. As a result of our

[1] Lord Kitchener was, in fact, stopped at Dover, whither he had motored from Broome Park.

conversation, Balfour agreed to write to Haldane and press the case for the immediate despatch of a 100,000 men, leaving a sufficient nucleus of regular troops in the country.

From Balfour's I went on to Bonar Law's, where I again met Lansdowne. Lansdowne had been convinced by the reasoning of Milner and Lovat and was ready to send a further letter to Asquith. It took some little time to bring Bonar Law to the same conclusion, and it was then too late to convey the letter to Asquith in time to be of any use, as we had been given to understand that the decisive Cabinet would be held at two o'clock.

Wednesday, August 5th.

Yesterday, in the House of Commons, Lloyd George and the Prime Minister asked me to join the Chancellor of the Exchequer in receiving a deputation of traders, bankers and others, to discuss the financial measures which it was necessary to take. We met again at the Treasury this morning and this afternoon, and in the absence of the Chancellor during a portion of the morning's sitting when the Cabinet was meeting, he asked me to take the chair and to continue the business in his absence.

Thursday, August 13th.

We have had some further meetings of the Treasury Committee, notably one to-day, when the Chancellor explained to the representatives of the great accepting houses, to the bankers, and to the traders, his proposals in regard to the purchase of Bills by the Bank of England. He appeared to announce these as a decision already taken by the Treasury in conjunction with the Bank. At a late period of the sitting Lord Mersey protested vehemently against the release of the banks and holders from all liability, but it appeared to me that it was then too late to consider the matter, as the offer had already been made by the Chancellor to the parties concerned and accepted by them. It was undoubtedly more favourable than any of them expected, and I think the Chancellor went too far.

VII

THE FALL OF THE ASQUITH GOVERNMENT IN DECEMBER 1916

THE future historian of the War years is more likely to complain of a plethora than a dearth of material. The latest additions to the mass which has already accumulated, and continues steadily to grow, is the second volume of Lord Beaverbrook's *Politicians and the Great War*, 1914–1916 and the *Life of Lord Oxford and Asquith*, by Mr. J. A. Spender and Mr. Cyril Asquith. The former book is of extraordinary interest, for Lord Beaverbrook relates events of which he might well exclaim "*pars magna fui*" and he has had at his disposal not only his own contemporary record but all the Bonar Law papers. His intimate relations with Bonar Law, his profound admiration for him, and his desire to win for his memory the high position in the eyes of history and in the hearts of his countrymen, which he believes his due, are the obvious motive of this contribution to the story of the crisis which led to the fall of Asquith's Coalition Government; but he has equally plainly been at pains to try and understand the motives of those from whom he differs, and his judgments of motive at least are generally kindly. He has, however, completely failed to understand the position of the Unionist Ministers with whom I co-operated.

Since I propose here to set out my own account of some of these events, it may be well to begin with a few words about my personal relations at *that time* with some of the leading characters in the drama.

For Asquith, as a man, I had warm personal regard and admiration, and with the foreign policy pursued by Lord Grey and himself I was in almost complete agreement. On all the leading questions of domestic policy on the other hand I had been in sharp conflict with him, and his handling of the constitutional crisis of 1910 and, more recently, of the Irish question, had gravely shaken my confidence in his judgment and power to ride the storm or even to foresee what lay before him. But at the outbreak of war he had given noble expression to the spirit and purpose of the nation and contributed powerfully to its union.

With Bonar Law I had, of course, been much more intimately associated. I had known him from the moment that he entered the House of Commons, had admired and rejoiced at his first successes and growing reputation, and had looked to him after my father's illness as the most powerful and convinced advocate of Tariff Reform. This led me, on Balfour's retirement from the leadership, to suggest to Walter Long that, as our rival candidatures to the succession so evenly divided the party at a critical time, we should both withdraw in Bonar Law's favour. Up to this time and, indeed, for some time longer, our association had been particularly close and I think he liked to have, and placed some reliance, on my advice. But as the Irish question became more acute and increasingly dominated the political scene, thrusting Tariff Reform into the background and causing him to drop the fight for the food taxes, he naturally turned more and more to Sir Edward Carson, with whose attitude in regard to Ulster he was in complete and passionate agreement, whilst he probably thought me lukewarm as I thought him rash and his language dangerous in the mouth of the leader of the Conservative Party, at some stages of the controversy. We thus saw less of one another, and I could not but feel that he had withdrawn some part of his confidence from me; but never, then or thereafter, did such differences of opinion or policy as existed between us weaken our personal friendship or alter what I think I may say was our mutual regard.

With Mr. Lloyd George, on the other hand, I had at that time never been in any closer relations than those which necessarily exist in the lobby or behind the Speaker's Chair between men of opposite parties who are yet obliged to do business together, as he and I had been obliged during the long discussions on his famous budget. I remember saying about that time to some of my colleagues who, by the way, were a good deal shocked by the observation, that if it ever became necessary in some great crisis again to form a "Ministry of all the Talents", Lloyd George and Winston Churchill were the first two Liberals I should pick; and on being challenged for my reasons, I said that both had courage, imagination and the power to act, and that I had found Lloyd George a good man to do business with, generous in concession where he felt able to concede, and never haggling over details when we had agreed on the main point. This view of him was strengthened when I sat with him on what was known as the Constitutional Conference after King Edward's death in which he showed these qualities in a very high degree. But he had been foremost in the attacks on the honour of my father and other members of my family during the South African War—an offence which I had neither forgotten nor forgiven; there had been both then and later much in his methods of controversy which I intensely disliked and I felt a great distaste for his ways and little confidence in his judgment. I have no doubt that he thought equally poorly of me. It was not till after Bonar Law's retirement in 1921, when I became leader of the Conservative Party in the House of Commons, that any real confidence or regard was established between us. Through the two anxious years which followed, I learned to know him at his best. Whatever mistakes he has made since, I bear witness to his courage and consideration for his Unionist colleagues in the Irish negotiations and his perfect loyalty to me during our two years close association. It is from that time that our friendship dates—a friendship which is independent of all differences of temperament or opinion. But I must repeat that in 1916 when the crisis came I had no reason to like him and did not in fact trust either his judgment or his methods.

At the time of Asquith's fall I was Secretary of State for India, but without a seat on the War Committee, which I attended only when Mesopotamian affairs were under discussion. My record of the events is contained in a private and personal letter which I wrote to the Viceroy of India, Lord Chelmsford, "for your own eye only," and one or two brief letters of comment to my brother. I have tried to confirm my recollections of the attitude taken up by Curzon, Cecil and myself, "the Three C's," as Lord Beaverbrook calls us, and of Walter Long, who acted with us, from other sources, but no reference to these days is to be found in Curzon's or Long's papers, and Lord Cecil was unable to trace two or three letters which he wrote or received.

For some time before the crisis we had all been getting increasingly anxious about the course of the War. The machinery of the large Cabinet of twenty-one members was ill-adapted for effective or rapid decision. The War Committee was hampered by the necessity of obtaining its approval for all large questions of policy whilst the Cabinet itself was saddled with responsibility for decisions which it could not really control. We felt, too, that the Prime Minister failed to direct its discussions or to show the qualities which the Chairman of any Committee, be it the Cabinet or a Board of Guardians, must possess if its discussions are to be business-like. It was not unknown for the Prime Minister to be writing letters while the discussion proceeded, with the result that in a Cabinet so little homogenous and composed of men of different parties so little accustomed to work together, complete confusion prevailed, and when he at last intervened with a statement that, " Now that that is decided, we had better pass on to . . ." there would be a general cry, " But *what* has been decided? " and the discussion would begin all over again. Asquith remained to the last a determined disbeliever in the appointment of a Secretary to the Cabinet and the institution of minutes of Cabinet decisions. After this practice had been introduced by his successor, I remember that he expressed his surprise at my warm approval of it, declaring that he had never found it necessary and that it was an inroad on established constitutional doctrine and practice. In matters of this kind he was sometimes extremely conservative.

Apart from these general criticisms some of us had felt strongly the delay in enforcing conscription and the sudden announcement of the Derby scheme [1] without previous consultation with the Cabinet at the very moment when we believed conscription to have become finally imperative.

[1] For voluntary enlistment by categories.

Some of us, including, I think, Bonar Law, were indeed at that moment meeting Lloyd George in discussion on the steps by which it might be secured and, if we felt that Asquith had been wanting in frankness to his colleagues, it must also be said that we thought that Lloyd George had let us down. So strongly were three of us impressed by the danger of delay that Selborne, Curzon and I only consented to remain in office after an exchange of letters with Asquith in which he definitely pledged himself to propose conscription if the Derby scheme failed to secure all the results expected from it.

Lord Beaverbrook sees in Lord Lansdowne's Memorandum the actual beginning of the crisis which culminated in December, and Lord Crewe, in the Memorandum printed in Asquith's *Memories*, inclines to the same opinion. To Bonar Law and Lloyd George Lansdowne's paper may have appeared as a weakening of the will to victory. It was certainly an accurate and formidable recital of the reports which were pouring into the Cabinet from all their advisers, but the effect on my mind, as on Lord Cecil's who wrote an able rejoinder, was not to persuade me that peace by negotiation was either necessary or possible, but to strengthen my conviction that our methods of conducting war were wholly unsuitable and must be radically revised. It was, indeed, the curse of this war that almost from its outbreak the stakes became so high that no nation could afford to cry forfeit and withdraw from the struggle.

We must then reorganize. When the War Committee was first appointed, I had myself suggested that it should be made the Cabinet and that other Ministers, heads of departments like myself, should work under it, but Asquith would have nothing to do with this proposal, insisting that responsibility must remain with the larger Cabinet, and I do not remember that at that time it received support from any other quarter.

Up to this point there was as far as I know no difference of purpose or attitude between Bonar Law and his Conservative colleagues. The desire to work with Asquith, the idea that the influence which he was supposed to possess with the Liberal, Irish and Labour parties was necessary to national union and the formation of a strong Government, and distrust of Lloyd George and his intentions were common to us all as well as to F. E. Smith, who was not then a member of the Cabinet and formed his views independently. Bonar Law's own attitude is thus summed up by Lord Beaverbrook [November 14th]:

"Bonar Law distrusted Lloyd George and his ambitions. He suspected that Lloyd George's plan of a new executive War Council was not a considered scheme for reorganizing the machinery of war. He suggested it was a scheme for side-stepping Sir William Robertson's authority under the Kitchener-Robertson agreement. In other words, whenever the War Secretary and the C.I.G.S. had a difference about strategy, Lloyd George would carry the matter to his own court of appeal, the War Council, and overrule Robertson there. Finally, the scheme was to exalt Lloyd George at Asquith's expense. This he was quite clearly not prepared to do—at least not without a great deal more thought and argument."

And so said all of us!

But Bonar Law's two most intimate friends and councillors, Carson and Beaverbrook' thought otherwise, and in the end they determined his attitude. Bonar Law had been seriously perturbed by the large following in the Conservative Party which had supported Carson against him a little earlier on some forgotten question about the treatment of German properties in the conquered colonies of West Africa, and he became increasingly restive under Carson's attacks and the response which they called forth from Conservative back-benchers. With all his qualities, Bonar Law had not the power to stand alone, and in the day of battle needed someone to stay up his hands. My first criticism of Lord Beaverbrook's story is that he wholly underrates his own influence with Bonar Law and the part which he himself played in determining Law's action at this and other decisive moments of his career. It is characteristic of Lord Beaverbrook's whole attitude to Bonar Law to represent himself as merely the clarifying medium which enabled Bonar Law to precipitate his own thoughts, and perceive them clearly. No one who ever saw them together, or even reads this book, can accept that account of their relationship.

Beaverbrook, like Carson, was resolved that Asquith must go. During the next few days he was active in the endeavour to bring Carson and Bonar Law into line and to link up Bonar Law with Lloyd George. The result was seen when Bonar Law for the first time summoned a meeting of the Conservative Ministers at his house on Thursday, November 30th.

By this time Bonar Law, Lloyd George and Carson had come to an agreement. Asquith was to retain the Premiership, to preside at the Cabinet and to lead the House of Commons, but all effective power was to be transferred to a War Committee of four, of which Lloyd George was to be chairman, and it was known that the other members were to be Bonar Law himself, Carson and Henderson. Asquith was to have the right to attend when he thought necessary and to refer decisions of the Committee to the Cabinet, but this proviso was plainly a face-saving device, the obvious result of which would be that the Prime

Minister would become a *roi fainéant* with Lloyd George as Mayor of the Palace. And not only would this have been the result, but it was equally plainly the intention of the authors of the scheme.

Bonar Law still [November 30th] desired to keep Asquith as Prime Minister; he still considered the influence which Asquith was supposed to wield indispensable to the creation of a stable government, but he had deeply committed himself to Lloyd George's plan, and his purpose in summoning his colleagues was to win their support for it. All the Unionist members of the Cabinet were present except Balfour, who was confined to his house by illness, and Lansdowne, and all except Bonar Law himself felt the strongest objection to this scheme.

I wrote my letter to the Viceroy on Friday, December 8th, that is three days after Asquith's resignation, which took place on the 5th, and the day before the constitution of the new Government was announced in the Press.

It will be convenient to reproduce that letter at this point of my story.

" *Private and Personal.*

" INDIA OFFICE,
" WHITEHALL, S.W.,
" *8th December* 1916.

" MY DEAR CHELMSFORD,

" In my last letter I undertook to give you some account of the events of the past week or two which resulted in the acute Cabinet crisis and in the resignation of Mr. Asquith's Government. I was unable to accomplish this in time for the last mail and perhaps that is just as well as, subject to the proverbial slip ' twixt the cup and the lip,' I can now carry the story to its end in the formation of a new Government.

" It had been for some time apparent to all of us that the late Government could not continue without some vital reconstruction of that part of the machinery which was specially concerned with the management of the war. Asquith has many virtues. He is a gentleman in the fullest sense of the word. Very pleasant to work with, very loyal to his colleagues, and with a great equanimity in good or evil fortune which is in itself a considerable asset in times like these. He had—or was believed to have—a very considerable influence among that section of the Liberal Party which was most addicted to peace, and in the Labour Party, and this influence has no doubt served throughout the war to keep down pacifist demonstrations and to secure for the Government the support of large bodies of opinion which would have viewed with suspicion, and probably with resentment, any Government which they considered of more naturally bellicose tendency, even though its policy had been exactly the same. On the other hand Asquith lacks the power to drive. Whether he was always deficient in it, or whether the habit of waiting on events and on colleagues has grown upon him in these later years, I cannot say. In any case the result was the same. Any Committee—call it War Council or Cabinet or what you will—is apt to dissolve in talk unless the Chairman keeps them steadily to the point at issue and makes it his business to secure from them a decision on each question as it is raised. Asquith never so understood his duties. He waited on others. He no doubt often averted conflict, but he never contributed a suggestion. He only once in my experience directly helped us to a rapid decision.

" Then, second to Asquith in the Cabinet, we had Lloyd George, a man of great energy and great resolution with quite extraordinary powers of gathering round him men of capacity, but himself uncertain in temper, very emotional, liable to be unduly exalted at one moment and unduly depressed at another; altogether a man in whose judgment I have no great confidence.

" Had either of these two been a little different, everything would have been different, and such reconstruction as became necessary, owing to their respective defects and qualities and as grew naturally out of our experience of war conditions, might have been carried out quietly and decently without any cataclysm. But you must take men as they are, and it is no use lamenting that they are not something else.

" About three weeks ago Bonar Law, who, as I think, throughout earnestly sought to keep the peace between them, told the Prime Minister that in his opinion a re-construction of the Government had become necessary. He made certain proposals with this object in view, to which he had previously obtained the assent of both Carson and Lloyd George; but his Unionist colleagues were not informed of them till later (Thursday, November 30th) and, when so informed, were unanimously of opinion that they were open to grave objection, and made certain alternative proposals. These did not commend themselves to Bonar Law who had, as was evident, committed himself too deeply to Carson and Lloyd George. Lloyd George, towards the middle of last week, presented to Mr. Asquith a proposal which was very much in the nature of an ultimatum; the whole Harmsworth press and the *Morning Post* were mobilized in support of him, and Asquith was bidden to stand and deliver.

" This was the situation on Saturday last (Dec. 2nd). On Sunday (Dec. 3rd) morning the Unionist members of the Cabinet, with the exception of Balfour, who was ill in bed, and Lansdowne, who was in the country, met at Bonar Law's house. The Sunday papers known to be in close relation with Lloyd George announced that he had presented his terms to the Prime Minister; that they had been rejected and that Lloyd George's resignation would appear in Monday's papers. It was obvious that the situation was quite intolerable. Lloyd George was in revolt and the controversy on his side was being carried on in the Press by partial and inaccurate revelations.

Asquith, Grey and Balfour were being openly denounced and told that they must go. No Government could continue to exist on such terms, and since the Prime Minister had failed to assert his authority and to reorganize his administration in time, we thought that the ordinary constitutional practice should be followed and the man who had made the Government impossible should be faced with his responsibilities. If he could form a Government, well and good. If not, he must take his place again as a Member of an Asquith Administration, having learned the limits of his power and deprived thenceforward of the opportunity for intrigue. In any case, power and responsibility must go together and the man who was Prime Minister in name must be also Prime Minister in fact. It seemed to us at that time that the only hope of a stable Government still lay in combining somehow or another in one administration the separate forces represented by both Asquith and Lloyd George. We were all of us of opinion that reconstruction had become necessary. We did not think that with a Parliament constituted like the present, a Unionist Government, or a Government under a Unionist Prime Minister, would have any chance of success. It was not for us to say which of the rival Liberals could secure the greatest amount of support in the Liberal Party and in the Parties which habitually worked with it. But we felt that the continuance of the existing Government had become impossible and that this question must be solved before any stable Government could be formed. Accordingly, we drew up a statement expressing our concurrence with the views expressed by Bonar Law about a fortnight previously, that reconstruction had become inevitable. We added that, in our view, the publicity given to Lloyd George's intentions had rendered internal reconstruction no longer possible, and we advised the Prime Minister that he should tender his own resignation carrying with it that of all his colleagues, and, if he was unable to accept this advice, we requested Bonar Law to hand to him our collective resignation. . . ."

The exact terms of this statement or resolution were:

" We share the view expressed to you by Mr. Bonar Law some time ago that the Government cannot continue as it is.

" It is evident that a change must be made and in our opinion the publicity given to the intentions of Mr. Lloyd George makes reconstruction from within no longer possible.

" We therefore urge the Prime Minister to tender the resignation of the Government.

" If he feels unable to take that step we authorize Mr. Bonar Law to tender our resignations."

My letter continues:

" The Prime Minister, who came up from the country that morning (Sunday), received Bonar Law immediately on his return. What passed at this interview is somewhat obscure. Bonar Law believes that he conveyed our whole mind to the Prime Minister; I have no doubt that he intended to do so, but I doubt if he ever really understood it. In any case it became evident subsequently that the Prime Minister had not at all understood our action which he regarded as a sudden desertion of himself, without warning and without cause, by all his Unionist colleagues. He asked for time to consider his decision and to consult Lloyd George. He invited Bonar Law to see him again after his interview with Lloyd George, and meantime Bonar Law consented not to hand him our resignation. This was comparatively unimportant, but unfortunately he refrained from handing him our resolution, which he had not even read to him. . . ."

This statement is specifically confirmed by Asquith. He says explicitly in his *Memories*: " the resolution (of the Unionist Ministers) was not shown to me." Lord Beaverbrook is wrong in supposing that any one of us then or afterwards charged Bonar Law with bad faith or suspected

him of it. We thought that he had blundered. We raised
no objection to his holding up the formal presentation of
our resignations for the few hours which the Prime Minister
asked for consideration, but we felt strongly that the actual
words of our resolution should have been communicated
to him and a copy informally given to him. The sequel
shows that we were right; for lack of this commonplace
precaution, misunderstandings followed which could easily
have been avoided. Our real complaint was that Bonar
Law was acting with Lloyd George and Carson to the
exclusion of his Unionist colleagues in the Cabinet, and
that we were not properly kept informed of the policy
which he was pursuing. On this point we had already
become uneasy when he first disclosed to us the direction in
which his mind was moving on November 20th, and Long
had then (December 2nd, not as printed in *Politicians and the
Great War*, " 2.10.16 ") addressed a strong appeal to him in
which, after declaring, " I am profoundly anxious about the
situation and believe that it must have a very serious effect
upon the prosecution of the War," he went on " to implore
you to do all you can consistently, of course, with your own
convictions, to carry your Unionist colleagues in the Cabinet
with you," and concluded, " what I care for is that we
should act together, act promptly and use our combined
strength to save the country from a grave danger."

My letter to Chelmsford continues :

" In the course of the afternoon Asquith saw Lloyd
George, and (I think under the reaction of what he considered our unjustifiable desertion) he accepted Lloyd
George's terms—no doubt they were put to him with
every consideration, and in as acceptable a form as possible—
in regard to the status, functions and number of the War
Committee, whilst reserving for further consideration the

question of its personnel. Lloyd George had proposed a Committee consisting of Bonar Law, Carson, Henderson and himself. I certainly would not have served under such a Committee nor would Curzon or Cecil. We have little confidence in Bonar Law's judgment and none in his strength of character. Carson was a great disappointment in the three months during which he sat in Asquith's Cabinet. He is an Irish sentimentalist as Lloyd George is a Welsh one. He and Bonar Law would merely have emphasized Lloyd George's failings whilst echoing his views, and these are known to have been at variance more than once with those of the General Staff and Command-in-Chief on questions relating to the larger strategy of the war. It was very proper to include Henderson as a representative of Labour. He is a very good fellow, but on all the larger issues of policy he would have been a cipher. Be that as it may, Asquith hereupon decided not to resign himself but to call for the resignation of all his colleagues and to reconstruct his Ministry, and we were so informed a little before eight (by Bonar Law who had arranged to meet us at F. E. Smith's house) by which time Curzon and Long had left town.

" On Monday (December 4th), however, Asquith changed his mind. This, I think, was due in the main to his finding the substance of Lloyd George's conversation with him in the morning papers and to the fact that it was there universally represented in the Lloyd George press as a complete surrender by the Prime Minister, who was to be left in his position only on condition that the whole conduct of affairs was placed in Lloyd George's hands. Some at least of Asquith's Liberal colleagues, under these circumstances, strongly urged him to reject Lloyd George's terms and to act upon the advice which we Unionists had already given him. By Monday night Asquith had definitely decided to inform Lloyd George that he could not accept his proposals and on Tuesday morning he received Lloyd George's reply [1] which, I need scarcely say, was his resignation, coupled

---

[1] See *Politicians of the Great War*, p. 262

with a perfunctory promise of support to Asquith's reconstituted Government and a very clear statement that he should proceed to agitate the country against him. Upon this Bonar Law announced that he had definitely decided to throw in his lot with Lloyd George. I have, I think, already said that Bonar Law was acting with Carson and Lloyd George throughout, even to the exclusion of all communication with the Unionist Ministers who were left in complete ignorance of his views till after he had definitely committed himself to these two."

I again interrupt the narrative of the letter to deal with the meeting in my room at the India Office on the morning of the decisive Tuesday. It was composed of Curzon, Cecil, Long and myself, and Lord Beaverbrook gives to the chapter in which he describes it, the title of " The Court Martial." This is simply ludicrous to anyone who knows the facts. I had gone to my office as usual at that time about ten in the morning. A little later, Cecil [1] came in to ask if I had any news ; he was followed a few minutes later by Curzon with the same question on his lips, and as the three of us had thus come together accidentally and without premeditation we telephoned to the Local Government Board to ask Long to join us. None of us had heard anything from Bonar Law since Sunday evening. We did not know what he was doing or what the Prime Minister had decided. Our responsibilities were great, and we were profoundly anxious and completely in the dark. The situation was intolerable, and Long agreed to ask Bonar Law to join us, or himself to call a meeting of all his Unionist colleagues at the earliest possible moment that day. Bonar Law fixed four o'clock that afternoon as the time and his room in the Colonial Office as the place for our meeting. I do not think that he conveyed to Long at this interview

[1] Lord Robert Cecil.

at all the impression which Beaverbrook's words suggest. At any rate it was not till three years later, and then by accident, that I learned the unfortunate inferences which Bonar Law had drawn from what was, as I have explained, this unpremeditated meeting in my room. We had no idea of ousting Bonar Law from the leadership; we desired, as Long's letter already quoted shows, to act with him and were only anxious that he should take us into his confidence so that we might speak and act in union.

My letter continues:

"On Tuesday afternoon the Prime Minister sent for Curzon, Bob Cecil and myself."

This is the first and only time the three of us met Asquith during these fateful days. Lord Crewe places this meeting on Monday morning, but Lord Crewe's memorandum was written on December 20th, twelve days farther away from the events than my own; Lord Beaverbrook follows him and states that the Tuesday meeting was our second appointment and that we "simply went over the old ground with reiterated emphasis." I am confident that my letter, written only three days after the meeting, is correct. We only once saw Asquith during these fateful days and that was on this Tuesday afternoon immediately before our four o'clock meeting in Bonar Law's room. The resolution passed at this meeting confirms the fact, for it begins, "Curzon, Cecil and Chamberlain have reported to us the substance of what passed at your meeting with them *this afternoon*. . . ." If the decisive interview had taken place the day before, we could not have failed to mention it. Lord Beaverbrook's mistake about the date invalidates his account of what happened on the Monday.

With this explanation I resume the quotation from my letter:

123

" On Tuesday afternoon the Prime Minister sent for Curzon, Bob Cecil and myself. He told us the whole story from his point of view, and we explained to him the meaning of our resolution, which he had not previously understood. He put before us the various contingencies in considerable detail, setting forth the pros and cons of the different courses open to us with great fairness. He asked whether we should be prepared to go on with him whilst Lloyd George and Bonar Law resigned. To this we replied that our only object was to secure a Government on such lines and with such a prospect of stability that it might reasonably be expected to be capable of carrying on the war; that in our opinion his Government, weakened by the resignations of Lloyd George and Bonar Law and by all that had gone on during the past weeks, offered no such prospect, and we answered this question therefore with a perfectly definite negative. This was evidently a great blow to him. Had we replied in the affirmative, he would clearly have been prepared to make the attempt and believed that he would have had the support of the great bulk of the Liberal Party and of the Labour and Irish Parties.

" He then asked us what our attitude would be towards Lloyd George if he attempted to form an administration. We replied again that our only object was to get a stable Government capable of conducting the war successfully. We had come under no obligation to Lloyd George, our hands were perfectly free, but we should be prepared to support, to join or to serve under any Government which offered a prospect of fulfilling our conditions. Whether Lloyd George could form such a Government we did not know.

" We told him that in our opinion the co-operation of himself and Lloyd George was really necessary. Bob Cecil had the courage to suggest to him that the finest and biggest thing that he could do would be to offer to serve under Lloyd George; but he would not allow Cecil to develop this idea, which he rejected with indignation and even with scorn.

" On leaving the Prime Minister we joined the rest of our Unionist colleagues in Bonar Law's room whilst the Prime Minister met his Liberal colleagues and Henderson. This time Lansdowne also was with us but Balfour was still confined to his house. After some discussion among ourselves we sent Curzon across to Downing Street with a letter in which we repeated the advice which we had given on Sunday, saying that in our opinion the resignation of the Government had now become absolutely necessary, and that it was imperative that it should take place that day.[1]

" We added that we believed the Prime Minister had come to the same conclusion, but, if this were not the case, we must ask him to act upon our resignations. It appeared that his Liberal colleagues, with some hesitation on the part of Crewe and Henderson, had given him the same advice earlier in the day. He called Curzon into the room where they were assembled, and, after asking a question or two about our attitude and views, informed him and the Liberals that he had decided to tender his resignation. Harcourt tells me that this was the first intimation the Liberal Ministers had of his decision.

" I am told, but I do not know this on trustworthy authority, that either the King did not ask, or Asquith declined to tender advice as to the name of his successor. In any case the King sent for Bonar Law. Feeling that there was a possibility that Asquith might more readily serve under him than under Lloyd George and being still anxious to secure the co-operation of both, Bonar Law did not at once decline. He proceeded forthwith to ascertain that Lloyd George would be willing to serve under him and, having ascertained that, he asked Asquith if he would do the same. He should of course have reversed the order of his visits, gone straight to Asquith from the Palace, asked

[1] The actual terms of this communication were : " C., C. and C. have reported to us the substance of what passed at your meeting with them this afternoon. After full consideration, we are unanimously of opinion that the course which we urged upon you on Sunday is a necessity, and it is imperative that that course should be taken to-day.

" We hope that you have arrived at the same conclusion, but, if this is not so, we are obliged to ask you to accept our resignation."

Asquith if he would serve under Lloyd George, and, on getting a refusal, made an appeal to Asquith to waive all personal considerations and consent to serve under *him*.[1] I think Asquith might have done it. He would have seen that Bonar Law was not a mere tool of Lloyd George and could act independently of him, and it was due to Asquith's position, if he was to be asked to serve under someone else after himself being Prime Minister, that he should be the first person approached by that someone, on receiving the King's Commission. But as Bob says, Bonar Law is an amateur and will always remain one. It is not by any means the only mistake he has made in these negotiations.

" As it was, he appears to have informed Asquith that he had first secured Lloyd George's assent since it would have been useless to invite Asquith if Lloyd George had declined! He was met by Asquith with a resolute refusal. He and Carson, I believe, or he and Lloyd George then proceeded to consult Balfour. I think it was at Balfour's suggestion that a conference was held at the Palace. According to the accounts that I have received of what passed, the proceedings were opened by Balfour who made a strong appeal for unity and offered suggestions for a basis of agreement. Lloyd George expressed his readiness to serve either under Bonar Law or under Balfour if Asquith would do the same, and it was thought by some of those who were present that some impression had been made on Asquith and that he would assent. After consultation, however, with his Liberal colleagues and on their advice, he definitely refused. Bonar Law then resigned his commission and Lloyd George was entrusted with the task of forming a Ministry. He at once asked Balfour, one of the proscribed of the week before, to take the Foreign Office. Balfour replied, ' You are putting a pistol to my head, but in the circumstances I say " Yes." ' He had already secured the co-operation of Carson, as I think I told you. Derby was acting with him, but none of the Liberal Cabinet Ministers would give him any support.

[1] *i.e.* Bonar Law.

By yesterday afternoon he had secured the support of the Labour Party and he had promises of support from about half the Liberal Party, some eighty of whom, he said would have joined with him in a campaign even against Asquith, whilst another fifty or so—a growing number—who would have supported Asquith if he had attempted to form a Government, were equally prepared to support Lloyd George, if he was the man to whom the task was entrusted.

" At this stage Curzon, Long, Cecil and myself were informed by Bonar Law of the position. We were shortly afterwards invited to see Lloyd George, and having put to him certain questions, and ascertained the position and constitution of the small body to whom the conduct of the war would be entrusted, and received answers to some other pertinent questions, we accepted his invitation to serve in his Government. There was not one of us who would not have been glad to escape from this necessity, but this is not the time when, on grounds of personal convenience, or indeed on any personal grounds whatever, one has a right to refuse such service as one can render to any Government which offers a prospect of the successful conduct of the War, still less to what appears to be the only possible Government of that kind.

" I deeply regret that the relations between Asquith and Lloyd George should have reached a point at which neither could serve under the other. I still more deeply regret, this being so, that Asquith should have definitely refused to serve under anybody. I think that in so doing he lost an opportunity of rendering great service to his country, and showing a magnanimity and public spirit which would have placed him high in public estimation. It was his definite refusal to serve under anyone and his apparent relapse into a state of complacent satisfaction with all the proceedings of the old Government, that definitely decided me—and, I think, my colleagues—that we had no choice but to accept office under Lloyd George. Once this general decision had been taken the two things about which I felt most strongly were, first, that it was necessary to have someone on the War Committee in whose strength and judgment I had sufficient confidence to be satisfied that Military opinion would not be disregarded or overruled in Military questions, and above all in questions of strategy; and, secondly, that this War Committee, necessarily having all real authority, should itself be in name as well as in fact the Cabinet, and that there should not be a great body of Cabinet Ministers without real influence on the general policy of the war and yet sharing the responsibility for decisions in which they were not consulted and exposed to constant criticism for acts of omission or commission in which they had no part. The former condition was fulfilled by the inclusion of Curzon in the War Committee, and the latter by making the Committee identical with the Cabinet. We pressed Lloyd George to include also Milner, either in addition to or in place of Carson, in this body, but we were told that his addition was impossible because it would necessitate the inclusion of another Liberal —even as it stood there was only one Liberal to three Unionists—and would upset Lloyd George's agreement with the Labour Party, who had been promised one seat in a War Committee of five. As to the substitution of Milner's name for Carson's, Bonar Law who was present at part of our interview, could only say that it was useless to discuss it as Lloyd George was pledged up to the eyes to Carson.

"This long story is for your eye only. I have not, hitherto, given you any similar political gossip, but I expect that at least your curiosity will be gratified by knowing something of the *dessous des cartes.*

"Yrs. very sincerely,

(sd) "AUSTEN CHAMBERLAIN."

"*December* 11*th.*

"P.S.—The list of the new Government is in the papers to-day except for the Under Secretaryships. You will see that some changes have been made. I am glad to find that Milner is, after all, a Member of the War Committee whilst Carson goes to the Admiralty. This new Committee, or Cabinet, got to work on Saturday, and I hope that we shall all now settle down to business again. At one stage of the business, when Lloyd George appeared bent on excluding both Curzon and Milner from the War Committee, I had clearly made up my mind not to take office. However, *dis aliter visum*. I should have been sorry to leave unfinished work in which I have been deeply interested. But I should have been a happier man if I could have regained my freedom."

A passage from a letter to my brother, written on the same day as this postscript, supplements it:

"It is amusing to think that part of Lloyd George's ultimatum to Asquith (the Sunday, or second edition) was that he must get rid of Balfour, and that he started out with the intention of turning Curzon off the War Committee and not putting Milner on!

"I told Curzon on Saturday the 2nd, when I first learned of Lloyd George's terms and their rejection, that tho' after the 'Die-hard' business, when I felt his desertion bitterly, I had said that I would not go tiger-shooting with him again, yet values changed and opinions had to be reconsidered. I had seen him at work and learned to appreciate his qualities and I would serve under the proposed Committee if he were added to it, but not otherwise.

"I added that I had long held the view that the War Committee should be the Cabinet, and I would not sit in a *Cabinet* with *no* power under a War Committee with *all* the power. I believe I originally stood alone in this view, which I urged when the old War Committee was formed. . . . We have got the three things I thought most necessary for the public service—the inclusion of Curzon and Milner in the War Committee and the formal constitution of the War Committee as the Cabinet."

It only remains for me to add, first, that Curzon had no authority from us to tell Asquith that we would not serve under Lloyd George or any man who could form a stable Government, and that the assertion that he did so is not borne out by his letter to Lansdowne recounting the meeting at Bonar Law's on Sunday the 3rd; and, secondly, to repeat my caution that my letter to the Viceroy does not express my final judgment on the men and events of which it treats. There are some phrases and expressions in it which I should revoke to-day, and which may shock some of those who chance to read them. But I have thought it best to print the letter word for word as it was written, while I was still under the immediate influence of the events related, so that there may be no suspicion that I have allowed my account of what I then did or felt to be biased by my subsequent knowledge or feelings.

It is fitting that I should close my story with Asquith's reply to the letter I wrote him when the die was cast. It shows the magnanimity of his mind—never more conspicuous than in the years which followed his resignation.

> " 10 DOWNING STREET,
> " WHITEHALL, S.W.,
> " Dec. 6, 1916.

" *Personal.*

" MY DEAR AUSTEN,

" I was much touched by your very kind letter. I have been treated by all my Unionist Colleagues during the last two years with unvarying loyalty, and I owe them a great debt of gratitude for their whole-hearted co-operation in most difficult times.

"None has been more helpful than yourself, and I hope and believe that the relations of real friendship which we have come to form will long outlast the ties of office.

"Yours very sincerely,

"H. H. ASQUITH."

No wonder that men served him gladly.

VIII

CABINET-MAKING AFTER THE WAR

THE small War Cabinet as finally established by Mr. Lloyd George in 1916 was certainly a great improvement on the unmanageable system which it succeeded. It gave a much more energetic direction to the War effort of the nation and its armies, it inspired a new hope and confidence in the country and among its allies. It was, I think, particularly successful where it established something like the dictatorship of one highly competent man, as the present Lord Maclay for Shipping and the late Lord Rhondda for Food, in place of the committees among which the control of these matters had previously been spread.

But the system was not without serious defects of its own. The Cabinet was overwhelmed with work; it was difficult to secure its attention for other aspects of national policy such as the rising problems presented by the Government of India; and though the Cabinet was small and in the last resort the decision rested with half a dozen men, the Cabinet room was often overcrowded with the ministerial representatives of other departments and their officials. In particular, Treasury control of expenditure, always most difficult in war-time, when everything else must be subordinated to the successful conduct of operations, became practically non-existent.

The Chancellor of the Exchequer had no time for anything except the highest problems of finance and was obliged to leave to Lord Chalmers, who was recalled to the Treasury, the duty of defending before the War Cabinet the interests in its charge, whilst in 1917 Lord Buckmaster and I, then both out of office, with Mr. Keynes as representative of the Treasury, were appointed a committee to control the dollar expenditure of all departments, which was causing anxiety both to the British and United States Governments, and to present the British case to an " Inter-allied Commission of Purchases and Finance " which was presided over by Mr. Crosby, ably assisted by Mr. Paul Cravath. It is pleasant to recall that Mr. Crosby asked for a memorandum on the way in which the British case was prepared, as our demands were found to be proportionately much more moderate and our estimates more trustworthy than those of the other Allies. I do not remember that we ever had an indent passed by us rejected, or even reduced, by the Commission, or refused by the United States Government.

It was obvious, in these circumstances, that when peace was made the problems of post-war finance would be among the gravest of those which would confront the Government of the day, and that the task of the Chancellor of the Exchequer would be at least as difficult as that of any of his colleagues, for, apart from the huge debt, internal and external, created during the War, war charges would remain long after war had ceased, the normal control of the Treasury over the expenditure of other departments would not be easy to re-establish, and the Chancellor would be forced to maintain taxation at the War level when in every quarter the taxpayer would be expecting and clamouring for relief. Obviously he would need in a very special degree all the authority with which his office could be invested and, in more than the usual measure, the confidence and support of the Prime Minister.

It was in such circumstances that on the morning of Friday, January 10th, 1919, I received from the Prime Minister, then in course of reorganizing his Government after the General Election, a letter saying that he had submitted my name to the King for the office of Chancellor of the Exchequer and that His Majesty had been pleased to approve the nomination. The letter seemed to me unnecessarily curt in the form of its announcement that Bonar Law would continue to occupy the house usually allotted to the Chancellor of the Exchequer and in the terms of the offer itself. It requested a very early reply as Mr. Lloyd George desired to have the matter settled at once as he was leaving that day for Paris. For the rest it contained a very sensible proposal that instead of bringing all Treasury disputes direct to the Cabinet they should be taken to a small committee consisting of the Prime Minister, Bonar Law, the Chancellor of the Exchequer and another colleague, like Lord Milner.

On receipt of this letter I called on Bonar Law. I told him that, as he was aware, I had no desire to return to the Treasury and that the stipulation about the house removed the one amenity which lent any attraction to the office. He replied, very stiffly, that his occupation of that house was a *sine qua non* with him—that he could not do his work as leader of the House unless he had the facility of access to the Prime Minister, which the occupation of No. 11 gave to him.

We had a rather stormy conversation. In fact we both lost our tempers for the first and last time in our long friendship, but the breach was healed by some kindly words from Bonar Law the same afternoon and left no scar on our relations.

As I was leaving he asked me what I proposed to do.

I told him that I proposed to consult my wife and that my inclination was, if she was prepared for such a course, to refuse the offer.

He suggested that I should in any case see the Prime Minister; and I replied that that would certainly be necessary if I did not refuse outright.

As I was leaving he overtook me in the passage, and added that perhaps in saying what he was going to say, he was not quite loyal to his Chief, but that he thought that I might fairly insist, if I took office, that it should carry with it a seat in the Cabinet.

"Do you mean," I said, "that the offer does not carry Cabinet rank? In that case I will not look at it for a moment"; and he replied that he did not know what the Prime Minister's intentions were—I must ask him.

After consulting my wife, I decided that in view of the strong reasons which there were for the retention of the Downing Street house by Bonar Law, I could not make that a ground of refusal, that I would see the Prime Minister, and that my answer should depend upon what he might say to me.

I accordingly called upon the Prime Minister by appointment at 2.15. I began by saying that I thought it better to speak plainly, and he asked me to do so. I then said that Bonar Law had probably told him—and in any case it was the fact—that I had never wished to go back to the Chancellorship of the Exchequer.

He said that he was not surprised at it; for though, as I knew, he had expressly stipulated when he went to the Ministry of Munitions that he was to have the right to return to the Chancellorship whenever he wished, he had quickly made up his mind that nothing would ever induce him to go back.

I said, " Then you will not be surprised that the office has no attractions for me. You have offered it to me in what I must consider a very curt manner at the very last moment—very much as you would throw a bone to a dog. I must say that I am not particularly flattered."

He interrupted me to say that he had come to town on Monday intending to see his colleagues personally, but his time had been so occupied on Tuesday and Wednesday with urgent problems of demobilization that he had had no opportunity of seeing any of them; and probably the others felt very much as I did. He was very sorry but it had been unavoidable.

I accepted this explanation and passed on to say that in offering me the office he had informed me that he proposed that Bonar Law should retain the Chancellor of the Exchequer's house. This, I said, was the one amenity of the office which for me had some attractions—owing to its proximity both to the office and to the House of Commons, and still more for the facility which it gave of constant and easy access to the Prime Minister, who was himself First Lord of the Treasury.

The Prime Minister here said that he understood my feelings, but that it really was impossible to carry on the arrangement by which the leadership of the House was held as a separate office on any other terms.

I replied that I appreciated the cogency of this argument— I made no complaint of the arrangement, though I thought it might have been expressed with more courtesy to me. But that brought me to the first condition of my possible acceptance. As I had said, the occupation of No. 11 placed the Chancellor in close proximity to the Prime Minister and afforded him the means of ready access to him at all times. Since I had rejoined Lloyd George's Government I had only once seen him outside Cabinet.

He interrupted me to say how much he regretted that he had not been able to see more of his colleagues, but his day's work had never begun later than seven—often at six—and lasted till ten at night. Even his meals were business meals: that very morning he had had people to breakfast and lunch to discuss business for whom he had been unable to find any other appointment, since his whole morning had been taken up by a deputation through which he hoped he had averted a railway strike.

Again accepting this explanation, I said that the office of Chancellor of the Exchequer was at all times a difficult one—that Bonar Law had told me that morning that he thought the situation at the present moment more difficult than it had been at any time while he had held the office. Even in ordinary circumstances the Chancellor was necessarily often involved in contention (even if it were friendly contention) with the Heads of other great Departments, and his position would be quite intolerable and indeed impossible, if he did not possess the confidence of the Prime Minister and receive his loyal support. Such support was naturally doubly necessary in times of such difficulty as the present.

The Prime Minister entirely agreed with my statement of fact and incidentally observed that Asquith had always given him that kind of support when he was the Chancellor of the Exchequer—" though not," he added, " when I was Minister of Munitions," and he interjected that he thought that that was the fault of McKenna, to whom Asquith's fall was due. As to the support for which I asked, his answer depended upon whether we were agreed about certain lines of policy.

I said at once that I recognized that the old Gladstonian Treasury tradition was quite unsuited to the moment—that we had got to take a much larger view of our responsibility; when I asked for his support I did not mean that he was to pledge himself always to be of my opinion, but that I must be assured that he gave me his confidence and that he intended to help me. I added that I recognized such a pledge could not be put into any tight form—no words of either of us could bind him in the future. The whole value of the assurance would depend upon the spirit in which it was given.

He then said that he agreed that a new tradition would have to be established at the Treasury. He thought that there would have to be considerable changes in the staff. The men at the top were clever men, but they were only the more powerfully obstructive for their cleverness. They were steeped in the Cobden-Gladstone doctrines of the *laisser-faire* school and that was not suited to these days. In his view there were four large policies with which we must proceed. The first was Housing; the second was the development of our Imperial Possessions; the third, Communications; and the fourth, Land Settlement. Did I agree with him as to the necessity for these measures?

I replied that I entirely agreed about Housing, and that unless we could make a really large effective start with it before the close of the new Parliament, we should be confronted with a wave of Bolshevism. I regarded it as a necessary measure for social security. As regards Empire development, that was (as he himself had indeed stated) my father's policy. I had what I might call an hereditary interest in it and I should be glad to do all I could to forward it. As to the other two, I agreed, subject, however, to the character of the financial situation which I might find on taking office and the possibility of obtaining the necessary funds. What the financial situation was, of course, I did not yet know. I could say nothing about it until I had got into the Treasury except to recall Bonar Law's description of its gravity, which I had already quoted.

He accepted this statement as perfectly satisfactory.

After some further conversation about the organization and staffing of the Treasury itself, I put my second condition to him. This was that whatever Cabinet be formed, large or small, the Chancellor of the Exchequer should be a member of it.

At this he pulled a wry face and said that was a difficulty. He had some ideas about an Imperial Cabinet and a Home Cabinet. He believed that Milner had communicated some similar plan to Bonar Law, but he had not had time to see it or to work out his own ideas. If he brought me into the Cabinet, he would have to bring in others—Long, Churchill, other Secretaries of State, etc.

I replied that I was sorry to make trouble and that no doubt he could find others who would take the Chancellorship of the Exchequer without a position in the Cabinet, but in my opinion nobody ought to do so, for he would never have sufficient authority for his very difficult and delicate task. I suggested that perhaps he would like to think the matter over and that I had better leave him to do so. If he decided against my contention, I would ask him to take my answer as a refusal.

He, however, preferred to continue the discussion. He asked how could there be a Cabinet at home when the Prime Minister, Bonar Law and the Foreign Secretary were all in Paris. They must to a large extent be plenipotentiaries—they could not be constantly referring to a Cabinet at home for instructions. His idea had been not to appoint any Cabinet.

I then inquired who would be responsible in his absence—who would be in a position to summon a meeting of Ministers if one was required—or to take decisions?

" Ah there ! " he said, " that is what the King asked. He is very gravely disturbed. I told him that I was prepared to support any decision which Bonar Law took."

" But," said I, " Bonar Law says that he is going to Paris with you as one of the Peace Delegates."

" Yes," said the Prime Minister; " he insisted that his party would not understand it if he were not included in the Delegation."

I replied that I thought that Bonar Law was quite wrong—that his business was to stay behind to preside over the Cabinet in the Prime Minister's absence and to take urgent decisions on his behalf.

The Prime Minister then sent for Bonar Law and reported to him the purport of our conversation.

Bonar Law replied that he was determined to go to Paris but that he did not expect to stay there more than a few days—very probably he might be recalled on Monday or Tuesday. He had intended to conduct the business by personal conference with individual Ministers or groups of Ministers.

I said that I doubted whether this would be acceptable to any of the Ministers or whether they would stand it. In any case it seemed to me an unworkable and unsound arrangement and I could not be a party to it.

We then went backwards and forwards over the old ground—Bonar Law feebly sympathizing with my claim that the Chancellor ought to be included.

The Prime Minister repeated that he could not do this without including others, and again went through his list; to which Bonar Law retorted, " that means a Cabinet of fifteen—and that is impossible! "

At this point I again offered to leave them to discuss the matter together, saying that if they decided against me, my answer might be taken as a refusal. Once again we went over very much the same ground. At last I observed that I myself did not believe that the Prime Minister could limit his Cabinet to ten members. I saw no great objection to fifteen, and raised none to the inclusion of the other people whom he had named; but that if he was not prepared for this step, it seemed to me that it would be possible for him to say, without raising difficulties, that the Chancellor of the Exchequer would continue to be a member of the War Cabinet as the holder of that office always had been. In recent times (though I thought it a mistake) the Heads of the fighting services and Foreign Office had not been members of the War Cabinet. He would, therefore, not be bringing in a new official.

He and Bonar Law at once replied that Bonar Law had sat in the War Cabinet not as Chancellor of the Exchequer, but as leader of the party and leader of the House.

I replied that the public would not make that distinction; I thought that, if the Chancellor were not in the Cabinet, it would be considered that the office was being placed in a position of unprecedented inferiority, and I repeated that I could not accept it on those terms.

Bonar Law then made the suggestion that the *personnel* of the old War Cabinet should continue unaltered: that this would mean that I should be a member of the War Cabinet—though I should not be specifically appointed to it as Chancellor of the Exchequer: this arrangement to continue at any rate until the Prime Minister returned from France and was able to make his final dispositions.

"Well," asked the Prime Minister, "will you accept that?"

I said, "Yes—on its being clearly understood between us that if at any time you form a Cabinet—big or small—without including the Chancellor of the Exchequer, I shall resign, and that you will not have any cause of complaint on my doing so."

"Very well," said the Prime Minister, "then we will try that," and thereupon the interview ended.

This arrangement was maintained in theory at least for some ten months. Only in the late autumn was the Cabinet reformed on the pre-war model, but in fact the principal Ministers, whether nominally members of the Cabinet or not, habitually attended its meetings on all important occasions and took part in its discussions, but constitutionally they had no responsibility for them. I do not think the plan had anything to recommend it. It would have been far better to form a representative Cabinet at once.

It is curious, as I re-read the notes which I made at the time of this conversation, to reflect that the project of two Cabinets—one for Imperial and the other for Home Affairs—to which both Bonar Law and the Prime Minister seem to have inclined at this moment, was but a revival in a different form of the project for a War Committee and a Home Affairs Committee put forward by the other Unionist Ministers during the negotiations which preceded the fall of Asquith's Government, and then so vehemently opposed by both Bonar Law and Lloyd George. The whirligig of Time brings its revenges. Looking back, I am clear in my own mind that it was well for the country that it was rejected on both occasions.

But if this inversion of our respective rôles is curious, it is still stranger to find not only Lloyd George who, at that moment, had certainly some excuse for taking an exaggerated view of his position, but also a man generally so sober in judgment and so little inclined to exalt his own position as Bonar Law, actually proposing to govern without a Cabinet and only to summon to their councils as and when they pleased such other Ministers as they thought necessary.

The War had, indeed, come near to upsetting the Constitution when it could be proposed by the Leader of the Tory Party to place England under a Duumvirate.

IX

THE SIGNATURE OF THE IRISH TREATY

THE Irish Treaty is little more than a dozen years old. It was signed on December 5th, 1921. Yet of the men who signed it four have already passed away. Arthur Griffith, leader of the Irish Delegation, died within a few months, worn out by toil and suffering. Michael Collins was murdered during the troubles which followed upon the establishment of the Free State and the withdrawal of the British forces.

Birkenhead and Worthington-Evans lived some years longer, and passed away in peace, but they, too, died midway in their careers, leaving to their friends not only the memory of fine service faithfully performed, but lasting regret for the work they might still have done had their lives been spared to the allotted span.

Birkenhead played a vital part in the negotiation of the agreement, upon which I could never have entered without his aid. I well remember a morning soon after the first opening of communications with Mr. de Valera, when Birkenhead walked into my room in Downing Street just as I was telephoning to say that I must see him.

" You and I," he said, " bear a great load of responsibility. Unless we are agreed, we shall smash the party and destroy any chance of settlement. It is time we each knew exactly where the other stands."

And then he proceed to explain his views with that clarity and brevity which always distinguished him in council. I found that he had come to say to me what I had meant to say to him, and thenceforth we co-operated without a shade of difference throughout the long negotiations, the many conferences, and the parliamentary struggle which followed.

To the public Birkenhead sometimes showed himself cynical, flippant and violent. To his colleagues in any time of difficulty or crisis he was a tower of strength—the most loyal and unselfish of friends, careless for himself but careful for them; gay and light-hearted in moments of ease; serious, cool-headed and with nerves of steel in time of stress and danger. The very fact that life was to him a gallant adventure, to be as gallantly encountered, created a link between him and Michael Collins without which we might never have reached agreement.

Arthur Griffith and Michael Collins were the outstanding figures among the Irish Delegation. United in their passionate love of Ireland, in all else they were as different as two men can be—Griffith, small, quiet, drab, almost insignificant in appearance, with the air of a tired scholar worn out by too much burning of the midnight oil; Collins, tall of stature, with swaggering gait, loud voice and noisy laughter, a figure that seemed to belong to the open spaces and the rough life of frontier settlements or mining camps.

What exact part Collins played in the murderous outrages of those troubled times, I do not know. There had been a price set on his own head, and he would have met with short shrift had he fallen into the hands of those who sought his capture. He bore us no malice for it; to him it was the fortune of war.

He told with humour the story of his narrow escapes,

and at such moments was the spirit of Irish recklessness and fun.

. The fighting and its grim accompaniment of murder and arson were to him but incidents in the battle for freedom. He held the lives of his enemies as cheaply as he held his own.

He had his own code of honour, and to it he was true ; but it was not mine, and between him and me there could be no real sympathy, and perhaps only partial understanding. It was not the least of Birkenhead's services in the Conference that he did enter into Michael Collins's mind, won his sympathy and secured his confidence.

To Arthur Griffith all this bloodshed was abhorrent. There was nothing of the swashbuckler or corner-boy about him. He had been a student of history and politics, and—if I mistake not—at one time a college lecturer.

He had thought that he could find a model for the future relations of Ireland and Great Britain in some modification of the constitution of the Austro-Hungarian Empire, and had published a thoughtful book in which he examined this possibility. But the Great War had intervened, the union of Austria and Hungary had been dissolved, and he had in the main ceased to regard their former relationship as a suitable model on which to base the future Irish settlement.

Some new solution had to be worked out, and he was ready, and even eager, to consider calmly and dispassionately any scheme which, whilst recognizing the national status of Ireland and securing freedom from British interference in its internal affairs, would continue its association with the British Empire and give peace to its distracted people.

He had, I think, no hatred of England in his heart ; he was ready, as so few Irishmen are, to forget and, therefore, to forgive, and though he stood firmly by what he conceived to be the rights of Irish nationhood, he was broadminded enough to understand, and within those limits to endeavour to meet the British point of view.

Differing as the two men did in outward appearance, in their outlook on life, in their previous training and in the methods by which they pursued their ends, they were united in their devotion to their country's cause and in their desire for peace.

Collins, for all his spirit of recklessness and devil-may-care ways, was not without a sense of realities.

In the hard school of experience he had been forced to recognize that, whilst he could continue the fight and inflict infinite trouble and loss on England and her friends, there could be but one end to the struggle if England persisted: and that, even if wearied of so much bloodshed and of so thankless a task, she finally abandoned the struggle, Ireland's ruin would have been accomplished before that end was reached.

In the offer of the British Government, if sincerely meant and loyally pursued, they saw the opportunity to realize all that was essential in their aims and to save their native land from anarchy and destruction. Collins, no less than Griffith, desired peace.

Far different was that dark spirit who accompanied them and their colleagues as secretary of the Irish Delegation. Erskine Childers was the nephew of a Cabinet Minister,[1] who in Mr. Gladstone's Governments had been successively First Lord of the Admiralty, Chancellor of the Exchequer, and Secretary of State for War.

He had become known before the Great War as the author of that brilliant story, *The Riddle of the Sands,* and in the War itself he had fought gallantly in the British Air

---

[1] The Rt. Hon. Hugh Childers.

Force. Thereafter—exactly how or why I will not speculate
—he had thrown himself into the Sinn Fein cause, and, as
is apt to be the way with converts, his new faith burned
with the intensest flame. Here was no will for peace, no
desire for conciliation.

Erskine Childers's love for England had turned to
inextinguishable hate. Once again the old adage was
illustrated in his person; he had become more Irish than
the Irish themselves. I see him sitting with his back to the
window behind Arthur Griffith's chair, aloof and hostile.

Is it a mere trick of fancy that when I try to conjure up
his features, his face is always in shadow—as dark as the
thoughts behind it? He, too, met a tragic fate as a rebel
against the Free State which issued from the Conference.

This is no place to write the history of the Conference.
It dragged on for weeks; more than once it was on the
brink of disaster. Its first sitting was held on October 11th;
the end did not come till December 5th.

On that day we sat morning and afternoon and late into
the night. The Ulster Parliament was to meet the next
day, and Mr. Lloyd George, the Prime Minister, had
promised Sir James Craig, now Lord Craigavon, that he
should know the result of the Conference before the opening
of its session.

Yet we seemed as far from agreement as ever; indeed,
the prospect of any agreement seemed to have receded
since we last met. All the old questions were reopened; the
Irish delegates appeared to have gone back on the decisions
already reached. The Conference adjourned for lunch.

Once again the chance of settlement seemed likely to be
shipwrecked on the position of Ulster.

Time was passing. It was already evident that the
messenger to Sir James Craig would be unable to catch the

boat train, and special arrangements were made for his journey.

Then Mr. Lloyd George appealed to Arthur Griffith, reminding him that he had undertaken that, if we consented to such a provision for Ulster as we now offered to him, he would not let us down.

Griffith answered, simply, " I said I would not let you down on that, and I won't."

Again the discussion was resumed, and roamed over many points. At last the Prime Minister put the decisive question : Were they prepared to stand by the agreement as now drawn ?

Griffith replied that he was, but he still spoke only for himself.

That, said the Prime Minister, was not enough ; if we signed, we should sign as a delegation and stake the life of the Government on our signature. Was the Irish Delegation prepared to do the same ?

" I have to communicate with Sir James Craig to-night. Here are the alternative letters which I have prepared, one enclosing the Articles of Agreement reached by His Majesty's Government and yourselves, and the other saying that the Sinn Fein representatives refuse the oath of allegiance and refuse to come within the Empire.

" If I send this letter, it is war—and war within three days ! Which letter am I to send ? "

And he concluded with a passionate appeal to them to think again before they rejected so generous a settlement.

It was now nearly eight o'clock. The Conference adjourned to meet again at ten. It was 11.20 before the Irish delegates returned ; what struggles had passed within the Delegation during those hours we could only conjecture, but the atmosphere had changed.

Some explanations were asked and given; the meaning of some passages was made clearer.

The Prime Minister thereupon asked whether, if these changes were accepted by the British Government, the Irish representatives "would sign as a delegation and recommend the agreement with their united strength to the Dail."

This time Griffith replied, in the name of them all, that they would.

"Then," said the Prime Minister, "we accept."

When all had signed and copies of the document had been exchanged between the two parties, we moved down our side of the table as the Irish representatives rose to leave, and shook hands with them for the first time, expressing our hope that we might together have laid the foundation of a permanent understanding and lasting friendship between our two peoples.

A braver man than Arthur Griffith I have never met.

Here is a problem for the psychologist. The day had been one of unrelieved strain. The tension reached its height during the long wait for the return of the Irish delegates in the evening. Peace or war—the issue still hung in the balance.

But there is a limit to human endurance; the reaction came. I recall that as we waited, our talk was of the merriest, and the room rang with laughter.

X

THE TREATY OF LOCARNO
BRITAIN'S GUARANTEE

THE people of this country are being invited in certain quarters to repudiate the Treaty of Locarno. The invitation is addressed to them in the name of Peace: Locarno, it is said, places the direction of British policy in the hands of France and our army and navy at the service of French policy.

It involves us—so the argument goes—in quarrels in which Britain has no conceivable interest, and exposes us to dangers from which, but for this unhappy entanglement, we should be completely immune.

The integrity of France or Belgium, it is urged, is no concern of ours; we are not interested in the existence of the demilitarized zone; we will not stir a finger to save the Polish Corridor. These are not British interests, yet for each and all of these the Treaty of Locarno would oblige us to fight. Thus our new Mentor in article and speech.

Before examining these assertions, it may be well to recall briefly the circumstances which gave rise to the series of treaties negotiated at Locarno in October 1925, and signed two months later in London, after being submitted to and approved by the Parliaments of all the countries concerned in them.

When the representatives of the Allied and Associated Powers met in Paris at the conclusion of the War to draw up the terms of peace, France, which had been twice invaded within the lifetime of them all, one-third of whose territory had been occupied and devastated by the enemy, and whose manhood had been decimated in the struggle, demanded the left bank of the Rhine as security for the future.

The representatives of Britain and America, determined not to create a new " Alsace-Lorraine," rejected this demand, but after prolonged negotiation offered France a treaty of guarantee as the price of her relinquishing it. The British Parliament approved the guarantee, but made their acceptance of it dependent on the approval of the United States. The American Congress refused its approval, and the guarantee therefore failed.

France, which had abandoned one form of security on promise of another, found herself without either. She was thrown back on such support as she could secure elsewhere.

Her Treaties of Alliance with Poland and Czecho-slovakia were the immediate result.

There followed four years of irritating and embittering friction between the Allies and Germany. The Peace Treaties were signed, but peace found no place in the minds and hearts of men or in the policy of States. Some of the conditions imposed by the victors on the vanquished were inexecutable and remained unexecuted.

Knowing that they could not discharge their liabilities in full, and fearing that anything they did would be construed only as evidence that they could do more, the Germans made no real effort to satisfy even the reasonable demands of the Allies. Refusal was followed by sanctions, sanctions by further resistance, and that resistance by still heavier sanctions.

Peace rested, not on good will or assent, but solely on the incapacity of the vanquished to renew the struggle.

Some day the wheel of fotune would turn. It would be possible for Germany to find an ally, and on that day, embittered by suffering, provoked by constant interference, seeing no other hope, however desperate the throw, she would stake all on a new gamble, and Europe would be faced with another and yet more appalling Armageddon.

This was the prospect which faced Mr. Baldwin's second Administration when it took office in 1924, but it is not to be supposed that there had been no previous effort to avert it.

In the endeavour to allay the fears and suspicions which were poisoning international relations and deflecting national policies, Mr. Lloyd George had reverted in 1922 to the idea of a treaty of guarantee, but in the then prevailing relations of France and England the idea was still-born. Next year the Assembly of the League of Nations elaborated a Treaty of Mutual Assistance in the framing of which Lord Cecil took a great part.

Lord Cecil, I think, at that moment represented the Government of the Union of South Africa presided over by General Smuts, but at Geneva he was generally regarded as expressing the mind of Great Britain.

Nevertheless, that Treaty was rejected by the Labour Government, which had succeeded Mr. Baldwin's, on the double ground that it would not, in fact, produce security, and that its acceptance would impose intolerable burdens on this country. The Dominion Governments equally rejected it.

In view of this rejection, the Assembly of 1924 set to work to devise a new scheme which might give the sense of security that was the necessary preliminary to any measure of disarmament by States which felt themselves threatened.

This time the " gaps " in the Covenant were to be filled

up; the aggressor was to be defined; every possible contingency was to be foreseen and provided for in advance and the obligations of the signatories were to be exactly stated. When the emergency arose, a majority of the Council would determine for every country what action it was its duty to take.

> " Theirs not to reason why;
> Theirs but to do or die."

The rest would follow automatically.

These proposals were embodied in a Protocol for the Pacific Settlement of International Disputes, usually referred to as the Protocol of Geneva. It was approved by the Assembly, at which the United Kingdom was represented by Mr. Henderson and Lord Parmoor, but before it could be considered by the Labour Government that Government was defeated and replaced by Mr. Baldwin's second Administration.

It fell, therefore, to Mr. Baldwin and his colleagues to determine the attitude of this country towards it, and in so doing to decide its fate; for it was recognized on all hands that the Protocol could not survive refusal by this country to assume the obligations and undertake the liabilities which it would have imposed upon us. Without the British Navy the Protocol was useless to those who had devised it.

The Protocol met immediately with a very critical reception in the Dominions. It was felt in some that it menaced their Sovereign rights, in all that it imposed excessive liabilities and exposed them to unnecessary dangers.

His Majesty's Government in this country shared these objections, and in the following March gave expression to them in a carefully considered declaration to the Council of the League.

"The Protocol," they said, "purports to be little more than a completion of the work begun, but not perfected, by the authors of the covenant. But surely this is a very inadequate description of its effects. The additions which it makes to the original document do something quite different from merely clarifying obscurities and filling in omissions. They destroy its balance and alter its spirit.

"The fresh emphasis laid upon sanctions, the new occasions discovered for their employment, the elaboration of military procedure, insensibly suggest the idea that the vital business of the League is not so much to promote friendly co-operation and reasoned harmony in the management of international affairs as to preserve peace by organising war, and (it may be) war on the largest scale.

"It certainly seems to His Majesty's Government that anything which fosters the idea that the main business of the League is with war rather than with peace is likely to weaken it in its fundamental task of diminishing the causes of war without making it in every respect a satisfactory instrument for organizing great military operations should the necessity for them be forced upon the world."

For these and other reasons, therefore, the Government of the United Kingdom, in full agreement with the Governments of the Dominions, declared their inability to accept the Protocol. Was no other course open to them? A mere negative, without the suggestion of any alternative, would have been disastrous.

Germany had not complied with the disarmament conditions of the Treaty of Versailles, and France was determined not to evacuate the occupied territory unless some other form of security was assured to her. As soon as it became known that the decision of Great Britain on the Protocol was likely to be unfavourable, a new wave of unrest spread over Europe, and the situation, already threatening enough, became even more menacing.

It appeared to His Majesty's Government, examining the situation, that:

" the brooding fears that keep huge armaments in being have little relation to the ordinary misunderstandings inseparable from international (as from social) life—misunderstandings with which the League is so admirably fitted to deal. They spring from deep-lying causes of hostility which for historic or other reasons divide great and powerful States. . . .

" What is feared is not injustice but war—war deliberately undertaken for conquest and revenge. And if so, can there be a better way of allaying fears like these than by adopting some scheme which should prove to all the world that such a war would fail? "

Rejecting, therefore, the Protocol, with its universal application and its incalculable liabilities on the one hand, and feeling on the other that it was equally impossible after all that had passed, to revert to the ideas of 1919 and 1922 and to revive the project of an alliance with France and Belgium directed against Germany, the British Government determined to try what could be made of a suggestion which had reached them from Germany whilst they were engaged in their consideration of the Protocol. In this they thought they detected the basis of a possible agreement, uniting Britain, France, Germany and Belgium in a common determination to maintain the peace of the West.

Their decision was announced in the following words :

" Since the general provisions of the Covenant cannot be stiffened with advantage, and since the ' extreme cases ' with which the League may have to deal will probably affect certain nations or groups of nations more nearly than others, His Majesty's Government conclude that the best way of dealing with the situation is, with the co-operation of the League, to supplement the Covenant by making special arrangements in order to meet special needs.

"That these arrangements should be purely defensive in character, that they should be framed in the spirit of the Covenant, working in close harmony with the League and under its guidance, is manifest.

"And, in the opinion of His Majesty's Government, these objects can best be attained by knitting together the nations most immediately concerned, and whose differences might lead to a renewal of strife, by means of treaties framed with the sole object of maintaining, as between themselves, an unbroken peace. Within its limits no quicker remedy for our present ills can easily be found nor any surer safeguard against future calamities."

More than once in the years preceding the Locarno Conference the rulers of Germany had suggested the possibility of a mutual pact for the preservation of peace. The first of these suggestions had been made by Dr. Cuno, then Chancellor of the Reich, in December 1922.

To relieve the fears which impeded the evacuation of the occupied territory, Dr. Cuno suggested that "Germany and France, in common with the other Powers interested on the Rhine, should enter into a mutual pledge, of which a Power not interested on the Rhine should be trustee" (the United States was intended), "not to wage any war against one another for a generation" (that is, for twice the length of the period of occupation envisaged in the Treaty of Versailles) "without a plebiscite."

The proposal was obviously inadequate in point of time and security, and, as importing the guarantee of the United States, unrealizable.

A similar, though different, offer was made by the German Government in May 1923, but it was again coupled with conditions unacceptable to the Allies and was refused by them.

Four months later, Dr. Stresemann, who had become Chancellor, made a further suggestion for a bilateral pact between the Great Powers interested on the Rhine, for a mutual guarantee of existing frontiers, but the proposal was curtly rejected by M. Poincaré.

In January 1924, Dr. Stresemann, who in the interval had ceased to be Chancellor but continued to hold the portfolio of Foreign Affairs, determined, in conjunction with the new Chancellor, Dr. Luther, to renew the attempt.

He was moved, as we know from his own papers, by three main considerations :

i. He feared that the new British Government might be contemplating a treaty of alliance with France and Belgium directed against Germany ;

ii. He had become convinced, largely by the arguments of Lord D'Abernon, the very able representative of this country in Berlin, that to attempt the reconquest of Alsace-Lorraine would be a hopeless task, and that in the question of security lay the only key to any possible solution of the recurring troubles with France ; and

iii. He dreaded a new occupation of the Ruhr and further coercive measures in default of agreement.

His first proposals were made to the British Government, but on their insistence were a few days later communicated to M. Herriot, at that time President of the Council and Foreign Minister.

The communication made by the German Government was to the effect that Germany desired a peaceful understanding with France.

She was prepared to negotiate a comprehensive arbitration

treaty and to enter into a mutual pact of guarantee with the powers interested on the Rhine. Similar arbitration treaties might be concluded with the other States which had common frontiers with Germany.

Further, a pact expressly guaranteeing the existing territorial status on the Rhine would be acceptable to Germany, and this pact might, in addition, guarantee the observance of the articles of the Treaty of Versailles, which established a demilitarized zone on the right bank of the Rhine.

I summarized the effect of these proposals in a passage which, to guard against all possibility of misunderstanding, was immediately communicated to the German Government. These proposals, I said, amount to this:

"That Germany is prepared to guarantee voluntarily what hitherto she has accepted under the compulsion of the Treaty, that is, the *status quo* in the West; that she is prepared to eliminate, not merely from the West, but from the East, war as an engine by which any alteration in the Treaty position is to be obtained.

"Thus not only in the West, but in the East, she is prepared absolutely to abandon any idea of recourse to war for the purpose of changing the Treaty boundaries of Europe, though she may be unwilling, or unable, to make the same renunciation of the hopes and aspirations that some day, by friendly arrangement or mutual agreement, a modification may be introduced into the East, as she is prepared to make in regard to any modification in the West."

It was in these proposals, if properly developed, that the British Government saw the necessary alternative to the Protocol.

The guarantee, which they were not prepared to extend to every country and every frontier, might properly be given in respect of a part of the world close to their own shores, which had been the cause and the scene of all our greatest struggles.

For a purpose so limited and in a sphere so circumscribed, Great Britain might rightly, and as a measure of self-defence, undertake a responsibility which would be intolerable and inexecutable if extended to the whole world. The German proposals went far beyond anything which they had previously suggested. But it was certain that they would be as barren of result as their earlier suggestions unless Great Britain was prepared to give her guarantee for the observance of the pact in the West. His Majesty's Government decided to offer that guarantee.

Could any British Government have taken the responsibility of refusing it? Such a refusal would have plunged Europe into chaos and made war certain sooner or later— and sooner rather than later.

In the months which followed, every effort was made to reach a settlement of the outstanding questions relating to the police and disarmament, and to prepare the way for a meeting of the representatives of the interested Powers. A first draft of the Treaty of Guarantee was prepared in the Foreign Office and, after being discussed with the French and approved by the Cabinet, was communicated to the Germans, so that their representatives might come to the Conference in full knowledge of the proposals which would be made to them.

The Conference itself met at Locarno in October 1925. Thanks to this careful preparation, its object was achieved in a little less than a fortnight. It was attended by the representatives of seven Powers—Germany, Great Britain, France, Belgium and Italy (at first taking part only as an observer, but presently announcing her adhesion to the Guarantee Treaty), and later Poland and Czechoslovakia.

nference was embodied in eight
f them, the Treaty of Locarno
in a party.

ual Guarantee between Germany,
itain and Italy. By it Germany
and France respectively covenant
nst each other, and to settle all
peaceful means. Also the five
ely and severally, guarantee the
l *status quo* resulting from the
and her two Western neigh-
f Versailles, and the observance
n for the demilitarized zone

cision as to whether the *casus*
to the Council of the League
on to this rule is the case of
violation of the stipulations
, if the guaranteeing Power
on is an act of unprovoked
her of the crossing of the
ies, or the assembly of
ction is necessary."

come at once to the
e ultimate decision
hich will be im-
to conform to

e time com-
rmany and
ermine the
s provided
Treaties

between Germany and Poland a
slovakia for the similar regulati
them by peaceful methods.

Finally, there are two treaties
and France and Czechoslovaki
guarantee to one another the
undertakings reached between
but the aid which each promise
with Articles XV and XVI o
to the case of unprovoked atta

This is a restriction of the
earlier treaties of alliance betw
the claim of either for assist
of unprovoked aggression so
with the guarantees given in
of the Covenant.

With the last-named trea
concern. They impose no
to no liability. They str
structure of Europe, but w
affect us only as signatori
the peace of the world
case of the Treaty
the guaranteeing P
the Council of th
the case of a fl
satisfy themsel
of hostility, a
immediate a

The obli
or more
taining p
employe

Daily Telegraph, a safety-curtain between Germany and her Western neighbours.

The Treaties initialled *ne varietur* at Locarno on October 16th, 1925, were signed in London on December 1st of the same year. In the interval they had been submitted to and approved by the Parliaments of all the countries concerned in them.

In the British House of Commons the Treaty of Guarantee met with general approval—only thirteen members were found to vote against it—and when the Imperial Conference met the next year, the assembled representatives of the Empire gave their blessing to it in the following resolution :

" The Conference has heard with satisfaction the statement of the Secretary of State for Foreign Affairs with regard to the efforts made to ensure peace in Europe, culminating in the agreements of Locarno; and congratulates His Majesty's Government in Great Britain on this successful contribution to the promotion of the peace of the world."

The conclusion of these treaties, in the negotiation of which this country had taken a leading part, undoubtedly enhanced British influence, but it did much more than this; it produced an immediate *détente* in international relations.

For the first time since the War Germany had been admitted to a conference with the former Allies on a basis of perfect equality, and the result had been agreement and the birth of a new spirit in their mutual relations.

At Locarno there had been no question of a dictated peace, imposed by overwhelming force and accepted under compulsion. Germany had voluntarily renounced all desire for the reconquest of Alsace-Lorraine, and of her own free will had guaranteed the inviolability of the frontiers of the

West and as freely accepted the establishment of the demilitarized zone.

What had once been dictated by the will of the conquerors had now been confirmed by treaties which owed their existence to a German initiative, and were the result of free and friendly discussion. As an earnest of the new spirit, the evacuation of the Cologne zone was begun on the day on which the treaties were signed and was rapidly completed, whilst large alleviations were introduced into the conditions prevailing in the two zones in which the occupation still continued.

But this was not all. If the Western treaties had stood alone, their conclusion might have increased the sense of insecurity in Eastern Europe.

It would have been unreasonable to expect Germany to renounce all desire for change in her Eastern frontiers, as fixed by the Treaty of Versailles—as unreasonable as it would have been, say, in 1875 to expect France to renounce all hope that she might one day recover her lost provinces. No such demand was therefore made, but Germany undertook never to attempt that alteration by force of arms, and to resolve all differences with her Eastern neighbours by peaceful means.

Again, the first suggestion of such agreements had come from Germany, and the treaties themselves were freely negotiated by her representatives and approved by her Parliament. To the Eastern Treaties Great Britain, as I have said, was not a party; they impose no obligation on her. Her guarantee was confined to the West, but her influence was used to secure their conclusion as an additional guarantee for the peace of the world.

We are now told that all this was a mistake, that Government and Parliament were alike wrong, and that the Treaty of Locarno, on which they received the congratulations of the Imperial Conference, will, if maintained, destroy the Empire.

What concern have we, it is asked, with the Continent of Europe, what interest in the frontiers of France and Belgium? What business is it of ours whether there is peace or war in Europe? Let other nations stew in their own juice and let us revert to a " splendid isolation."

It might be sufficient to reply that we have signed the Covenant of the League, and cannot divest ourselves of the responsibilities it imposes; that the Dominions and India share those responsibilities, for they, too, are members of the League, and that they have throughout shown, and continue to affirm, their attachment to the League.

It might be recalled (for memories are short) that the signal for the Great War was given by the murder of the Archduke at Serajevo, and that remote from our shores as the origin of the conflagration was, it spread like a prairie fire after a summer drought, and quickly involved not only these islands and the Empire, but even the United States.

It is true that we have no direct interest in the Polish Corridor or Upper Silesia, and certainly we are not called upon to assume any particular responsibility in regard to them. But who can predict with confidence that if they gave rise to conflict, we should remain entirely unaffected, and that the experience of 1914 might not be repeated?

It is a truism of politics that Peace is a British interest— almost the greatest of British interests. Since that is so, we do right to use our influence to maintain it, though it is no part of our duty to make ourselves in every case its guarantors.

Our concern with the West is far more direct. There have been many fluctuations in British foreign policy, perhaps many inconsistencies, but through all our long history from the time of the Spanish Armada to the present day there has been one principle to which we have persistently clung. Separated as these islands are from the western shores of the Continent only by the narrow waters of the English Channel and the North Sea, it has been a cardinal principle of British policy in all times, and under all governments, that we could not allow the Low Countries to be dominated by the greatest military Power of the day.

For this cause we fought Spain under Philip II and France under Louis XIV and Napoleon. It was the invasion of Belgium which united this country in the early days of August 1914, and finally determined our intervention in the Great War. From first to last the independence of the Low Countries has been recognized as a British interest, for, in truth, their frontier is our frontier, and the destruction of their independence would be a fatal blow at our own.

The lesson which we learned in the days when sea power was a secure defence is doubly impressed on us when aviation has annihilated space and bridged the waters. Our safety lies not in abstention till war has broken out but in throwing our weight beforehand into the scale of peace.

It may well be—German as well as French authorities assert it—that if the German Government had known in time that this country would join in repelling any attack on France or Belgium, the Great War would never have been begun.

Germany, though at present disarmed, is still potentially the greatest military Power on the Continent. It is from that quarter, and that quarter alone, that danger has menaced us since 1870, or might menace us again.

The fate of Belgium is inextricably bound up with that of France, our safety with both. All must be in danger if war should again break out in Western Europe.

Is it not better to recognize the danger in time and guard against its occurrence, rather than sit idly by until the world is again in flames?

Of one thing we may be sure. There could be no more perilous policy than to declare that we were henceforth indifferent to events in Europe. The British Empire covers a vast area of the globe. Its growth has been watched not without envy by other nations; it offers splendid pickings for the hungry. The one thing which might make possible Napoleon's dream of a Europe combined against us—a dream which haunted also the Kaiser's imagination, as his notes show—is that we should announce our intention to take no further interest in the affairs of the Continent.

In such a case other nations might see their only chance of salvation in union, and we might well awake to find that we had to pay the costs of their feast of harmony. In truth, our choice is not between participation and isolation, but between helping to shape events and becoming their victim.

It is objected that by the Treaty of Locarno we obtained no guarantee for the United Kingdom in return for the guarantee which we gave to France, Belgium and Germany —or, in other words, that we took additional risks without gaining any additional security. It is true that we neither sought nor obtained any reciprocal guarantee; it is not true that we gained no additional security.

As long as the existing territorial settlement of Western Europe is maintained these islands are in no danger. Our peril would arise only if that settlement were upset, but then it would arise immediately. We made by the Treaty of Locarno a great and significant contribution to the peace of the world, but in making that contribution I have never pretended that our motives were purely altruistic and that we took no thought for ourselves. On the contrary, it was because the peace and security of these islands and their immunity from attack are closely bound up with the independence and integrity of the Low Countries and France that we felt justified in giving in that sphere alone a guarantee which we refused to make general. In guaranteeing those frontiers we insured our own.

There remain two specific allegations to which it may be worth while to give the answer.

First, it has been alleged that the Treaty of Locarno, though it does not guarantee the maintenance of peace between Germany and Poland, does indirectly commit us to war if war breaks out between those two nations.

The argument, as I understand it, is as follows : If war breaks out between Germany and Poland, France is bound by her alliance to support Poland and will attack Germany in the West. In that case the Treaty of Locarno obliges us to go to the assistance of Germany to repel the French attack.

If this be the argument it rests on a double fallacy, for if Poland makes an unprovoked attack on Germany the Franco-Polish Alliance, as modified at Locarno, absolves France from any obligation to go to her aid. If, on the other hand, Germany wantonly attacks Poland, in defiance of her pledges at Locarno and of her signature of the Kellogg Pact, no sane man will suggest that the action of France in going to the assistance of Poland is an act of unprovoked aggression such as alone brings our guarantee of the western frontiers into operation.

This is not an allegation that can be sustained by reference to the Treaties.

The second allegation is of a different character. The attack on the Treaty of Locarno began with a demand for its denunciation; in other words, for the repudiation of the pledge contained in it. But those who engineered the attack have now discovered that the word repudiation does not sound well in English ears, and that a policy of repudiation will never be accepted by their countrymen.

So they have changed their ground, "The Treaty," they now say, "is already null and void for want of performance."

The object of the Treaty, they argue, was to procure the disarmament of France. France has not disarmed. Germany and Great Britain were deceived. The consideration in return for which the British guarantee was given has not been paid. "The Treaty of Locarno cannot be repudiated because it no longer exists."

Again the argument will not bear examination. The object of the Treaty was to preserve peace, not to secure disarmament, and, whether disarmament be secured or not, the preservation of peace is as much a British interest to-day as it was eight years ago.

Further, disarmament was not a condition of the Treaty, and no deception was practised on the Germans in this respect.

It is true that the representatives of the seven Powers who met at Locarno felt and expressed the firm conviction that the conclusion of the Treaties would hasten disarmament, as it would facilitate the realization of other German aspirations, notably, the evacuation of the occupied territory; and in fact the evacuation was completed in the first half of 1930, five years in advance of the Treaty date.

Disarmament has proved more difficult of achievement, but it is too early to assume that the attempt has failed. Indeed, the prospects of the Conference seemed more hopeful than ever before at the very moment which Germany chose for her withdrawal. But whatever the result, neither evacuation nor disarmament were conditions of Locarno, and the representatives of the Allies expressly refused to give any pledge about them, even going so far as to warn the Germans that they regarded the German claims to equality in armaments as unreasonable, just as they warned them that no German claim for the return of the colonies could be entertained.

The Treaty of Locarno remains, therefore, in full vigour, and the attack upon it has so far resulted only in the emphatic reaffirmation of the loyalty of this country to its pledged word. It is well that it is so, for Locarno is still the safety-curtain of Europe. To cast doubt upon its maintenance would be to encourage hopes and ambitions which can never be realized except by war; and if such a war breaks out in such a cause, those who think that we shall be able to remain idle spectators of the contest, indifferent to its issue, have either never read English history or never learned its plainest lesson.

One word in conclusion. The purpose of the Treaty of Locarno was to preserve peace and to promote reconciliation. It was not aimed at Germany any more than at France or Belgium. The guarantee given to France and Belgium was given in the same terms to Germany.

The enemy, if enemy there should arise, was not this country or that, but the aggressor—the nation which should break its pledges and make an unprovoked attack upon its neighbour.

I first me
in October
sometimes
it possible
whom we
was lunchi
from Lonc
asked, and
should go ;
You will n
impression
of the Con
degrees tha
to apprecia
The cir
peculiar ar
He had n
mutual gu
similar pro
Cuno to
municated
of France,
at first rai
more acro
to be mer
a wedge
Governme
serious con
ment that
guarantee
ratified A
country a
long mon

There is in my mind no thought of hostility or ill will to Germany. There is, I admit, serious anxiety as to the trend of policy of the present German Government, and the effect of their daily propaganda on their people.

Against this we set Chancellor Hitler's repeated declaration that he earnestly desires peace. Can he not reassure the world by deeds as well as in words?

work which had to be done—had convinced us of Dr. Stresemann's sincerity, and had evolved from his first sketch a practical scheme (already communicated through their legal adviser to the German Government) which was probably more definite and more far-reaching than Dr. Stresemann had contemplated.

But German opinion was highly suspicious; the public had not yet grasped the meaning or possibilities of the new orientation which Stresemann desired to give to German policy, and, apart from all the bitter feelings remaining from the War and the quite-recent Ruhr occupation, was perhaps as much afraid of Western " entanglements " as any American has even been of becoming involved in European alliances. The Chancellor (Dr. Luther) and Dr. Stresemann left Berlin amidst extraordinary police precautions. They came to Locarno knowing that the successful issue of their Locarno negotiations would only be the beginning of a long and difficult domestic campaign.

In these circumstances it is not surprising that at the outset they were exceedingly susceptible and prone to suspicion. I had done my best to make it clear that on this occasion we met not as victors and vanquished but as equals. With the memory of the rather humiliating conditions of previous Conferences as fresh in my own mind as I knew it must be in theirs, I had sought to secure for our Conference room a round table where there should be neither top nor bottom. One of sufficient size was not available, but failing this a square table had been procured with no sign to differentiate one place from another.

Nevertheless, even before the Conference met difficulties arose. I reached Locarno about midday on the Sunday preceding the opening of the Conference. The French, Belgian and Italian delegations were established in the same

There is in my mind no thought of hostility or ill will to Germany. There is, I admit, serious anxiety as to the trend of policy of the present German Government, and the effect of their daily propaganda on their people.

Against this we set Chancellor Hitler's repeated declaration that he earnestly desires peace. Can he not reassure the world by deeds as well as in words?

XI

GUSTAV STRESEMANN

WHEN the remains of Gustav Stresemann were laid to rest amidst the mourning of the people whom he had served so well, his patriotic labours were sincerely and rightly acclaimed. Even more remarkable was the universal recognition outside Germany that in him passed away the greatest German since Bismarck. Called to power at a moment of almost indescribable calamity for his country, his death found her restored to the comity of nations, one of the most influential and respected members of the League and with the date fixed when the last occupying forces would leave her territory. We may well pay our tribute of profound respect to the great qualities of foresight, insight, courage, loyalty and patience by which so much was achieved.

I was lunching on the yacht of a friend in Barcelona Harbour when Reuter's representative sent in his card with the request for my comment on Dr. Stresemann's death.[1] The news came upon me like a thunder-clap, for though no one who had seen him during the previous two years could fail to recognize that he was a very sick man, I had had no warning of any special danger. To the sense of the tragedy which had thus befallen his country and Europe there was added my personal sorrow at the death of a man for whom, in the converse of recent years, I had come to feel not only a profound admiration but a sincere personal affection.

[1] Oct. 3rd, 1929.

I first met Dr. Stresemann at the Conference of Locarno in October 1925. Nine months of slow, laborious and sometimes exasperating negotiations had at length made it possible for this meeting to take place between those of whom we still spoke as Allies and their former enemy. I was lunching with Asquith a little before my departure from London. "Do you know Dr. Stresemann?" he asked, and on my replying in the negative, he added, "you should go and see John's portrait of him—a proper *junker*! You will not have an easy time." This, too, was my own impression when I first met him face to face at the opening of the Conference on a Monday morning. It was only by degrees that I learned fully to know him and, in knowing, to appreciate him.

The circumstances of the Locarno Conference were peculiar and his position one of extraordinary difficulty. He had made his first tentative proposal for a pact of mutual guarantee in the previous January. A somewhat similar proposal had been suggested earlier by Chancellor Cuno to the American Government, who had communicated it to Monsieur Poincaré, then Prime Minister of France, but nothing had come of it. The new proposal at first raised some suspicion in Great Britain, and even more across the Channel. It was thought in some quarters to be merely a skilful diplomatic move intended to drive a wedge between our two countries. But the British Government felt at once that it demanded their most serious consideration, and represented to the French Government that it was on these lines, and on these only, that the guarantee of French territory originally offered in the non-ratified Anglo-American treaty could be renewed by this country after all that had occurred in the interval. The long months of negotiation—not too long for the important work which had to be done—had convinced us of Dr. Stresemann's sincerity, and had evolved from his first sketch a practical scheme (already communicated through their legal adviser to the German Government) which was probably more definite and more far-reaching than Dr. Stresemann had contemplated.

But German opinion was highly suspicious; the public had not yet grasped the meaning or possibilities of the new orientation which Stresemann desired to give to German policy, and, apart from all the bitter feelings remaining from the War and the quite-recent Ruhr occupation, was perhaps as much afraid of Western "entanglements" as any American has even been of becoming involved in European alliances. The Chancellor (Dr. Luther) and Dr. Stresemann left Berlin amidst extraordinary police precautions. They came to Locarno knowing that the successful issue of their Locarno negotiations would only be the beginning of a long and difficult domestic campaign.

In these circumstances it is not surprising that at the outset they were exceedingly susceptible and prone to suspicion. I had done my best to make it clear that on this occasion we met not as victors and vanquished but as equals. With the memory of the rather humiliating conditions of previous Conferences as fresh in my own mind as I knew it must be in theirs, I had sought to secure for our Conference room a round table where there should be neither top nor bottom. One of sufficient size was not available, but failing this a square table had been procured with no sign to differentiate one place from another.

Nevertheless, even before the Conference met difficulties arose. I reached Locarno about midday on the Sunday preceding the opening of the Conference. The French, Belgian and Italian delegations were established in the same hotel, and the Germans had already taken up their quarters in another. My first step was to leave cards upon them, a civility which I believe had not been paid at any of the previous Conferences. In the course of the afternoon Monsieur Briand called upon me to discuss the arrangements for the morrow and to ask me, at the desire of the Italians and the Belgians, as well as himself, to preside at the Conference. I accepted on the condition that the Germans joined in the invitation, but this, after some hesitation, they felt unable to do. In the state of German public opinion, they considered it impossible to accept a permanent President chosen from the Allies, and, whilst willing that I should preside on the first day at the request of the Allies, they demanded that the presidency should be held by each Power in turn. I refused this suggestion as unpractical and ridiculous, and not without some difficulty it was arranged that they should join in the invitation to me to preside on the first day, and that when we had settled our procedure I should declare that all was now so simple that in future we could dispense with a chairman!

Even to the last moment these difficulties persisted. The last differences had been settled, the initialling of the Treaties had been fixed for the morrow, when I received a message that the Chancellor and Dr. Stresemann wished to see me at six o'clock, and begged that I would summon Monsieur Briand to a meeting in my room at that hour. We met, and for four hours we travelled over again an oft-repeated discussion. We could advance no further, we had made our ultimate concessions. Reparations and evacuation were not on the programme of the Conference. These subjects must be left to time and the new spirit which we hoped that the Treaties of Locarno would create.

At ten o'clock we broke up, exhausted by the last-

minute revival of painful and difficult discussions when we
had supposed that final agreement had been reached. Only
much later did Stresemann reveal the secret: the Chancellor had received a telegram from certain of their colleagues
in Berlin forbidding the two Ministers to initial anything
till they had discussed the draft with the German Cabinet.
To have obeyed this injunction would have destroyed all
chance of success; to part without agreement would have
made agreement in future still more difficult. "When the
Chancellor read the telegram," said Stresemann later, "he
buried his face in his hands. For two minutes he sat silent;
then suddenly raising his head, 'Tell them to go to Jericho!'
he said. 'I initial all the same.'"

In pursuance of the arrangement we had reached, when
the Conference met for the first time I seated myself beside
the Syndic, and the other delegations found their places at
the table naturally and without difficulty. Except for the
speech of welcome by the Syndic and the brief answer
which I made on behalf of the Conference, no speeches
were made, and we proceeded at once to read a first time
the draft upon which the British and Allied Governments
had agreed as modified by our jurists in consultation with
the legal adviser of the German Government during a visit
which he had paid to London at our invitation.

The simplicity and business-like character of this opening,
together with the long and careful preparation, laid the
basis for the success of the Conference. Chancellor Luther,
speaking fluent French, contributed not a little to our
understanding of one another, but the brunt of the German
case fell upon Dr. Stresemann. None of those who were
present will ever forget the lofty character of the debates
conducted between him and Monsieur Briand. The
conversational tone which was carefully preserved in the

discussions detracted nothing from the weight or power of their arguments. The courage, the resource, the tact, and the consideration shown by these two representatives of two powerful nations seeking to put an end to their secular animosities raised the discussion to the highest level of practical eloquence and moved the hearts of all who listened.

I cannot here trace the progress of the Conference from day to day or tell the story of Monsieur Briand's party of pleasure on the lake in the little steamer named *The Orange Blossom*, to celebrate my wife's birthday, during which we surmounted our greatest difficulties. But I must recall the final scene when the various treaties had been initialled and Stresemann made his last appeal. The German representatives, he said, had initialled with a full sense of their responsibility, intended to make this treaty their own, determined to stand or fall by it, and on their return to Germany to use their utmost endeavour to secure its acceptance by the German people. And then in tones of deep emotion which moved us all, he added that in so doing they acted in the confidence that from this treaty we should develop its natural and logical consequences in the political and economic spheres.

Not less moving was the response of Monsieur Briand. He said that he, too, had initialled with a full sense of his responsibility and, he could add, with the certainty that he spoke the mind of the French Government and the great mass of the French people; and then with a grateful acknowledgment of Dr. Stresemann's restraint, he added that now, his mandate exhausted, and speaking only for himself, but still confident that he represented the opinion of the great mass of the French people, if this were to be the end and no further consequences were to follow he would have thought it dishonest to embark on the negotiations at all, and he pledged himself to do his utmost to realize those unspoken aspirations which he was grateful to Dr. Stresemann for not expressing but which he knew lay nearest to his heart.

A few more moments and we had parted, but not before the Chancellor and Monsieur Briand had appeared at the window before the great crowd now assembled in front of the Court House and had shaken hands before the people in token of the new relations established between their countries.

To those of us who were Stresemann's associates in this first hour, it came as some consolation in our sorrow for his death that he lived long enough to gather the fruits of his far-sighted policy and to fix the date for the total evacuation of German territory. When the secret history of the conference at The Hague comes to be written, it will not be surprising if it be found that his was the hand which finally averted disaster. It is a comfort to us that he who took such risks and showed such courage lived to see his purpose accomplished, and was mourned by his own people as one whose immense services to the Fatherland were recognized, and who was respected by other nations as a great statesman, a loyal partner and a true friend of peace.

By his death a great German patriot passed to his rest.

XII

ARISTIDE BRIAND

SINCE the death of Gustav Stresemann the world has suffered no loss comparable to the passing of Aristide Briand.[1] He had witnessed the horrors of the War, and the cries of the widowed and the fatherless had struck deep into his soul. Peace had become with him a veritable passion; he was indomitable in its pursuit, and his presence at the Quai d'Orsay was a guarantee that the policy of France would be peaceful. "There will be no war while I remain Minister." That pledge he gave to the world; how faithfully he kept it all men can bear witness.

My first meeting with Briand after I became Secretary of State for Foreign Affairs was at the Council of the League of Nations held in Rome in December 1924. I set myself at once to win his confidence, and through him to regain for my country the confidence and sympathy of France, for I was profoundly convinced then, as I still am, that it is only by the maintenance of this mutual confidence and by close co-operation between our two nations that the rehabilitation of Germany and the restoration of Europe can be achieved.

The occupation of the Ruhr had followed on our differences; the evacuation, first of Cologne, and then of the whole Rhineland five years in advance of the Treaty date were the fruits of our agreement. Briand shared my point of view and was quick to respond to my advances.

Next year he became President of the Council of Ministers

[1] March 7th, 1932.

179

and Foreign Minister of France. Thereafter our co-operation was constant as long as I remained Foreign Secretary, and our friendship ripened into a close and affectionate intimacy. We had tried one another out in long and exhausting negotiations, and each had complete confidence in the good faith and loyalty of the other.

What manner of man was this who, amidst the rapid changes of French Governments, was not only twelve times Prime Minister, but held the portfolio of Foreign Affairs for seven consecutive years, until failing health forced him to resign; who won the confidence of Stresemann as completely as my own; who was throughout perhaps the most powerful single personality in the League of Nations, and became in some sort the living embodiment of its spirit?

Physically a man of medium height, with broad, stooping shoulders, deep chested, his head crowned with an untidy shock of greying hair. A heavy drooping moustache half hid a slightly crooked, full-lipped mouth, whose ugliness was redeemed by an enchanting smile that matched well the bright eyes dancing with an often slightly malicious wit. He was, indeed, incorrigibly witty; he could not help it. The good things sprang irresistibly to his lips in graver discussions no less than in his lighter moments. "Tell me Briand's latest," was the greeting with which Lord Balfour used to receive me on my return from my visits to Geneva, and we used to enjoy together the feast which Briand had provided.

The famous game of golf at Cannes which upset his Ministerial coach provided an example. Lord Riddell was at that time acting as a sort of super Press-agent for Mr. Lloyd George. Briand's first drive, as might be expected, had not sent the ball far. When Lord Riddell drove off with a skilled stroke: " *Tiens!* " exclaimed Briand, " *il lance sa balle comme une fausse nouvelle* " (" He sets his ball flying like a bit of false news ").

This is delightful chaff, but his thrust on occasion could be deadly. On his return to Paris he found that his colleagues had already decided his fall, and that the friend to whom he had especially entrusted his interests during his absence had joined his foes. Seizing the situation at a glance, he thrust his papers back into his portfolio and, rising from the Council table, announced that he was going to tender his resignation to the President of the Republic. Then, with his hand on the door, he turned to the friend who had failed him: " By the way, my dear X, can you tell me the value of thirty pieces of silver at the exchange to-day? "

But Briand had not only wit; he had a sense of humour also, and this gift was richly shared by Stresemann. It did much to smooth over the difficulties of our first meetings at Locarno, and helped to turn many a dangerous corner in later discussions at Geneva. Both men could keep discussion on a quiet conversational level, even when treating of the gravest subjects, and both could enjoy a joke at their own expense as richly as a joke at another's.

One day in the lobby of the Assembly at Geneva the Press correspondents remarked the two men sitting apart engaged in a lively and apparently very merry conversation. " What were you two conspirators plotting behind my back? " I later asked of Briand. It appeared that Stresemann had been anxious to explain the circumstances in which a high personage in Germany had made a rather provocative reference to war guilt and to invoke Briand's influence with the French Press to prevent them making heavy weather about it. Briand was able to say that Monsieur Poincaré and himself had already taken steps to this end, and then continued: " But why can't you let the question alone? As to the wisdom of putting this clause into the Treaty, I have my own opinion; but I can't alter it now. Why can't you leave it to the judgment of history? "

" But what," asked Stresemann, " will history say? "

" Ah," replied Briand, " I am no prophet, and will not anticipate her judgment. But there are three things which I think she will not say—she will not say that this time France was the aggressor; she will not say that Belgium invaded Germany; and she will not say, like Bethmann-Hollweg, that a treaty is only a scrap of paper." [1]

When people ask me what is meant by " the atmosphere of Geneva," I tell this story. It is no small thing that it should be possible for the representatives of France and Germany to be able to treat so grave an issue with so light a touch.

I recall another occasion at Geneva when a *bon mot* from him helped to quiet nerves and to restore good temper. The Council had been sitting morning and afternoon; the day was hot and sultry; the long room in which we met had been crowded with representatives of the Press and a public attracted by the dramatic quality of the debate which had been in progress; the atmosphere grew more and more oppressive as the afternoon wore on, and when at last the debate ended and the room was cleared in order that the Council, which had not felt able to accept the resolution drafted by its *Rapporteur*, might evolve another which should secure the assent of both parties, everyone was exhausted and nerves were on edge. There is no more

[1] This story has been printed in an incomplete form without the last phrase. I insert it here because it is certain that it was precisely that phrase to which Briand attached the greatest weight, as being most pertinent to our post-War problems.

Chamberlain with Stresemann and Briand

hopeless task than for fifteen or twenty men to try to draft a document. In a few moments the Council had as many drafts before it as it contained members. Whatever was accepted by one party to the dispute was rejected by the other, and the Council itself seemed as hopelessly divided as the parties themselves. I happened to have been the *Rapporteur* whose proposal had been rejected. I thought I had done my share and, leaving my colleagues to their task, I retired into the background to await the result of their united efforts. Presently I was joined by the representative of the Netherlands. " *Ouf!* " he exclaimed, " *c'est comme un accouchement dans une gare!* " and indeed the scene was one of not less embarrassment and confusion. Later we resumed our places at the table. The heat was oppressive. Only one member of the Council seemed insensible to it ; he who never seemed warm enough had sat all day in a thick overcoat which at this moment he was wrapping more closely around him. "Look at our friend," said Briand ; " I am sure that when he dies he will leave directions that he shall be cremated and, as they push the coffin into the furnace, you will hear his voice crying, ' For God's sake, shut that door. There's an awful draught ! ' "

We all laughed, the victim included—and reached agreement.

I cannot think of Briand without my mind reverting to Locarno. That was the culminating point of his career, and no lesser men than he and Stresemann could have made it a success. I have already described the closing scene of the Conference when Stresemann appealed to us all, but most of all to France, that this should be not the end but the beginning of a chapter in our relations and that we should draw from it the consequences, political and economic, which it logically implied.

None who heard them will ever forget the noble words of Briand's reply or the deep feeling with which he pledged himself henceforth to work unremittingly for peace. As I listened I felt my love for France justified, for in Briand's words I heard the voice of all that is noblest and most generous in the soul of the French nation. Is it permitted to me to add a note more personal to myself? As he left the room Briand found my wife waiting for me, and, taking her two hands in his, and deeply and visibly moved, he said again and again, " Ah, Madame, without your husband I would never have attempted it." I ask no other epitaph. Is it strange that I loved him? "

Other memories crowd upon me—the first meeting of the German and French statesmen in the Conference Room, the long and weighty discussions chiefly carried on between Stresemann and Briand, but often aided by the fluent French and softer speech of Luther; the more private conversations in my room, and, above all, the trip on the lake in the *Orange Blossom* to which Briand invited us, and at which we found the solution of one of our gravest difficulties.

In starting, we had evaded the vigilance of the Press, but when we finally returned to Locarno after nightfall the whole 150 correspondents present there were massed upon the quay. " What have you to tell us, Monsieur le Président? " they asked eagerly. But we had agreed that we could say nothing until we had reported to our colleagues and secured their consent. Briand was equal to the occasion. " Gentlemen," he said, " we have been studying ichthyology. In the shallows near the shore we found some little fish which we identified without difficulty. Further out we came upon bigger ones; they gave us more trouble, but we managed presently to classify them also. Then in the middle of the Lake were one or two really big fish. Ah! they offered a more difficult problem; we have not yet quite solved it, though we are on the way to putting them also in their proper place; but there was one quality possessed by all these fish which greatly impressed us—their silence"; and with a smiling "Good evening, gentlemen," he hurried off to the shelter of his hotel.

In this country we have ceased to cultivate oratory, but in France it is an art which is still studied, admired and practised. Briand was a great orator with a style all his own. He possessed a deep, melodious voice which could sink to a whisper or ring out like a deep-toned bell, but whether raised or lowered, whether you were seated beside him or at the farthest end of the hall, it was always audible and never noisy. I think that the adjective which best describes it is *caressing*, and this was the character of the speeches themselves.

Though he used no notes, he did in a way prepare for a speech, but the speech which he made was not the speech which he had prepared. He was singularly sensitive to the atmosphere of the moment and the mind of his audience, and the speech as delivered was in form and substance the result of his reaction to the feeling and mood of his listeners. I have heard a more perfect and sustained effort of oratory in the Assembly from Monsieur Paul-Boncour —one, indeed, which the skilled translators of the League confessed themselves quite unable to render into English —but I have never listened to a speaker so *persuasive* as Briand.

He was not a great reader; he hated writing. It was in talk that he expounded and, I think, not infrequently formed his ideas. These were large and generous, but seldom worked-out and often in advance of the possibilites of the moment. He consciously took Time for an ally and counted on its aid in overcoming difficulties.

I remember an occasion when he was hurriedly recalled from Geneva by a Cabinet crisis in Paris. He returned after seventy-two hours, having formed his ninth Government. " Yes, my ninth," he told us, " and it's always the same thing. So many portfolios to this section, and so many to those others, but always I reserve one portfolio to my own absolute discretion. That portfolio I allot to Time. He is my most useful colleague." Patience was one of his great instruments. If his hopes were disappointed, then " Patience, and shuffle the cards."

He had a deep sympathy with the countryman and with the sailors and fishermen of his native Brittany. He loved the sea and the countryside—above all, the sea, and the sea most of all when the waves ran high. " My barque," he once wrote to me after a stormy debate in the Chamber, " has not, I admit, been sailing on calm seas. It was pretty well tossed about by the waves, and certain rocky points on the surface were affording me matter for serious un- easiness. . . . The deck is not yet too steady under my feet. Happily, I do not suffer from sea-sickness. . . ."

Such was the man as I knew him—simple in his tastes, warm in his friendships, a charming companion in a leisure hour, a colleague of splendid loyalty in time of difficulty. He loved France passionately, yet was ever in his own phrase " a good European "; he served the cause of Peace with all his might and in some measure it claimed him for its victim. Only a few weeks before his death I sent him the cartoon with which *Punch* saluted him on his retirement. I cannot do better than close this article with his reply (the original is, of course, in French) :

" COCHEREL,
" *February 6, 1932.*

" DEAR FRIEND,

" I have been greatly touched by your thought. You know what value I attach to our friendship.

" I shall keep this drawing from *Punch*, which goes straight to my heart. There is, in truth, in the art of the English humourists a feeling of delicacy and exquisite international courtesy of which ' *le vieux Punch* ' may be proud of maintaining, in our time, the tradition.

" In the attitude in which I am represented in the drawing one sees clearly that the English artist has felt how heavily a simple dove bearing an olive branch can weigh upon a man's wrist. You know something of this matter, dear friend, you to whom this bird is not less familiar. Believe me, the dove of Locarno will always symbolize for me, across all the difficulties of the present hour, the truth of a political thought to which you are as faithful as I am.

" I send you my best wishes for you and yours, and beg you to transmit to Lady Chamberlain my very respectful homage.

" I remain always very affectionately yours,

" ARI. BRIAND."

He could well be content to leave his cause to the judgment of history.

Thus I wrote on the morrow of Briand's death. The three years which have since passed have not provided a successor to the particular place which he held in world politics ; still less have they dimmed the affection and esteem which I felt for him. Yet our friendship, measured in years, was a brief one. It was not its length but the character of the man which gave to it its value—his large sincerity of heart and mind, his courage, his patience under difficulties, his indifference to self, his far-sighted vision, his loyalty and truth, his honest striving for appeasement and reconciliation in a world bled white and scarred with suffering, yet still tossed and driven by the old hates and fears.

I am told that there is to-day in France some reaction against his fame; that passages selected from the Papers of Stresemann are used to represent him as the dupe of a Prussian Mephistopheles who trapped him with soft words while all the time plotting repudiation and revenge.

The charge is absurd to anyone who like myself collaborated with them both from day to day for the happiest years of their association. It is as unfair to Stresemann as it is unjust to Briand. There was neither knave nor dupe, but a great German and a great Frenchman who, from amidst the blood-soaked ruins of the past, sought to raise a new temple of peace. Each knew that the gulf which separated them and their two Nations could not be bridged in a day; for both of them Locarno was not a fulfilment but a beginning. It is perhaps because too much was expected from it that their fame has suffered a temporary eclipse; but their work stands and is the corner-stone of the arch of peace in Europe to-day.

XIII

RAYMOND POINCARÉ

MANY judgments were formed of Poincaré in the course of his career and found their echo at the moment of his death,[1] for strong characters like his, if they command the confidence of their followers, can scarcely escape becoming the objects of fierce attack by their opponents who may respect the man but cannot forgive the policy—least of all when it is successful. In the case of a man like Poincaré the last word was not spoken on the morrow of his death. The final judgment rests with history, for to history he belongs.

It is always rash to attempt to anticipate the verdict of history. "I sometimes think," my father once said in reference to Gladstone, "that great men are like great mountains: one cannot realize their greatness till one stands at some distance from them," and it may well be that history, when the time comes for it to be written, will find much to modify or change in the judgments which we form to-day.

Perhaps my only qualification for attempting an appreciation of the man and his work is that I stood at a little distance from him, in space if not in time, and that, though my life so nearly covered the same years and was so largely influenced by the same terrible events as his, I saw them from a different angle and in some measure from a position of greater detachment. My personal intercourse with him was slight and, after his illness, was confined to the receipt

[1] October 15th, 1934.

of messages of friendship and regard, which, from such a man, gave me the more pleasure because we had sometimes differed seriously on policy and they were therefore as unexpected as they were welcome.

In whatever society one had met him, the stranger would at once have recognized Poincaré for a Frenchman, and under his rather cold demeanour there burned a passionate love of France. It was something more fiery, perhaps more aggressive, than the common love of a man for the country of his birth. It was the love of one old enough to have realized all that was happening in 1870, who had seen his country invaded, his native province torn asunder and a large part of it transferred to an alien rule. Who shall blame him if this passion of love seemed sometimes to turn to hate? He could neither forget in defeat nor forgive in victory. Can one wonder that the youth of that generation grew to manhood with the hope that one day those wrongs would be redressed and the lost provinces restored and that their supreme purpose in life was to secure that, when that moment came, France should be prepared. It was in this faith that men like Poincaré and Clemenceau were bred; by it and for it they lived and toiled. It is to the lasting credit of Poincaré that at the most critical moment of the War, subordinating all personal feeling to the public interest, he called Clemenceau to the helm. It was a triumph all the greater that in one respect it was a triumph over himself, for to a man of his temperament the very restrictions which his position, as President of the Republic, imposed upon his actions and utterances, must have made more difficult co-operation with a man of such dominating and autocratic habit of mind as Clemenceau.

Surely these two men, bitterly as they were divided *ont bien mérité de la Patrie*—and not of France alone, but of all who cherish the freedom of the human soul, to whatever country they belong.

Poincaré brought to his task in those war years indomitable courage and a steadfastness of purpose that nothing could shake. He showed the same qualities in his last great ministry of National Union and perhaps it was at that moment that he rendered his greatest service to France. Such was the confidence which his name inspired that his mere presence " was worth an army corps." We do well to pay honour to men of such courage and integrity; they are not numerous in the world of politics but it is to them that in hours of crisis the people turn for guidance, and never turn in vain.

No portrait can be true to life which has no shadows. Men have the defects of their qualities and Poincaré was no exception to the rule. The force of his own convictions rendered him at times insensitive to the feelings of others and intolerant of all other points of view. I believe that he was a sincere friend to the *Entente*, yet his insistence on the occupation of the Ruhr in the face of repeated British objections caused a rift between the two nations which has perhaps even now not been completely mended. I met him in council at that time. So unyielding was his attitude, so sharp his language that I remember exclaiming to the Prime Minister: " But what Monsieur Poincaré proposes is not an ultimatum to Germany; it is an ultimatum to us! " At such a moment, his firmness was not far removed from obstinacy, and the French lawyer seemed to have assumed the uniform of a Prussian corporal.

I said something of the kind to a French friend who was his staunch admirer. Poincaré was, I complained, so fixed in his own ideas, so rigid and uncompromising in his expression of them and so unwilling to make any concession even to an ally that co-operation became impossible. I have never forgotten my friend's reply which, indeed, once served me as a mirror in which to show a German in what light German policy appeared to the rest of the world: " *Il faut vous rappeler que Monsieur Poincaré est Lorrain, et qui dit Lorrain dit moitié Prussien.*"

But it is not on this note that I would close. During life he never rested. His work is done. France honours a great Frenchman who subordinated all else to the greatness of his country and we join France in her memory of one who, in helping to save France, helped also to save the liberties of mankind.

XIV

LORD MORLEY OF BLACKBURN

TURNING over the few letters from Lord Morley which I possess, all written in the later years of his life, I found this note penned when I had just been appointed Secretary of State for India :

" MY DEAR AUSTEN,

" You were, I believe, laying down the law on my hearthrug some thirty years ago. I was not yet in the H. of C. Who'd have thought that our humble roof sheltered two individuals destined to be Secretary of State for India. Somehow, I like to think of you sitting in my august chair. It is a grand and profoundly interesting office. . . ."

The letter is dated May 27th, 1917, but the incident to which it refers must have occurred nearer forty than thirty years before. Indeed, I think that I shall be right in saying that it took place in the summer of 1876, when I was not quite thirteen years of age. Morley had invited my father to spend two nights (it would be an anachronism to call it the week-end) with him at Brighton and Mrs. Morley had given my father permission to bring me with him. I was then at a private school at Hampstead, founded by a former assistant-master of University College School and carried on after his death by his widow. For convenience in educating her two youngest daughters and to provide companions for them, this lady had added some six or eight girls to the twenty or so boys who composed the bulk of the school.

I remember my feeling of shyness at thus going to a strange house which mingled with the joy of being with my father, but Mrs. Morley soon put me at my ease though I remained rather afraid of Morley himself. In any case I sat during dinner becomingly silent in the presence of my elders, who discussed amongst other things the subject of education. Morley declared himself in favour of the co-education of boys and girls. I felt that I could have put him right on a subject on which he was obviously very ill-informed, but I did not think my father would approve my intervention in the conversation; so, for the time, I stifled as best I could my indignation and remained silent; but Mrs. Morley confided to my father after I had gone to bed that when she had carried me off to the drawing-room, I had taken my stand on the hearth-rug and poured out my indignation at this monstrous heresy, declaring that it was all very well for theorists to declare that it would improve our manners, teach us chivalry and humanize school-life, but that I, who had practical experience of the system, knew that it did nothing of the kind. The girls were a nuisance at games, they worked harder than we did in class, and were constantly held up to us as an example; they wouldn't conform to our standards and so forth and so on. I picture myself as a kind of infant Winston Churchill, becoming an orator in the stress of my emotion and making up for my enforced silence in the earlier part of the evening by the violence of my denunciation of what I felt to be rank heresy born of ignorance. It must have been my first speech, delivered it is true to a small but kindly audience of one who enjoyed the humour of the spectacle of which I was quite unconscious at the time.

My elder sister, who liked long words (and never had any difficulty in spelling them), complained of me in my

infancy that I had " no conversation "; but I must soon
have made up for this early deficiency of speech, as this
incident shows. I might have forgotten it had it not been
so useful to my brother and sisters when it was told to
them in later years, and there was added a later anecdote
dating from my Rugby days. Charlie Howard, then my
fag (and afterwards, as Lord Morpeth, M.P. for one of our
Birmingham seats and later still Lord Carlisle) wrote to
his mother a description of life at school which she was
unkind enough to repeat to some member of the family.
The account ended only when the lights were put out in
the dormitory. . . . " Then," he wrote, " we discuss
politics and things—at least when I say discuss, Chamberlain
jaws us and tells us what we ought to think." Apparently
a lifelong habit had already formed itself!

When one revives old memories one ceases to be master
of one's thoughts. The mind wanders from incident to
incident and one forgets the purpose with which one set
out. Who shall say what fixes some unimportant trifle
in one's memory and keeps it living, whilst much that is
more important escapes remembrance? The Brighton
hearth-rug has led me far from my theme. It was of
Morley, not of myself, that I wanted to write.

Morley and my father met for the first time in 1873.
It was that gallant sailor and eager, though luckless politician,
the late Admiral Maxse, from whom George Meredith drew
the hero of *Beauchamp's Career*, who made them known to
one another, and the acquaintance thus begun ripened quickly
into the closest friendship. It was well for my father that
it did so, for two years later he was again a widower, his
hearth was desolate and his whole world lay in ruins.
What Morley's friendship had already come to mean to
him may be guessed from a sentence in a letter from Morley

to me soon after my father's death. He sent me, "for such use as you may desire," nearly four hundred letters written by my father to him: "Two or three of them, written when he was *in deep domestic sorrow*, are of a sacred sort and perhaps should hardly be seen by anybody but yourself and Beatrice" (my sister). And a year later in July 1876, the month in which, on his fortieth birthday, my father was first elected to Parliament, he wrote to Morley, "I value your friendship very much and it is the only bright spot in my new life."

Thereafter they met frequently. They visited Paris together or made longer tours on the Continent in their summer holidays, and Morley would visit my father first at Southbourne and afterwards at Highbury, his Birmingham homes. Notes passed between them frequently, making appointments for breakfast and a morning visit to the Royal Academy or for an early dinner and the theatre afterwards.

I remember one such occasion at a later time when my father accepted Irving's offer of a box at the Lyceum to see *Faust*, and between the acts discussed the consequences of Randolph Churchill's resignation and the possibilities of the reunion of the Liberal Party by a Round Table Conference; but by that time the differences had struck too deep a root and the Conference ended in failure. My father in thanking Irving for the box and telling him how much they had enjoyed the performance, ventured the criticism that Irving's *Mephistopheles* had rather too much of a French *petit-maître* about him to be a convincing German devil. Irving admitted the charge but asserted that a true representation of Goethe's *Mephistopheles* would be too coarse to please English taste.

When, in 1880, my father entered the Government and took the house in Prince's Gardens which thereafter remained his London home, I suppose that a week seldom passed in which Morley did not dine there at least once, and often more than once. When they first met, Morley was editor of the *Fortnightly Review*; by this time he was editor of the *Pall Mall Gazette* and in 1883 he entered the House of Commons as member for Newcastle-on-Tyne. When I came home during school holidays or university vacations it was one of my greatest pleasures to be present at these dinners where the talk ranged over art, literature and history, but dwelt above all on the political questions of the day. I wish I had tried to Boswellise some of these conversations, for the two men were among the few really good talkers whom I have known—and both could listen. When they held these symposia their talk was a liberal education for a youth like myself.

There is an echo of what my father thought of Morley's share in these talks in a letter written to me long afterwards (December 29th, 1914) by my great friend and Rugby Housemaster, Henry Lee Warner:

" I have been reading Burke's *Reflections* to my wife lately and we turned to Morley's remarks in the *Men of Letters* and came on his page on the political estrangement of Fox and Burke and Fox's generous words. It reminded me so of your father's remark that one evening with John Morley would do more for his son than many days' teaching at Rugby."

I sent this letter to Morley, who replied:

" I am delighted with that remark in L. W.'s letter. I am full at this moment of the old Tabagie Parliaments at Southbourne and Highbury. It is all very much alive in my memory."

The fact is that they had each opened a new world to the other. Morley, the university man, the disciple of Mill, the uncompromising author of the essay on " Compromise," the biographer of Voltaire, Rousseau and Diderot and the student of Burke, was a stimulating companion to a man who had left school at sixteen and, though he had afterwards read widely for himself, had no pretensions to be a scholar.

" I have always thought," I wrote to Morley after my father's death, " that the special attraction of your friendship to him was that while you were in general sympathy on the politics of the day, you opened many windows through which till then he had had no chance of looking."

And to Morley, the scholar and philosopher and publicist, the intensely practical life which my father led, immersed in the work of administration whether of city or country, was something equally new. Though in theory Morley gave the highest place to letters and declared that he would sooner have been the author of *The Decline and Fall* than Mr. Pitt, he had what almost amounted to a craving for a public life. He was equally ready to be either hero or martyr, to be crowned with laurels or to be burned at the stake, but the author's life did not satisfy him; he longed for the limelight and the perils and the triumphs of the platform.

After my marriage, I wanted my wife to know him and invited him to dine quietly with us as soon as we had settled in our new home. He accepted cordially and Sir William Anson completed our small party. In the course of dinner Morley, who was then Secretary of State for India, told us of his morning's work at the office. The Zakka Khel were giving trouble on the India frontier; was there to be a punitive expedition or not? Of course the soldiers wanted one; so did the Political Officer; so, too, the Government of India; so in fact did everyone. Jupiter-Morley was not convinced. "I called in Sir Richmond Ritchie, had a few final words with him and then decided finally against it. It had only taken a quarter of an hour, but I said to Ritchie, 'Do you remember Lord Justice Bowen's definition of hard work? It was answering yes or no on insufficient information. I'm tired!'"

Later, in the drawing-room, the conversation turned on the choice of careers. I suggested, not perhaps without a spice of malice, that to be a great writer would be the best gift a fairy godmother could bestow on an infant in its cradle. Morley vehemently repudiated my suggestion. The work of composition was the vilest drudgery and left one exhausted after an hour or two. "No, I'd rather be a great singer or a great actor."

"Or a great orator," Anson suggested. "He, too, is something of an actor."

"Yes," said Morley, "or a great orator. I'd sooner sway great audiences and sit down, as the reporters say, amidst prolonged applause than decide in my cabinet whether or not there is to be an expedition against the Zakka Khel."

Human nature is full of such contradictions. One night when I sat next Asquith at Grillons something led him to say to me: "What a book, Austen, you or I could write about the *real* men as we have known them, contrasted with the man the public thinks it knows."

"As for instance, so and so," I said, naming a man we had both known and who had been a colleague of Asquith's in Mr. Gladstone's Government.

"Yes," rejoined Asquith, "or John Morley!" for this

man of high purpose, with the lofty forehead, small deep-set eyes, strong mouth and commanding nose and face so deeply lined as to give in repose the stern and almost ascetic appearance which earned him the sobriquet of " Honest John," was not without his full share of human weaknesses. He had really beautiful hands and displayed them with as much coquetry as any fine lady. He was very sensitive, and cared curiously for the outward show and trappings of power. At this moment when he was going to the House of Lords and giving up the Secretaryship of State for India, he was insisting, greatly to Asquith's embarrassment, on receiving the Lord Presidency of the Council instead of the Privy Seal, since the former took precedence of the latter, and threatening to resign if his wish were not gratified. " I have a drawer full of his resignations ! " Asquith exclaimed impatiently.

But to return to Morley and my father. Morley himself has told us the story of that friendship in his *Recollections*,[1] and has sketched with the hand of a master both my father himself and the principal figures in the circle of friends whom he had gathered around him in his Birmingham home. As in one of Franz Hals' great Company pieces at Haarlem, you see the company gathered around the central figure, but each head stands out clearly from the crowded canvas and a few deft strokes give to each its special character and quality.

I had once said to Morley that I wished he would write some account of that remarkable circle and he had answered enigmatically, " Perhaps I have." Some years later he asked me whether I would be willing to read through the proofs of a fragment he had written about those early days, but on re-reading it himself, he wrote (December 4th, 1915) :

[1] Vol. I, Book II, Chap. 1.

" Since getting your pleasant assent to a bold proposal of mine, I have travelled over the ground of my draft of the fragment, and it will never do even for vision so friendly as yours. It needs much polish and reconstruction. So I will not do anything to make your Xmas other than a merry one."

A year later, on November 20th, 1916, he wrote:

" With some misgiving, I send you what I promised. It will read to you cold and meagre. The only excuse is that it is a part of my *Recollections*, and has no pretence to deal essentially and amply with him and his career.

" Please look at the episode on p. 116.

" Do not trouble to *write* me any remarks: you are too busy. I will come to you at I.O., if you should wish.

" Will you let Beatrice see it, if you please? Of course *sub sigillo*.

" Thank Mrs. Chamberlain for her most pleasant meal.

" Yr.

" M."

" Of course, I should be really grateful for any suggestions that may occur to you or your sister. There is no urgency."

I kept no copy of my reply, but he wrote again on November 23rd:

" A thousand thanks for your kind letter. But I feel no little remorse at the idea of throwing this load upon the hands of a man so intensely occupied as you are. I only beg of you not to let it get in your way. Remember it is not *his* biography and only in a very fragmentary and superficial way a piece of my own poor affair. I only want you to say, when you are ready, whether there is any blunder that strikes you, or any piece of an unfair implication.

" I hope Mrs. Chamberlain and you said ' How true,' of the lines of Mr. G. to Granville as to your father's merits as a talker of business. I thought it really good.

201

" The omissions were intentional. I was really afraid of sending more.

" Don't trouble to *write* when the time comes. It will be a delight to me to *attend* you, as the lawyers say.

" Yours always sincerely,

" M."

" You will know that I have not a shade of literary *amour-propre*, and *in one* sense the more faults you find, the more valuable for me."

In his *Life of Gladstone* he had quoted from a letter from Gladstone to Granville (October 8th, 1885) :

" Chamberlain has been here. He is a good man to talk to ; not only from his force and clearness, but because he speaks with reflection, does not misapprehend, or (I think) suspect, or make unnecessary difficulties, or endeavour to maintain pedantically the uniformity and consistency of his arguments," and Morley had added the comment, " No description could be more exact."

I was not entirely reassured by the statement that he had none of an author's *amour-propre*. No doubt he meant what he wrote, but would he in fact like it if I took him at his word and how would he receive my comments? I was not quite happy about the task I had undertaken. There was so much in what he had written that gave me pleasure and yet there were some things in which I thought his words were open to misconstruction, and two passages which showed a real misunderstanding of my father's attitude. However, I took him at his word and wrote fully and frankly.

Morley's reply was more than generous and showed how wrong I had been to doubt the spirit in which he would receive them. He wrote (January 3rd, 1917) :

" MY DEAR AUSTEN,

" Influenza has knocked me off my perch, and my recovery of strength is horribly slow. But I flew eagerly to the box when it was brought to me, and I have thoroughly digested both the letter and the spirit of all you say. To every one of your points I assent, and the result will be to lessen the chance of *jar*, and to make the whole picture richer, and more worthy of the best and truest sides of the original.

" This is the first letter written out my bed for a month, so forgive clumsiness and believe that I do most heartily appreciate your kindness, judgment, and honest candour. I may recast a good deal, in the light of your letter and an excellent one from your sister.

" The caucus oysters provided me with a good laugh, and several capital meals much approved by the medicos.

" All happiness to you and your house for the year.

" Yours always sincerely,

" M."

The " caucus oysters " need a word of explanation. In reading my father's letters to him I had been reminded that it was my father's custom for many years to send him a barrel of oysters every Christmas and the first gift of the kind had, I suppose, been recommended by my father as being of the " caucus brand." I thought it would be pleasant to revive this old custom and had sent them with the explanation that I must revive the old name for, writing from what he had called his " august chair " in the India Office, I dare not call them " natives."

When his book was published I wrote to him again and asked for a few words from him to paste on the fly-leaf of my copy. He replied :

" I am sorry you have had a ' sympathetic ' or other cough ; but it is at all events a comfort that when you were in Paris you were not infected with the desire to make a sympathetic *speech*. Don't you think so? . . . I enclose a word or two for your copy. There is nobody whose acceptance of the book gives me more contentment than yours. All possible good wishes to you and your household.

" Yours always,

" M."

The inscription enclosed was:

To

AUSTEN CHAMBERLAIN

———

From John Morley
with cordial regards
and a host of
cherished memories
November 1917.

The oysters reappear in other letters. They were the symbol of those cherished memories. With the gift of Christmas 1918 I must have recalled some of them, for he replies:

" I have not for many a day had a letter that gave me better pleasure than yours. It awakens a host of the most delightful memories that still linger in my mind, and your kind words move me to the core.

" I retain my lifelong attachment to the Bivalve, without fear of any disaster; and we will drink the health of the giver of them with infinite cordiality, you may be sure."

My last letter from him was written on December 20th, 1920, when I had become Chancellor of the Exchequer for the second time:

" Thank you, with all my heart, Dear Austen, for your letter and the gift. They recall in these last days the earlier and the happiest days of all my long life. Warmly do I wish you and your household all the good you want.

" Irony is hard to keep out of our poor human affairs, and the same post that brings your letter, brings from my accountant an assessment for Income Tax, amounting to ―― Thousands of pounds, and including the unholy item of Super Tax! All the same, I remain your grateful friend,

" MORLEY OF B."

Surely such friendships are rare. It was a cruel turn of fortune's wheel which parted the two friends in 1886 and made them protagonists in opposite camps. The strife was bitter for a time; hard words were spoken on both sides and for a time these rankled and kept the friends apart; but Time the Healer closed these wounds and the old feeling revived. When I wrote to Morley from Highbury at Christmas 1913, he answered:

" The happiest days of my life were passed in the house from which you write. If you think your father would care to hear it, I wish you would assure him that old memories are unabated with me and always will be."

In the same letter Morley wrote:

" Ah 1914! ' Oh that a man might know the end of this year's business ere it come!' I see not a patch of blue sky—not for the country, as you rightly put it."

He was thinking of Ireland, but his words, like the irony of a Greek tragedy, had a deeper meaning. In August war broke out. My father had died in the preceding month.[1] The last words exchanged between the two old friends were messages of peace.

[1] Lord Morley died September 1923.

XV

ARTHUR JAMES BALFOUR

I

" BALFOUR has the finest brain that has been applied to politics in our time." So Birkenhead, himself no mean judge, said to me as we walked away from a Cabinet meeting in which Balfour had taken a leading and decisive part, and such, I believe, would be the general verdict to-day. Yet in the obituary notices published on the morrow of his death,[1] his Prime Ministership was generally written down a failure; at best it was treated as the least satisfactory part of his public life.

This judgment needs revision. Balfour's premiership lasted less than three years in all; it began when the Unionist Party had already been in office for seven years and when the reaction from the " Khaki Election " and the South African War was already in full force; the Tariff Reform controversy broke out within a year and thereafter tended more and more to overshadow all other questions. Within six months it led to the resignations of the two most powerful figures in the Cabinet [2] and of three other Ministers at the head of first-class Departments of State.[3] Yet Balfour's courage never failed; he maintained consistently the line he had marked out for himself and he accomplished successfully and by his own force of will three great

---

[1] Died 1930.
[2] Joseph Chamberlain and the Duke of Devonshire.
[3] Lord Balfour of Burleigh, Mr. C. T. Ritchie and Lord George Hamilton.

reforms which, however criticized at the moment, have stood the test of time and still dominate the scene to-day. Simultaneously he carried through a revolution in our foreign policy. It is not easy to find a parallel to such an achievement accomplished in so short a time and amidst such difficulties.

Let me justify these words:

i. He established the Committee of Imperial Defence.

The conception was his; the form and manner of its constitution was his, and his was the direction given to its first steps, to be developed indeed later but never to be changed in any material respect. For the first time in its history our country was equipped with a body competent to examine the problems presented by the defence of the Empire as a whole and to work out schemes embracing in one common view the parts to be played by the army and navy acting on a common or co-ordinated plan prepared beforehand, instead of an imperfect co-operation hastily arranged when the crisis was already upon them. Nor did the change end there, for by the elastic constitution which he gave to the Committee, not only the fighting services but also the civil departments could be and were represented as required on the Committee and its sub-committees, and thus learned for the first time what would be required of them in war whilst they brought their special knowledge and experience into the common stock.

It is impossible to over-rate the service thus rendered by Balfour to the country and the Empire. Without this Committee and the work done by it under him and his successors, the outbreak of the Great War would have found us wholly unprepared for the problems with which it at once confronted the Government, and, humanly speaking, victory would have been impossible. It may be added that apart from the service which he rendered by creating such an organ, it would be difficult to overstate Balfour's personal contribution to its earliest inquiries. It may be sufficient on this head to say that when, more than twenty - five years later, the Government of the day appointed a committee with Birkenhead as chairman to review the problem of Indian defence, it was the unanimous view of all its members, including the chief military advisers of the Crown both in this country and India, that, though changed conditions naturally required some alterations in the tactical application of the strategical principles which Balfour had laid down, his statement of the strategic principles themselves could not be bettered.

ii. After a series of fruitless efforts by others to deal with the educational problems of the day, he devised and framed the Education Act of 1902 which, however disastrous its immediate effects on the fortunes of the party (and it nearly destroyed the Liberal-Unionist wing, driving masses of Nonconformists back into the Liberal fold), has held the field for thirty years. As Sir Charles Trevelyan confessed when Minister of Education in the late Labour Government, after the first revival of controversy had cleared away it was found to have removed the sectarian difficulties which had stood in the path of educational reform ever since Forster's Act of 1870, and the solution which Balfour provided has remained practically unaltered down to the present day. Without this measure every effort at the reform and development of primary education might still have been rendered abortive, as so many previous efforts had been, by the old religious controversies.

iii. He reformed the Licensing Law, making for the first time systematic provision for the reduction of redundant licences throughout the country. I believe that he found the basis for his Bill in a scheme which had worked for a time successfully in the City of Birmingham, but had then led to disagreement and been finally destroyed by a decision of Quarter Sessions. That the Bill was wholly his work I can testify, for I was a member of the Cabinet Committee which was appointed to draft a Bill and the draft which that committee produced bore no resemblance to Balfour's scheme which replaced it. This Act also has stood the test of time.

In each of these three matters the initiative, the conception and the execution of the new plan were wholly his own and so was the force of will which carried them through the Cabinet and Parliament. After the resignation of the five Ministers in the autumn of 1903 it may be said with truth that the Government existed only by and through him; yet it lasted another two years.

No Prime Minister ever took a closer interest or, except when also Foreign Secretary, as had been the case with Lord Salisbury and was again to be the case with Mr. Ramsay MacDonald in his first administration, a more active part in the conduct of foreign policy. At decisive moments when Salisbury was absent or unwell, Balfour had acted for him, and when he himself became Prime Minister it is safe to say that Lansdowne took no important step and sent no important despatch without first consulting him. It does not detract from Lansdowne's services as Foreign Secretary to say that his chief accomplishments would never have been achieved but for the constructive mind of Balfour and the constant support he gave him, not only in executing his foreign policy, but in conceiving and shaping it. To them, and to my father in the earlier stages, were due the Anglo-French *Entente* and the Anglo-Japanese Alliance—two events of the first order of magnitude which fixed the lines of our foreign policy for the next ten years and, conserved and developed by Lord Grey after the defeat of the Conservative Party at the close of 1905, were—I think it is not putting the case too high—decisive for our own fate and it may well be for the world's, when the day of Armageddon came.

It is true that, whilst all this was being accomplished, the Government was steadily declining in popular favour, and less and less able to rely even on its majority in the House of Commons until at last, as Lord Grey remarked, though he had known governments which had lost public favour without realizing it, and others which had realized it without admitting it, this was the first Government which openly avowed that it no longer possessed the confidence of the country but nevertheless asserted its determination to continue to govern as long as it retained the support of its parliamentary majority. Balfour himself openly justified this position as sound constitutional practice, but it is now no secret that his real reason and purpose were to conclude the Anglo-Japanese negotiations and to see the Treaty ratified before he surrendered power to Campbell-Bannerman, in whose policy he felt no trust. The result, when the elections at last came, is not likely to tempt any of his successors to carry on in similar circumstances.

To what was this debacle due? I have already called attention to the fact that when Balfour succeeded to the Premiership, the reaction against the Unionist Party, bred of seven years of office and the mistakes and losses of the South African War, had already begun. The Education Bill, great and enduring as has been its success when once in operation, deprived the Liberal-Unionist wing of the party outside Birmingham of the great bulk of middle- and working-class nonconformity, which had been its main source of strength in the towns and villages. Even in Birmingham itself the situation was only saved by my father's influence and the extraordinary exertions which he made to prevent a similar disaster befalling the party in that stronghold of Unionism. Thus the cohesion of the Government supporters was already badly shattered before ever my father's speech of May 1903 evoked that wide and immediate response which took him as much as others by surprise, and at once placed Tariff Reform in the front rank of the questions of the day.

This is not the place to write the history of these events which must be told by Mr. Garvin in his *Life of Joseph Chamberlain*. It is sufficient to say here that that history would have been very different if, during my father's absence in South Africa, the then Chancellor of the Exchequer [1] and those who acted with him, had not repudiated the decision to retain the Corn Duty and use it for the purposes of Imperial Preference, a decision taken by the Cabinet before my father left England in the previous autumn. It was from that repudiation that all our subsequent troubles sprang.

I do not pretend that I think Balfour's subsequent handling of the situation wise, but it was certainly not lacking in courage. He was not then or thereafter, so far as I know, a full-blooded Protectionist, but he was definitely a " fiscal reformer." The old Free Traders were consistent advocates of the principle of *laisser-faire* in fiscal and social questions alike. Balfour was neither a Protectionist nor a Socialist, but he did not believe that the old dogmas on which our

---

[1] Mr. (afterwards Lord) Ritchie.

Free Trade policy was founded were theoretically sound. He had always desired the power of retaliation or bargaining in negotiations with foreign countries, and believed that the time had now come definitely to break with the doctrine of *laisser-faire* in trade questions just as it had long been abandoned in industrial affairs. As regards Imperial Preference he clearly appreciated (as some of his colleagues did not) the vital importance of the problems which the development of colonial nationalism was creating. When the question was definitely raised by Laurier's pronouncements, he was, as usual with him, a little sceptical and very questioning, but never for one moment did he minimize its importance and he was quite determined not to bang, bar or bolt any new doors. His view on this matter was clearly stated in a letter to the Duke of Devonshire:

" If, as seems certain, Canada and other Colonies are prepared to employ their tariffs in order to further an Imperial ideal, and if, as seems probable, the rejection of their overtures will lead to their withdrawal and we become worse off as an Empire than if those overtures had never been made, I should be sorry to think that I belong to a Government or a Party which hastily rejected them." [1]

But—and this is vital to an understanding of his action then and throughout the controversy—the purpose which was dominant in his mind from the first moment that such a danger appeared was to prevent the break-up of the party. He thought Peel's action in 1846 inexcusable. Praise of Peel at any time drew from him the same sharp condemnation. " He committed the unforgivable sin; he broke up his party." Balfour himself was determined not to repeat the fault. He felt that, on becoming leader, he

[1] See Bernard Holland's *Life of the Duke of Devonshire*, Vol. II, p. 328 (Longmans).

had accepted a trust and that his first duty was to maintain intact what had been committed to his charge. He understood and sympathized with the hopes and the anxieties of those who placed the Imperial problem first. He would go with them as far as he could without breaking up the party, but he would not go beyond the point at which he thought that party union could be maintained.

So he chose his position and refused to be driven from it. He made no effort to keep the colleagues who were not prepared to break definitely with the old hampering dogma; he accepted Chamberlain's resignation, not because he objected in principle to Imperial Preference, but because he did not believe it to be as yet within the range of practical politics. He made great efforts to retain the Duke of Devonshire, but his course was not shaken by his secession a few weeks later. No man ever faced greater difficulties with greater courage. He was not a successful party leader, but on a calm review of the obstacles which beset his path from the first and of his achievement, who shall deny his title to be named among our great Prime Ministers?

2

What, it has been asked was his real attitude to Politics? Was he merely a dilettante who had been seduced into the political arena by the accident of his relationship to Lord Salisbury, one who found pleasure in the dialectical duels for which the House of Commons afforded an opportunity, but at heart cared for none of these things? Was his real passion for philosophy, or natural science or some other study of his active and questioning mind? He cared for all these things; he cared for them intensely. It was said of Mr. Gladstone that he could talk on almost any subject so well, and with such wealth of knowledge that he appeared an expert on that subject to all except the experts in it. Balfour's knowledge was of another kind. It was the men of the profession, the experts themselves, who most delighted to discuss with him their own subject; and he himself loved to talk another man's " shop." " The man who talks shop," he once said, " never bores me, for he is talking of something that he knows. What I can't stand is the man who insists on talking about what he doesn't know." His intellectual interest was in fact almost as wide as the universe, but though other studies might have claimed him in his earliest years and were never completely abandoned, I am convinced that, at least from the time when he became Chief Secretary for Ireland, politics became his ruling passion to which, in the measure which their pursuit made necessary, he was prepared to, and in fact did, subordinate all the others.

As leader he had a very high sense of his duty to the party which had entrusted its fortunes to him, but he was very far from being a typical party man. I cannot do better than apply to him the description given by Sainte Beuve of the first Duc de Broglie: " He is one of the most original minds of his time; this is seen above all in the form, the method and the means of demonstration which he employs; even when he thinks what everyone else is thinking, when he reaches the same conclusions, he reaches them or convinces himself of them by reasons peculiar to himself. He has his own reasons for everything, perhaps true, sometimes subtle, always ingenious and never common."

Therein lay his weakness both as a leader and as a speaker. Things which seemed important to him often appeared of little consequence to his followers and to his opponents (as for instance in the Tariff controversy) a mere splitting of hairs, a quibble unworthy of the ingenuity with which he sustained it and of the serious issues at stake. He was not content to make a broad statement of his views without at the same time giving expression to all the qualifications which to his mind it required. In the course of the Tariff controversy after my father had left the Government, I once asked Balfour to put together in a single speech at the Albert Hall three simple statements of principle which were to be found separately in as many of his previous speeches. I assured him that if he would do this, he would make it much easier for my father to co-operate heartily with him. He readily agreed; indeed he drew from a drawer in his writing-table a couple of those long envelopes on which he was accustomed to make his notes and showed me that he had already jotted down two out of the three points which I had mentioned for incorporation in his speech. I reported to my father what had passed between us, who replied that if Balfour would do that, it would be very satisfactory and helpful.

The sequel is curious. My father rang me up on the telephone the morning after the Albert Hall meeting. "Well," he said, "Balfour has let us down. He hasn't said what he told you he would say."

"Oh yes he has," I answered and recited the three points, adding that he had made them all, and I proceeded to read them out from *The Times* which lay before me. "That's all right," said my father, but where do you find that?" Alas! there was the rub. The first statement came near the beginning, the second in the middle and the third near the end of the speech. The effect which I had hoped they would produce was wholly lost in the mass of intervening matter. In my despair I told Balfour of this conversation. I urged that it was useless to exhibit an easel-picture from the platform of a mass meeting; the details, instead of making it clearer, simply rendered its meaning indistinguishable. The speaker in such circumstances must work like the scene-painter; he could only get his effects by painting in the broadest outlines. Balfour sighed and confessed that that was doubtless true, but he could not change his ways. He was in fact always strongest in attack and weakest in exposition, much better in the House of Commons which had learned to know him, than in a mass meeting which was puzzled by his ways and often found it difficult to follow his argument and extract its meaning.

His power over the House was never more amazingly shown than in the months which followed his return to it as member for the City of London after his defeat at Manchester in the disastrous rout of the party in 1906. A mere remnant of his followers in the preceding Parliament had survived the debacle. The House was full of strange faces. The majority, flushed with victory after ten years of defeat, was intolerant and rude to him. It was not so much that they disliked him as that they despised him, and contempt is less easy to conquer than hatred. They openly jeered at him and constantly interrupted him when speaking. In the midst of it all he remained unmoved even when his friends were provoked to fierce indignation and remonstrance, and before the year was out, he had won the respect of every one of his opponents. However much they disagreed with him or smarted under his rapier thrusts, they felt that he gave distinction to the House and brought qualities to its service which no other of its members possessed in a like degree.

3

To the charm of his character and the pleasure of his converse, all who knew him bear witness. To me he was always the kindest of friends and the most helpful and encouraging of chiefs and colleagues. He gave freely and always of his best alike in council and in conversation, and his conversation had a peculiar charm for the men of a younger generation, for he was not only an admirable talker but a most encouraging listener. I have found many besides myself to confess that, after an evening spent in his company, one left with the feeling that one had been at the top of one's form and really had talked rather well. A night's reflection showed one that it was he who had worked the miracle, listening with such interest, drawing out one's thought and often transmuting it to more precious metal by his own alchemy. Only to pretension and conceit was he without mercy.

What was the real Balfour—the inner man whose secrets he guarded so jealously from prying eyes? Was he at bottom heartless and indifferent, as some have suggested, both for himself and others? I do not believe it. He was far more sensitive to any charge which touched his honour or pride than his contemptuous "I do not read the newspapers" would suggest, and I, who was at his right hand during the last two years of his Prime Ministership, know what it cost him to part with George Wyndham and Hayes-Fisher.[1] "Are you going to the Eton and Harrow match?" I asked him in one of his later years, and he answered almost with a shudder, "No; there are too many ghosts!" and I remember with what deep feeling he spoke

---

[1] Mr. George Wyndham, M.P., Chief Secretary for Ireland in Balfour's Government, resigned in May 1905. Mr William Hayes-Fisher, M.P. (afterwards Lord Downham) was Financial Secretary to the Treasury, but resigned in April 1903.

to me of George Wyndham and Alfred Lyttelton in the early months of the War when his thoughts turned naturally to the friends with whom he had worked in the past. Whatever others may think, I at least am convinced that he not only needed the sympathy and affection with which he was surrounded but that he returned it.

Lord D'Abernon, in one of those brilliant "appreciations" which he prefixed to his account of his Berlin Embassy, asserts that Balfour "was hampered by no passionate convictions." It may be a bold thing to differ from so shrewd an observer, but in this instance I cannot follow his judgment. Indeed to me the most remarkable thing about Balfour is that with a mind so critical, so little inclined to expect great results from any accomplishment within the power of man, he yet did take so passionate an interest in all mundane affairs. He was as keen as a boy about the sports which interested him. Though he constantly reminded us that Parliament could achieve little, and that the best that could be hoped from legislation, even his own, was that it would do no harm and might even do a little good, he fought his battles with a passion that I have seen elsewhere only in men of far more positive and sanguine temperament. It is his distinction, to quote a phrase of Lord D'Abernon's, to have "held towards life an attitude attained only by the truly philosophic," to have seen the littleness of man's life and his struggles and yet never to have allowed his sense of this littleness to paralyse his arm or to prevent him from doing with all his might that which his hand found to do. He may have cared little for much which other men thought important, but he fought passionately and tenaciously for that which he held to be true.

Lord D'Abernon poses many questions about the inner

man and concludes, " all these are problems which have remained insoluble during his life and will probably remain insoluble for posterity." Yet it is Lord D'Abernon who writes of him, " his general theory of life appeared to be that happiness is close to us, in freedom from bondage to imagined good, and in emancipation from the things of sense. No one less than he sought happiness in regions where happiness is not to be found."

To have combined the practice of so lofty a philosophy with so active and so combatant a life is given to few indeed.

XVI

ANDREW BONAR LAW

Mr. Baldwin, when unveiling a portrait of Bonar Law, said of him that he had a personality "lovable, elusive and wistful." No better words could have been chosen to describe him.

He was essentially a lovable man. It is the first word which springs to my mind when I think of him. It was not merely that in his own family he was surrounded, as so many of us are, with the most watchful and devoted affection; in a wider circle he won friends, as it seemed without seeking them, by the kindness of his heart, and perhaps not less by the rather pathetic solitude in which the inner man appeared to dwell, especially after the death of his wife, and by that air of wistful longing for it seemed he knew not what, of which Mr. Baldwin spoke. Again, as leader of the Conservative Party, he won the confidence and affection of his supporters in an unusual degree, and in difficult times, when other parties were breaking up under the stresses and strains of a revolutionary period, he retained their unbounded trust and kept them united.

How great was his influence with them may be illustrated by three cases in which his action was decisive. He precipitated the formation of the first Coalition Government under Asquith, and his action in allying himself with Lloyd George was a not less important factor in its fall. He it was who decided, I believe without any previous consultation with his Unionist colleagues and against the wish of some of them, to fight the " Coupon Election " after the Armistice on a Coalition basis; and, finally his attitude at the Carlton Club meeting of 1922 and his readiness to assume the Premiership, determined the attitude of the majority of the party towards the Coalition and brought it to an end. It is part of the irony of life that I should have wished to end the Coalition with the War, and that he should then have decided to continue it only to bring about its destruction when I had fallen heir to his inheritance and felt myself bound in honour by the ties which he had created. I saw him late in the afternoon of the day preceding the Carlton Club meeting. He was then still undecided as to his course, and spoke sadly and with much sympathy for me. It was a hateful position, he said. He thought he would plead the state of his health and keep away from the meeting altogether, but in that case he must leave Parliament and give up public life. If he came to the meeting, he must speak against me. I told him that his speech would be decisive; the vote would go in his favour, the Government would have to resign and he would have to form a new one. " Well," he said again, as I took my leave of him, " it's a hateful position; I expect that if I had remained in your place I should have acted like you."

Such apparent inconsistencies were not unusual with him and are not easily explained. His was indeed an elusive personality. Mr. Baldwin thought he had found the explanation in a childhood passed in very straitened circumstances in a lonely New Brunswick Manse, but he was at once taken to task by a Glasgow correspondent, who wrote that Bonar Law had left New Brunswick in early boyhood and had been brought up by relations in

Glasgow in ease and comfort, if not in luxury. Be that as it may, the picture of the New Brunswick home which Mr. Baldwin drew seemed the fitting background for his life and character. Whatever his creed in later days, his early Calvinistic training had left deep traces on his attitude to life. Of such things he and I never spoke. The nearest we came to them was one morning when we walked away together from the memorial service held at St. Margaret's for Alfred Lyttelton. We were silent for some moments and then, turning to me, he spoke: "If such things can so move you and me, Austen, who do not belong to that Church, what must not they mean to those who were brought up in its fold!"

Something of the bleakness and the solitude of the long winters of the land in which he was born seemed to cling to him through life. He did not care for society and, unless in a familiar circle, was shy and reserved. I have often seen him smile, but I cannot recall having ever heard him laugh outright. Mirth seemed a stranger to him. Even his pleasures were for the most part of the sedate and studious kind. I do not think he read much poetry or ever quoted it, but he would have found his kindred spirit in " Il Penseroso " rather than " L'Allegro."

> " Hence, vain deluding Joys,
>   The brood of Folly without father bred!
> How little you bested,
>   Or fill the fixèd mind with all your toys!"

And he might well have ended with the same appeal:

.   .   .   .   .

> " These pleasures, Melancholy, give;
>   And I with thee will choose to live."

Melancholy indeed seemed his chosen companion even when I first knew him before the happiness of his home

222

The work of the Conference was embodied in eight Treaties. To only one of them, the Treaty of Locarno *par excellence*, is Great Britain a party.

This is the Treaty of Mutual Guarantee between Germany, Belgium, France, Great Britain and Italy. By it Germany and Belgium and Germany and France respectively covenant never to resort to war against each other, and to settle all disputes between them by peaceful means. Also the five Signatory Powers, collectively and severally, guarantee the maintenance of the territorial *status quo* resulting from the frontiers between Germany and her two Western neighbours as fixed by the Treaty of Versailles, and the observance of the conditions laid down for the demilitarized zone constituted by that Treaty.

In all cases but one, the decision as to whether the *casus fœderis* has arisen is entrusted to the Council of the League of Nations. The only exception to this rule is the case of actual invasion, or a flagrant violation of the stipulations regarding the demilitarized zone, if the guaranteeing Power is itself satisfied that " the violation is an act of unprovoked aggression, and that by reason either of the crossing of the frontier or the outbreak of hostilities, or the assembly of armed forces in the zone, immediate action is necessary."

In this case each party undertakes to come at once to the help of the victim, but even in this case the ultimate decision is left to the Council of the League, which will be immediately convoked, and all parties agree to conform to its judgment.

The subsidiary treaties concluded at the same time comprise the arbitration conventions between Germany and Belgium and Germany and France, which determine the methods for the peaceful settlement of all disputes provided for in the Treaty of Guarantee; and Arbitration Treaties between Germany and Poland and Germany and Czechoslovakia for the similar regulation of all disputes between them by peaceful methods.

Finally, there are two treaties between France and Poland and France and Czechoslovakia, in which these Powers guarantee to one another the faithful observance of the undertakings reached between Germany and themselves; but the aid which each promises to the other in accordance with Articles XV and XVI of the Covenant is confined to the case of unprovoked attack on either by Germany.

This is a restriction of the obligations involved in the earlier treaties of alliance between these countries, limiting the claim of either for assistance from the other to cases of unprovoked aggression so as to bring them into harmony with the guarantees given in the West and with the spirit of the Covenant.

With the last-named treaties Great Britain has no direct concern. They impose no obligation on us and subject us to no liability. They strengthen and extend the peace structure of Europe, but we are not a party to them. They affect us only as signatories of the Covenant, concerned that the peace of the world should not be broken. Even in the case of the Treaty of Guarantee, Great Britain and Italy, the guaranteeing Powers, must, as permanent members of the Council of the League, be parties to its decision, or in the case of a flagrant violation of the treaty be able to satisfy themselves that there has been an unprovoked act of hostility, and that the circumstances are such as to render immediate action necessary.

The obligation could not be more carefully safeguarded or more certainly directed to the sole purpose of maintaining peace. The treaty forms, to use the apt phrase employed by Professor Gerothwohl in the columns of the had been laid low by his wife's early death. The air of sadness which was native to him seemed to call for sympathy and drew men's hearts to him; yet it was not easy with such a nature to give that sympathy except mutely. He did not wear his heart upon his sleeve or encourage others to do so. It was, perhaps, one of the ties which bound us to one another that we could understand and sympathize with each other without the need to put our feelings into words.

What was the secret of his hold upon the Party? He was a brilliant debater and a most effective platform speaker. He had a marvellous memory, a great and unequalled capacity for the lucid and logical presentation of his case. He had, in addition, a way of clinching his argument and driving it home to the mind of his audience which recalled to members of my family the speeches of my father. These qualities are sufficient to explain his parliamentary and platform successes; but they are not sufficient to explain the confidence which the party, and later the country, came to repose in him. That must be sought less in his gifts than in the character which he gradually and unconsciously revealed to them.

It was, indeed, the opening of a new chapter in the history of the Conservative Party when he became its leader. He had no connection with the great Tory families; he was unknown outside political circles; he had never held high office nor even sat in a Cabinet. To the ideas of the landed gentry, so influential and still so numerous in the Tory ranks, he was a stranger. He had singularly little regard for tradition and even less for the forms in which it was enshrined. Even to me, brought up in boyhood among advanced Radicals, he sometimes appeared an iconoclast, and in England at least he was a Nonconformist.

He once said to me, before the War had stirred deeper emotions, that he cared intensely for only two things: Tariff Reform and Ulster; all the rest was only part of the game. The success of such a man as leader of the Tory Party presents one of the paradoxes of our political life.

He was already forty-two when he was first elected to the House of Commons. Not very long afterwards he was sitting alone with me in the old smoking-room of the House of Commons, a prey to one of those moods of depression which beset him from time to time throughout his life. I tried to cheer him up. " No, Austen," he replied, " this is no place for me. It's all very well for men like you who came into it young; but if I had known then what I know now, I would never have stood for Parliament." So, many years before, when I had just become a candidate for the Border Burghs, W. H. Smith had said to me that I did well to begin young, for the House was no place for a man who, like himself, had come into it for the first time when he was already over forty. Yet W. H. Smith was then, as Bonar Law was later to become, the leader of the House and one of its most trusted and respected figures.

Bonar Law was endowed with far more brilliant parliamentary gifts than W. H. Smith, but the secret of success in both cases was the same; it lay in character—in their natural simplicity of life, in the absence of all pretension and affectation and in their single-minded devotion to duty.

This is not to say that Bonar Law was without ambition. Asquith once spoke of him as " mildly ambitious." This was entirely to mistake the man. He was not mildly but intensely ambitious—I sometimes think he was the most ambitious man whom I have known in politics. I once confessed to him that I had made many attempts to read Gibbon's *Decline and Fall*, but had never succeeded in persevering to the end. He was astonished and declared at once that he found that great procession of ambitious men, realizing their ambitions only to be cheated of their hopes, the most fascinating of all studies. He knew that he was ambitious and could not understand why others did not perceive it. " You make a great mistake about me," he once told the members of the Press Gallery at the House of Commons when they entertained him at luncheon. " You think I am a modest man with no ambition. I am really very ambitious." [1] And when he had to deliver his Rectorial Address at Glasgow University, he chose " Ambition " for his theme, and recalled how as he listened many years before to Mr. Gladstone's Rectorial Address, he had resolved that one day he too would be Lord Rector.

In another man, such ambition might have been his ruin. Bonar Law was saved by his strong sense of duty. When the first Coalition was formed, he would not permit his friends to press his claim to the Chancellorship of the Exchequer, and allowed Mr. McKenna to be appointed to it over his head. I know that he felt the slight to his position which Asquith's choice implied, but he would suffer no remonstrance to be made. Ambitious he was, but there was nothing mean or selfish about the ambitions which he entertained.

He and I had our differences; we did not always see eye to eye, and I confess it pained me when it was he who, emerging from his retirement, struck the blow which put an end to my leadership. But there was no bitterness in

[1] I had this story from the late Sir Alfred Robbins, who was among the hosts.

our divisions, no loss of mutual respect and affection, and I was glad indeed when his family put, as it were, the seal upon our friendship by choosing me to be one of the pall-bearers at his funeral in the Abbey.[1]

He was indeed a most lovable man.

[1] Mr. Bonar Law died October 1923.

XVII

FRENCH AND ENGLISH

No two nations have greater need to understand one
another than England and France; and yet no two peoples
find national understanding more difficult. "It is not,"
wrote Monsieur de Madariaga in days when he was still a
member of the Secretariat of the League of Nations, "it
is not that it is impossible to bring France and England to
see eye to eye; only their eyes are so different." The clarity
of the French mind which shines so brilliantly in its noble
prose, is alien to the more slovenly habits of English thought.
The stern logic which Frenchmen require is not only alien
to the English character but repugnant to our experience.
All our history is a compromise. The Thirty-nine Articles
of the Church of England balance as delicately between
conflicting dogmas, as the resolution which declared the
throne of James II vacant and united in its support Whigs
and Tories, High Churchmen and Independents, supporters
of Passive Obedience and the right divine of kings and the
sons of those who only a generation earlier had cut off the
head of James's father. The men of the French Revolution
proclaimed a new faith and sought to bring into existence
a new order. It has been the claim of English reformers
from our earliest days that they sought no innovation, but
only the restoration of ancient liberties which had fallen
into disuse. It was a wise saying that in Europe every man
is born two thousand years old. We cannot escape from
our past. Frenchmen and Englishmen alike are what

227

history has made them. The French constitution has been made and remade. The British constitution has grown. The one is a structure carefully planned where every stress and strain has been calculated by the builders and provision made against it in advance—a classic building begun and finished in a single style. The other is a Gothic building bearing evidence, in the varying styles of nave and clerestory, of transepts and choir, of its slow development, and still resting on the rounded Norman arches of an earlier structure which themselves, not improbably, rise on Saxon foundations. There is much of history and character to be read in old buildings.

As in big things, so in small there is much which makes mutual comprehension difficult. The difference of manners, the different key in which the emotions are expressed are apt to lead the Englishman to think the Frenchman exaggerated and insincere, and to make the Frenchman judge the Englishman cold and unsympathetic even when he feels most deeply and most desires to show his friendliness; and more deadly still, the Englishman's absence of logic alike in thought and deed supplies the foundation for the charge of national hypocrisy to which he too often retorts against his critic, the charge of national cynicism.

It is easier to state these differences and to recognize the difficulties and misunderstandings to which they give rise, than to suggest a remedy. By contrast with the first approach of Englishman and Frenchman, generally uneasy and constrained, the first meeting of German and Englishman is usually easy and deceptively cordial. For one thing, the Englishman in general is no great linguist and knowledge of the English language is far more general among Germans than among Frenchmen. At first sight, too, their habits and modes of thought seem not very dissimilar; it is only as one goes deeper, that the profound differences appear. Our growth is rooted in a different soil and watered by different rivers. The deeper Englishmen and Frenchmen penetrate into each other's nature, the more they will find they have in common; the deeper Englishman and German go, the greater the divergence of faith and spirit which will be revealed between them. It is not without significance that it was precisely those Englishmen who knew Germany best, who had lived there or had formed German connections, who first foresaw and warned their countrymen of the coming peril. "What has been, may be." If the peril ever revives, the same deep forces will be at work, the same great issues at stake. England and France will need each other. Pray God they stand together or our common civilization will perish.

Our common civilization, yes, for we have a conception of the dignity of man and of the freedom of the human mind which is our common birthright. Alone, among the Great Powers of Europe, France and England still champion ideas deep rooted in their national character which elsewhere have lost their attraction. In the country of Goethe his lofty and inquiring intellect and his free spirit would find no home to-day; the passionate love of liberty which inspired Schiller would be silenced or driven to seek elsewhere the right to think its own thoughts and to express its soul. "According to plan" has become "According to pattern." Conform or perish! is the new law. Mr. Baldwin's words have a wider application and a deeper meaning than that which he gave them: "Our frontier is on the Rhine."

I am an Englishman. If ever, which God forbid! strife should break out again between France and England, I am with my country, right or wrong, and all the time. But

I hold, with deep conviction, that such a struggle between the two great democracies of western Europe would be not only fatal to them both, but a calamity for the world. I ask of Frenchmen nothing which I do not ask equally of my own countrymen. I plead with both for a closer study of their neighbour, for a willing recognition of the limits set by history and geography, by temperament and circumstance beyond which neither people can advance.

In such larger comprehension lies the beginning of wisdom and in the wise direction of our relations lies the safety of us all.

XVIII

ANGLO-AMERICAN FRIENDSHIP

BESIDE the Mall, near to the Admiralty Arch, there stands a monument erected by the officers and men of the Royal Marines in memory of their comrades who fell in the South African War and the Boxer troubles in China. It represents a private of the corps standing at bay with a fallen comrade at his feet.

On the pedestal are two bronze bas-reliefs. The one shows a party of marines working the big naval guns at the defence of Ladysmith; the other depicts an episode in the defence of the Peking Legations, and the moment chosen is one when, all the British officers being disabled by wounds or illness, the detachment was commanded by a United States officer, easily distinguishable by his uniform from the British troops in whose midst he stands. The scenes to be depicted were chosen by the marines themselves.

Is there in any other country a monument erected by soldiers to their fallen comrades where they have deliberately selected from a crowd of glorious memories that one moment which shows them fighting under the command of an officer of another country than their own? No words of mine could so well express the sense of comradeship and kinship which Britons feel for Americans.

Perhaps we sometimes exaggerate the kinship. No Englishman in common parlance would speak of an

American as a foreigner. It comes to us naturally to think of Americans as kinsmen from whom we have parted, with whom we have, alas, twice quarrelled and not infrequently disagreed, but still as kinsmen—men who shared all but a small fraction of our history, who speak the same language, who read the same Bible, who are co-heirs with us of the glories of English literature,

> " who speak the tongue
> That Shakespeare spake, the faith and morals hold
> That Milton held."

We are apt to forget how large a part of those who went even from our own islands went with bitterness in their hearts. Still more, perhaps, are we apt to forget how large a part of the population of the United States to-day is drawn from other sources with different habits, sympathies and traditions. But when all due allowance is made for the differences that do exist, we believe that we are nearer to Americans than to any other nation outside the British Commonwealth and that in fundamentals we stand for the same things.

It is a truism of British policy that the greatest British interest is peace, but a war between the United States and ourselves seems to us different in kind from any other war, so fratricidal, so unnatural that we refuse to contemplate it even as a possibility, and that for as long as I have known anything of British Governments it has never entered into their calculations of what was necessary for defence. The three-thousand-mile frontier between Canada and the United States is unfortified. It is policed rather than defended by such forces as either nation maintains in its neighbourhood. The British Islands from the Bermudas to the Caribbean tell the same tale of trust and confidence.

No European frontiers are so unguarded, nor do those who dwell on them live in such care-free security.

But, as I have said elsewhere, a mere negative statement of this kind would be a very inadequate description of our thoughts and policy. We desire not only to live at peace with the United States, but to cultivate the most cordial and the closest relations with them, and this desire has increasingly affected the course of British policy in recent years. In the Spanish-American War British sympathy was from the first entirely on the side of the United States. In China we stood with America in the early years of this century as supporters of the Open Door and as peaceful but determined opponents of the annexation of Chinese territory by particular Powers; at the Conference of Algeciras the objects of the British and American representatives were the same and they rendered one another reciprocal support, whilst more recently at the Conference of Versailles our delegations were habitually found in agreement on points on which both differed from the rest of the Allies.

These are cases in which common interests, common traditions and similar habits of thought caused our two nations to act in general agreement. A more direct instance of the influence of American opinion on British policy is seen in the termination of the Anglo-Japanese Alliance of 1905, or rather, in its conversion at the Washington Conference of 1921 into a quadruple treaty to which the United States and France as well as Great Britain and Japan are parties.

The case is an interesting one. The Anglo-Japanese Treaty had been for twenty years one of the sheet-anchors of British policy. Together with the conclusion of the *Entente* with France it marked the definite abandonment of the policy of " splendid isolation " which both English parties had followed towards the close of the last century. It was, moreover, considered as a particular guarantee of their security by the Commonwealth of Australia and the Dominion of New Zealand, and it was regarded by all of us as a bulwark of peace in the Pacific. Nevertheless, it was terminated because it gave rise to misunderstanding in America and was felt to be an obstacle to the friendship and confidence which we desired to see existing between us. It is not without significance that the strongest opposition to its renewal came from the Dominion of Canada, and that Canada, whose interests have not infrequently been the bone of contention between London and Washington, was on this occasion the connecting link between British and American opinion, just as Great Britain has at other times served as a bond of union between the United States and Europe.

This, I would claim, was conspicuously the rôle played by Great Britain in relation to the Pact of Paris, more commonly known among us as the Kellogg Pact. It is true that the idea of a treaty outlawing war was first broached by that great Frenchman and friend of peace, Aristide Briand, but it is not, I think, too much to say that the French were surprised and even alarmed when they saw their bantling presented to them in its American clothes. Mr. Kellogg's extended plan was warmly welcomed by all sections of opinion in Great Britain and the Dominions, but the first reaction in France was less favourable and the reply of the French Government seemed to English no less than to American ears less cordial than we should have expected. I believe that in the communications which followed, Great Britain played a useful and important part in interpreting the intentions and anxieties of either party to the other and, by the friendly explanations she invited and received, removed misunderstandings and secured agreement.

The very fact that the British Empire belongs to no continent but is represented on them all, gives to us a certain detachment which approximates our position in European affairs to that of the United States and fits us to be a connecting link between the Old World and the New. It is, indeed, my conviction that the wider American interests spread and the more the United States accept the consequences of their attainment to the position of a world power, the better shall we understand one another and the more shall we find ourselves driven by common interests and a common outlook to pursue a parallel policy.

It is, therefore, without jealousy that we have watched the phenomenal growth of the United States since the close of the Civil War, and we could give no greater proof of it than in accepting the doctrine of naval parity. To no other nation should we have made that sacrifice, to no other nation are we now prepared to make it. The sea has been our bulwark; it has been to us alike a defence and a highway: it is the sole means of communication between Great Britain and the rest of the Empire.

For historical reasons, a standing army has never held the place in the affections of the English people which it holds in most continental countries. On the other hand the navy has always been the popular idol and our naval supremacy has been the Ark of the Covenant, as sacred to all British parties as the Monroe Doctrine to the American people. Nevertheless we have accepted without hesitation the principle of parity with the United States, and the scale of our naval defence has in fact always been determined by other standards of comparison, whether the measure was, as at one time, equality with the fleets of the next two European Powers or, as in later times, a fixed superiority over the largest continental navy.

That the readiness and unanimity with which the principle of parity with the United States has been accepted in Great Britain is in part due to the sentiment of which I have already spoken is no doubt true, but sentiments may change and it is, therefore, well to note that in this case it has a solid basis of reasoning to support it.

The truth is that since the War of Independence there has only been one subject on which our respective views of public law have clashed, namely, the extent and limits of the rights enjoyed by a belligerent at sea against neutral commerce; and, at any rate at the point we have now reached in the world's development, the strength of the American Navy is not, paradoxical as it may seem, the decisive factor in determining how far in case of war we should press what we believe to be our rights against American opinion.

It is only in those wars in which all our resources are strained to the uttermost that the rigorous enforcement of our belligerent rights becomes a matter of high consequence to us. If in such a war the United States are engaged with us, as was the case in the later years of the Great War, no difference of interest or practice arises between us. If, on the other hand, they are neutral as in the early years of that struggle, it would be simple madness to drive them into the ranks of our enemies. The plain truth is, and we may as well frankly acknowledge it, that we could not afford to do so. It would not be necessary for them to send out a fleet or even to move a ship; it would suffice that they should place an embargo on supplies to us of money and munitions of war.

As Lord Grey of Fallodon says in his *Twenty-Five Years*:[1]

" The blockade of Germany was essential to the victory of the Allies, but the ill-will of the United States meant certain defeat. . . . The Allies soon became dependent for an adequate supply on the United States. If we quarrelled with the United States we could not get that supply. . . . The object of diplomacy, therefore, was to secure the maximum of blockade that could be enforced without a rupture with the United States."

We are, therefore, obliged by self-interest to refrain from pressing our rights beyond the point at which American acquiescence can be secured lest we should be deprived of the resources which are necessary to our defences.

Thus far I have spoken of the feelings of Britons toward America. What are the feelings of Americans toward Britain? It is a momentous question and on the answer much depends, both for our own peoples and for the world. America has become a world Power. She speaks as such and expects to be listened to as such; but no man and no nation can permanently maintain rights unless he or it accepts the responsibilities which flow from them. *Noblesse oblige;* in every privilege is inherent a corresponding duty. Unless the duty is accepted, the privilege cannot be sustained —good democratic doctrine, surely, which should appeal to the great republic.

The United States may still avoid entangling engagements in Europe. They may isolate themselves, but they cannot immunize themselves, as the course of the Great War shows. Their concern with Europe grows greater

[1] Hodder and Stoughton.

and their co-operation tends to increase as their commerce grows and their interests widen. Must not Americans sometimes ask themselves whether it would not be wiser—and safer—to try to guide events rather than merely to suffer their consequences?

I put the question only. I do not attempt to answer it. I venture only the prediction that if ever Americans are led by events to answer it in the affirmative, common interests and common habits of thought will make Great Britain and America the supporters of common ideas and associates in the cause of freedom and of peace.

Perhaps of more immediate interest to Americans than the dangers and difficulties of the Old World are the problems of the Pacific. New currents are stirring in the Far East; a new and, it may well be, a decisive era is opening. What is to be the attitude of the United States to these developments? American policy is obscure and perhaps not yet decided. Yet it is with America that the decision rests. It is by her that the lead must be given.

An Englishman can only say that the declared policy of the United States and Great Britain is the same—the maintenance of the integrity of China and of the Open Door for the trade and enterprise of all nations. Will this common purpose suffice to produce a common policy?

On the answer to that question peace may well depend, but the answer can be given only by America.

PART II
IDLE HOURS

XIX

OFF THE STAGE AT THE PEACE CONFERENCE

I

AN EVENING WITH LLOYD GEORGE

It must have been in March 1919, I think. I was Chancellor of the Exchequer and was summoned to Paris on some question of post-War finance, and travelled with Lloyd George. He had just paid his first visit to London since the reorganization of his Government after the general election of 1918. He had intended to employ that week in consultation with his colleagues as to their domestic policy, but he had found us in the midst of industrial troubles which threatened to involve us in a general strike throughout the South Wales coal-fields. He had to sacrifice everything to this emergency and had spent the week in continuous and harassing conferences with the warring representatives of masters and men. I expected to find him worn out. I myself who had taken but a small part in this business was tired and glad enough when, as the train started, Lloyd George settled down to read the morning's papers. At Dover I went to my cabin for a nap whilst Lloyd George, at the Captain's invitation, went up on the bridge and chatted with the Duke of Connaught and Sir Henry Wilson throughout the passage. In the train to Paris I joined the three at luncheon, and Lloyd George kept us all lively with his amusing talk, straying from the present to the past and back again, full of fun and good humour and wisdom, and apparently as free from care as a schoolboy on holiday. Then, with an apology to the Duke, he carried Wilson and me off " to talk business." As we approached Creil, he said, " And now I am going to have a nap." He was asleep almost before we left his compartment.

Arrived at Paris, I had just time to find the rooms assigned to me in the Hotel Majestic and to dress, before going to his apartment for dinner. There I found a party which included Balfour, such other Ministers as happened to be in Paris, and Sir Maurice Hankey. Lloyd George showed no sign of the anxieties and labours of the last few days and at the moment when I entered was assuring Balfour that there were at least six poets then writing in Welsh who, could the world but understand the language in which they wrote, would be recognized in all countries as poets of the highest order. Balfour observed dryly that it was a pity they did not give the world an opportunity to appreciate their merits!

We moved in to dinner and Lloyd George told admirably a moving story of the last Eisteddfod, how the seal of the envelope containing the name of the successful competitor had been broken and his name called that he might come forward and be crowned and installed in the Bardic chair. But no answer came. Silence succeeded to the burst of cheering which had greeted the announcement of the winner, a shepherd from the mountains. The name was called again, and in the breathless silence which followed came presently a piteous cry: " Killed on the Somme "; the chair was draped in black and crowned with the laurel wreath he should have worn, which was later carried to the lonely cottage where his mother dwelt in one of the mountain valleys.

Lloyd George finished, and turned rapidly to Balfour to ask what had been happening in the Peace Conference during his absence. Balfour could not report much progress. "After all, you have been away only seven days. I have been an exile from England since Christmas. Tell me what is happening there. What, for instance, is the new House of Commons like?"

"I'll tell you," said Lloyd George, his eyes sparkling with fun and a smile spreading rapidly over his face. "I made a speech to them. I addressed myself at first to the Opposition benches in front of me. They were very cold and hostile; I couldn't get a cheer. This, said I to myself, is not the House of Commons; it's the Trades Union Congress. So I turned as one does in such circumstances to the benches behind me, but neither was that the House of Commons; it was the Associated Chambers of Commerce."

2

My Last Meeting with Botha

The draft of the Treaty of Peace had been handed to the Germans and their reply had been received. We were again in Lloyd George's apartment—Lloyd George himself and Balfour, all the Dominion representatives and such British Ministers as were available. We had met in the morning, adjourned for lunch and met again in the afternoon. The question was should any concessions be granted, and if so, what; or should we insist that the treaty must be accepted as it stood. There had been much discussion as to what concessions could be proposed to the Allies with any chance of acceptance, but no difference as to the wisdom of conceding what we could. It must have been past six and I had to leave by the eight o'clock train for London, for my presence was needed in the house of Commons next day. "Well," I said, "I think we all seem agreed on the main question. You will not need me any more and I am content to leave further details to you."

"Wait a moment," said Lloyd George. "General Botha, you have not yet spoken?"

"Oh, I agree with the rest of you. It pays to be generous," and, laying his hand gently on Milner's shoulder, beside whom he was seated, he added with a friendly smile, "even a small country, driven to desperation, can give a great deal of trouble, as my good friend Milner knows."

That was the last time I saw Botha. He died [1] a few months later.

3

A Dinner with Balfour

The Peace Conference was in progress. We were a party of four dining in the Majestic, the headquarters of the British Delegation—Balfour and Ian Malcolm, then his Parliamentary Private Secretary, were the guests of Oliver Locker-Lampson, who served me in the same capacity, and myself.

In a momentary lull in the talk, Oliver suddenly asked, "Mr. Balfour, what do you think of the Prime Minister's brains?"

"Well," said Balfour after a moment's hesitation, "I'll tell you one thing about them. I've often been surprised when Lloyd George has come to what I thought the right decision on some complicated issue, to discover afterwards how little he appeared to have known about the essential

[1] August 1919.

facts. All I can say is that if I had known as little as he appeared to do, I should certainly have gone wrong."

This instinctive judgment, more like a woman's than a man's, accounts for some of his greatest successes—and no small part of his failures.

The talk turned to books. Again it was Oliver who spoke. " Mr. Balfour, if you were banished to an island and allowed to take with you the works of only one novelist, which would you choose? "

I suggested Thackeray.

" No, not Thackeray," said Balfour, waving aside my favourite novelist without discussion. " Dickens, perhaps, but certainly not Thackeray."

Other authors were discussed—Fielding, Scott, the Brontës. Then Balfour suggested Bulwer Lytton, whom he thought grossly underrated. I expressed my surprise, confessing that I found him unreadable. Balfour protested; " Look at *My Novel*, to take but a single instance—full of faults, no doubt, but what a bold conception and how great, even with all its faults, the measure of achievement! "

I was interested by the selection, for the last time I had been to stay with my father at Cannes, I had found him re-reading *My Novel*, and he, too, praised it for the same qualities, and declared Bulwer to be much underrated. Will Mr. Michael Sadleir bring him into vogue again?

I set up another of the authors whose fame Mr. Sadleir has revived—Anthony Trollope. I thought that not only the *Barchester Towers* series were perfect of their kind, but that the political novels—*Phineas Phin* and the rest— were equally good. They gave a perfect picture of political society at the close of the Palmerstonian period. Balfour seemed interested; he must look at them again. Finally he agreed with Oliver rather than stated for himself, that as a Scotsman he could not do better than choose Walter Scott, but he accepted the suggestion with less warmth of approval than I should have expected.

Then I raised another and a more delicate question. Recalling Andrew Lang's delightful Introduction to his *Old Friends*, that entertaining volume of imaginary letters from one character of fiction to another, I asked Balfour who was his lady-love among the heroines of romance.

" Well," he said, " there's a girl in a book that you fellows will never have heard of, called *The Initials*." [1]

" Arthur," I exclaimed, " not Hildegarde ? "

" Hildegarde, Hildegarde—was her name Hildegarde ? Anyway the girl in *The Initials*."

It was so characteristic that though he knew he loved her, he could not remember the name of the lady of his affections.

Again I was interested. All my family were brought up on this now wholly forgotten book, published some-time in the 'sixties of last century. My father also had succumbed to the lady's charm. I remember an occasion when we were driving from Innsbruck to Cortina and had stopped to lunch in the hotel at the top of the Brenner. There was no one but ourselves in the restaurant when we arrived, but presently a train disgorged a crowd of German tourists. Suddenly my father exclaimed," There's Hildegarde ! " I had my back to the new arrivals and turned to see the lady. " Don't stare at her like that," said my father, almost angrily, " you'll make the girl quite uncomfortable and she'll sit with her back to us ! "

The story has a sequel. I told it on some occasion to Sir Alfred Hopkinson. I happened to meet him some time later. He reminded me of it. He had, he said,

[1] By Baroness Tautphœus, 1850.

with difficulty and only recently procured a copy " and I, an old man of eighty, have fallen head over ears in love."

I re-read the book after the conversation with Balfour but I could not share these transports. If, in my thoughts, I am ever unfaithful to Ethel Newcome, it is to Beatrix Esmond that they stray. Becky Sharp would have been a delightful companion at a dinner party, and if she cared to take the trouble, would have almost swept a man off his feet, but I couldn't marry Becky Sharp though, as Andrew Lang reminds us, her " kindness was so great that she even condescended to be amusing to her own husband."

XX

HOW GREAT SPEAKERS PREPARE
THEIR SPEECHES

A CORRESPONDENCE in a Sunday paper led me some years ago to write a note on the use made by my father in his public speeches of poetical quotations, and, if I may judge by the expressions of opinion which reached me, that glimpse into the methods of work of one of the great speakers and the greatest Parliamentary debater of his generation was not without interest. The newspaper itself remarked that " it is always fascinating to look into a prominent man's workshop," and this observation, spurring my own curiosity, has led me to try to carry the matter further.

How do great speakers prepare their speeches? Is there, or has there been, any uniformity of practice? Is there any golden rule which will lead the beginner to success? It is improbable, but, except among contemporaries, it is not very easy to collect the materials for an adequate answer. Notes of speeches are apt to be torn up as soon as they have served their purpose, or, if retained for a time, to be destroyed at the first overhaul of papers. Even if the notes themselves are by any chance preserved, they do not necessarily reveal the extent or the character of the preparation which went to their composition. Descriptions of the effect of historic speeches upon their listeners are common enough, but we more rarely get a glimpse of the craftsman at his bench sharpening his tools or shaping his work.

Yet the subject is surely a fascinating one. Nearly forty years ago I begged of John Bright the notes of the last great speech that he delivered in public, and I have often been tempted to make this the basis of a collection among my contemporaries. But the fear of being importunate, and the formidable frown with which Mr. Bright greeted that first request (though a couple of days later it was most kindly granted), have deterred me; and, apart from speeches of my father, I have but few examples.

There is another difficulty. Every successful Parliament man must be a debater, able to speak without preparation and without notes, or with only such notes as he may hastily jot down while listening to the opponent to whom he is about to reply. But some of our greatest speakers never use notes even for speeches that have been the subject of careful preparation; and in such cases, unless they themselves have disclosed their secret or some friend has observed and recorded it, we are thrown back upon speculation and guesswork. I suspect that in the more leisurely and rhetorical days of the late eighteenth century and of the early and middle part of the nineteenth century an ampler preparation than is usually practised to-day was in most cases both possible and necessary.

A good deal of information can, however, be gathered if one takes the trouble to search for it, though I do not think that anyone has yet sought to bring it together. Of Chatham's method I can find no account, and of his notes, if he used notes, none have survived. In the case of the younger Pitt we are more fortunate. His success in Parliament was immediate and decisive. Not even the memory of Chatham's lofty eloquence could lessen the fame at once acquired by his favourite son. " He is not a chip of the old block; he is the old block itself!" Burke exclaimed after listening to his maiden speech, and Lord Stanhope has preserved for us not only Pitt's own account of the training that he had undergone at his father's hands, but also a description of his method and examples of his notes. Chatham, he tells us, was not only accustomed to send the young Pitt specimens of oratory to study, but "bade him take up any book in some foreign language with which he was well acquainted, in Latin or Greek especially," and "to read out of this work a passage in English, stopping where he was not sure of the word to be used in English, until the right word came to his mind," [1] whilst "to train his son in sonorous elocution, Lord Chatham caused him to recite day by day in his presence passages from the best English poets, especially Shakespeare and Milton." When after this training in his boyhood he came to speak in the House of Commons, "he did not prepare the structure or the wording of his sentences, far less write them down beforehand. The statement of his friends upon this point," Lord Stanhope declares, "is much confirmed by his own notes, as scattered among his papers. These notes,[2] which are in his own handwriting, are all extremely brief, at most some figures for his finance, and some headings for his argument." And then Lord Stanhope gives as instances "his only written preparation for two of the most remarkable among his many great harangues."

[1] But then Pitt, as I would beg our schoolmasters to observe, had from first to last been encouraged to read the Classics for their inherent beauty and interest. "He had never, indeed, according to the fashion at Public Schools, applied himself to Greek or Latin composition. He had never mastered the *laborious inutilities of the ancient metres*." (My italics). Stanhope's *Life of Pitt*.

[2] These notes seem to have disappeared. The present Lord Stanhope tells me that nothing is now preserved at Chevening except a single sheet of notes, apparently scribbled by Pitt across his knee as he listened to a debate, and therefore useless for any elucidation of his practice on a set occasion.

Here are the notes as printed by Lord Stanhope for Pitt's speech on the renewal of the war in 1803 :

NOTES OF SPEECH (MAY 23, 1803)

Acts since the Preliminaries.
    Elba.
    Etruria.
    Louisiana.

Since definitive Treaty.
    Black Sea.
    Piedmont.
    Germany.
    Switzerland.

Cases which may arise.
    Encroachments on Austria or
        other parts of Continent.

On powers guaranteed by us   .   Portugal.
        Naples.
        Malta.
        Turkey.

On Maritime Interests   . .   Spain or S. America.
        Portugal or Brazil.
        Holland or its Colonies.
        Egypt or Maritime Possessions
            of Turkey.
        N. America.

On objects immediately British .   Shutting Ports of Europe.
        Sending forces to India, or
            advancing claims there.
        Press.
        French emigrants.

General state of Naval and Military
    preparation.

Finance system.

System of Foreign connection.

This is the speech of which Fox said that " if Demosthenes had been present he must have admired and might have envied," and which Lord Stanhope placed among the three best that Pitt ever made.

To me these seem the perfection of what notes should be, if (but what an *if*!) from such bare headlines, the speaker can make, I will not say a speech that Demosthenes might envy, but one which is at all adequate to the occasion. But for a set speech of immense consequence, both alike from the position of the speaker and the circumstances of the moment, the very baldness of these notes suggests to my mind careful preliminary thought and concentrated mental preparation.

Fox, on the other hand, appears to have given little thought to preparation and to have used no notes. The late Sir George Trevelyan describes him as " an extempore speaker," and attributes no small share of his facility to his early fondness for amateur theatricals. " The pains which he had bestowed on learning to speak the words of others, enabled him to concentrate his undivided attention upon the arduous task of improvizing his own. If only he could find the thing which required to be said he was sure to say it in the way that would produce the greatest possible effect." Thus his biographer; but then we have Fox's own confession that he acquired his pre-eminence in debate by speaking at least once every night for two sessions, an example which no possible victim of the practice would commend to aspirants to a like fame.

Of Sheridan's method I can find no trace; but Windham, whom Erskine May describes as his superior in education and attainments, and little inferior in wit, and to whom he assigns a higher place as a debater, is shown, by papers preserved in the Additional Manuscripts at the British Museum, not only to have made full notes, but, on some occasions at least, to have written out in full all that he intended to say. The manuscript of his speech on the

Rohilla charge against Hastings is preserved together with much material that went to its preparation.[1]

The Additional Manuscripts also contain similar drafts and notes of speeches by Charles Yorke and Huskisson,[2] and some of the first Lord Liverpool's speeches in the handwriting of his secretary. These, like the others, are written out in full even to the " Mr. Speaker " or " Sir " which opens the speech or introduces a paragraph. Lord Liverpool was certainly no orator, but it would be unkind and doubtless untrue to infer that his speeches were made by his secretary, though such things have been known to occur. I remember a Member of Parliament in my early days who made some very polished speeches, full of good things. " How do you hit on these things? " I once asked him. " Well," he said, " I have a very clever secretary, and I shut him up in one room, and myself in another, and we each write a speech. Then we compare notes and I take the best of both ! " *Sic vos non vobis*, oh ! private secretaries and Civil Servants ; but how you must suffer when your chief bungles your arguments and blunts your points !

In such cases as I have been describing, the preparation was evidently very careful and complete. But what is preparation? [3] My father once said to the late Sir E.

---

[1] Windham's Diary records on the occasion of this speech an experience which many a later Member must have shared :

June 1st, 1786.—Day of motion on the Rohilla War. . . . I have seldom found myself more clear than during my visit to him (Sir Philip Francis), and afterwards, *till I went to the House : but somehow, by the time I got there, my mind had got into some disorder, and my spirits into some agitation ; and by the time Burke had finished, I found myself in no good state to speak.*

[2] The Peel Papers, now in the British Museum, may show what Peel's practice was, but they fill, I think, nearly two hundred volumes and have not yet been catalogued.

[3] And what, it may be asked, is an impromptu? I have just come across the following entry in Anne Thackeray's Diary : *Wednesday (March 1st, 1854).* " I had an invitation from Mrs. Thomson Hankey, but Papa could not take me, having a public dinner to attend, at which he made the most beautiful impromptu speech, as I have good reason to know, as he delivered it to me from his bed the day before."—*Letters of Anne Thackeray Ritchie.*

Hamilton, then Mr. Gladstone's private secretary, that Mr. Gladstone told him that he did not prepare his speeches, unless it might be some peculiarly important and delicate announcement on foreign affairs. "I don't know what he means by preparation," retorted Sir Edward. "If he means that he doesn't sit down and write, I daresay it's true, but he lies on a sofa and *wombles* it in his inside. And I'll tell you this, Mr. Chamberlain, none of us like to go near him the day before he makes a great speech!" As a very wise parlourmaid once said of my father on a similar occasion: "No, Mum, it's not what he says, but what he looks!" What private secretary could not tell a like tale? I do not believe that any man ever made a good speech without feeling the strain beforehand *if he had time to think about it*.

No doubt in these busy days when the occasions for speech are so numerous and the opportunities for thought so few, much of the preparation is only semi-conscious or sub-conscious, the result of "wombling" at odd moments and amid other preoccupations, and much is left to the hazard of the moment. "Sir," said Dr. Johnson, "it concentrates a man's mind wonderfully to know that he is to be hanged in a fortnight," and a man's knowledge that in another moment he will be on his feet addressing three or four thousand people, or the fact that he is already doing so, is equally stimulating to his faculties. Under this pressure ideas that have been vaguely floating in the mind suddenly take shape and scattered thoughts fall as suddenly into place. "Why do you worry, Chamberlain?" Mr. Bright once said to my father who was lamenting the fate that compelled him to deliver three speeches "each with a beginning and a middle and an end" to three great mass meetings on one Saturday afternoon—"why do you

worry? there is always inspiration in a great crowd."
No doubt in such circumstances some things worth saying
will be forgotten and the *esprit de l'escalier* will torment
the speaker with the vision of lost opportunities as soon as
he sits down. But this matters little. Those are the happy
ones who, on such occasions, can resume their seats without
having said something that they would wish immediately
to recall.

Disraeli was as independent of notes as his great rival.
"He was," says Mr. Buckle, " gifted with a marvellously
retentive memory, which often, indeed, betrayed him into
plagiarisms of a sustained character in speech and writing,
but which, at any rate, enabled him altogether to dispense,
in his ordinary practice, with the use of notes." Disraeli
himself justified his practice by saying, "if I once used
notes, I should lean upon them; and that would never do."
"He depended," we are told, " in some degree on catching
inspiration from his hearers; he told Delane, he was ' much
influenced by my audience and the impromptu.' This
does not, of course, mean that there was not careful preparation before any great effort, or that, in particular, the biting
phrases by which he will always be remembered were not
deeply studied in his mind, and assiduously polished before
they were launched, apparently at random, upon the world.
In preparing the few speeches of importance which he
delivered outside Parliament he often made use of a highly
original method; he privately rehearsed them, either in
whole or in part, to an experienced reporter of The Times,
J. F. Neilson, in whom he placed especial trust."

In like manner Macaulay, when he spoke " had no notes
in his hand and no manuscript in his pocket," but his
speeches were most carefully prepared and were repeated
without the loss or omission of a single word. " If a debate

were in prospect he would turn the subject over while he paced his chamber or tramped along the streets. Each thought as it rose in his mind embodied itself in phrases and clothed itself in an appropriate drapery of images, instances and quotations; and when, in the course of his speech, the thought recurred, all the words which gave it point and beauty spontaneously recurred with it." [1] Macaulay's memory was, of course, phenomenal and has become proverbial. But it is curious to find how many men, who prepared their speeches carefully, yet used no notes.

The late Lord Salisbury and Mr. Bonar Law were of this number, and Lord Salisbury at least was not only a most effective but a most polished speaker. In answer to my inquiry, the present Lord Salisbury writes: " It is quite true that my father always spoke without notes. He had nothing in the shape of papers in his hands unless he was going to quote someone else. . . . He once told me that the epigrams (though he did not use the word, I am sure), or it may be the illustrations—for both of which his speeches were notable—occurred to him only as he was speaking. . . . I remember also that he was accustomed to use some *memoria technica* in place of notes." Towards the close of his last Administration Lord Salisbury told me that he regretted that he had not accustomed himself to the use of notes in his younger days, for by that time he had begun to feel the strain of being wholly dependent on his memory for the substance and arrangement of what he meant to say. It may be that neither he nor Mr. Bonar Law ever attempted verbal preparation unless of some passage of singular importance, but, even so, the strain of composing the whole speech without putting pen to paper, of marshalling the arguments, of arranging the order of presenta-

[1] Trevelyan's *Life of Macaulay.*

tion of the facts, or remembering that this thought or argument had been rejected and that other substituted in the course of preparation, must have been immense. Mr Bonar Law himself told me that two hours of such work left him as exhausted as a twenty-mile walk.

But if some men use no notes and some forgo preparation altogether, we can set against their example the practice of others not less illustrious. Of Canning's custom in his earlier years we have no certain knowledge, but it is not likely that he was less careful then than later, when he had long established his reputation as an orator and his position as a statesman. " Certainly during his last tenure of office when he was about to make an important speech, his whole mind was absorbed with it for two, or, perhaps, three days, beforehand. He spared no labour in obtaining and arranging his material. He always drew up a paper (which he used in the House) with the heads, in their order, of the several topics on which he meant to touch, and these heads were numbered, and the numbers sometimes extended to four or even five hundred. At these periods he was not easy of approach; interruption irritated him, except it related to the matter in hand." [1] Once again the private secretary reveals the strain of long preliminary labour which produced the smooth delivery and glowing rhetoric of the speech itself.

So, too, with Bright. Though he said that he had once written a speech and then found its delivery so great a strain that he had never attempted it again, he became, I think, by his slow and leisurely method of preparation almost word-perfect in what he intended to say, and could probably have repeated a speech the moment after its delivery with very little change of language. He was

---

[1] Stapleton's *Canning*.

accustomed, I have been told, to try in conversation the effect of his arguments and sometimes even of his phrases, but he had a fine ear for the cadences of language and an unfailing instinct for the right word which must have been a natural gift. "If my manner of speaking is good, it may have become so from reading what is good," he once wrote to a correspondent, and probably few could rival his knowledge of the Bible and of Milton and, rather surprisingly, of Byron. An aunt of mine, in whose house he was staying, once asked him to read some Browning on a Sunday afternoon towards the close of his life. He consented, but he did not care for Browning's poetry, and in a few moments had laid the volume aside and was reciting from memory long passages of Byron's poetry to which he was attracted, perhaps, as much by its rhetorical character as by its passion for liberty.

The mention of Byron and Browning recalls to my mind two stories of Bright that are worth telling. Bright and Browning dined one evening at my father's house in Prince's Gardens about the time of the publication of Donelly's *Cryptogram*. Half-way through dinner the lady who sat between them said, "It is time that you intervened, Mr. Chamberlain. Mr. Bright and Mr. Browning are coming to blows." It appeared that Mr. Bright, who enjoyed legal puzzles, and was said to know the evidence in the Tichborne trial better than any layman, had professed his belief that Donelly had succeeded in proving that Bacon wrote Shakespeare; and Mr. Browning's temper had not been proof against the strain. As, later, I held the door open for the guests to pass out of the dining-room, I caught the echo of the storm. "Stupid old man!" growled Bright to my father; "I don't believe he understands his own poems." And a moment later, as Browning passed

out, " Obstinate old fool ! " he muttered, " I don't believe
he ever read a play of Shakespeare in his life." And,
indeed, I do not think that Bright ever showed any great
appreciation of Shakespeare.

The second story I was told by my father. Bright was
addressing the annual meeting of his Birmingham constituents in the Town Hall. He was speaking of the horrors
of war (I do not know the occasion) and began quoting,
" Lo ! where the Giant on the mountain stands," throwing
up his hands as he did so in anticipation of the coming
image, when a look of agony crossed his face, and, turning
to the chairman, he demanded fiercely, " What's the next
line ? " The chairman, poor man ! was unequal to the
occasion—how many of us would have done any better ?—
but the line was at once given by Mr. Sam Timmins (a
well-known Birmingham figure of the time, whose name
is recorded in the Free Library as one of its principal
benefactors) and Mr. Bright sailed on :

> " Lo ! where the Giant on the mountain stands,
> His blood-red tresses deep'ning in the sun,
> With death-shot glowing in his fiery hands,
> And eye that scorcheth all it glares upon."

But this is a digression. Mr. Bright's notes were very
full. His biographer prints a facsimile page of the notes
of a speech made in 1860. " Each idea in its order," says
Mr. Trevelyan, " is represented by a few words or figures,
while the 'key sentence' or 'island,' as he used to call it,
is written out at full." I possess the notes for two of his
speeches, one as chairman of a Rochdale meeting in 1877,
and the other the only speech he made on Mr. Gladstone's
first Home Rule Bill. It was addressed to his constituents
in the Birmingham Town Hall on July 1st, 1886, and was,
I think, the last speech but one of his long public life.

The earlier speech must have occupied fifteen or twenty minutes in delivery, the later one more than an hour. The notes for the former cover three sides of small-sized letter paper; those of the latter, nine. Both are in small but very clear handwriting, and almost every word is underlined. Long sentences are written out in full, or nearly so. One page is here reproduced.

The first four lines conclude his examination of the Land Bill. Then he turns to the exclusion of the Irish members from Westminster and to the alternative suggestion that they should attend only for Imperial business. It will be seen how detailed all this is, even to the very characteristic aside " and rather commend them," which is followed up on the next page with the equally characteristic "Vote of censure —or two-pence income tax to pay for new Bombardment— or blunder on Afghan frontier." If these are "islands," Mr. Bright sailed amidst a veritable archipelago. The earlier notes are almost equally detailed, and hardly bear out Mr. Trevelyan's conclusion that he wrote out " only the heads of his argument with an occasional ' key sentence,' " and " ending up with the peroration transcribed in full."

The mention of a peroration reminds me of the advice of an old parliamentary hand—I think Lord Palmerston— to a beginner in the House. " You need not bother about the beginning of your speech because that will naturally arise out of the debate. Nor will the body of the speech give you much trouble, for that will be concerned with the subject under discussion, and unless you were fully conversant with the matter you would not speak; [1] but you must know your peroration or you will never be able to sit down."

[1] I suspect that Lord Palmerston—if Palmerston it was—was an optimist even for his own day.

where your security. Ask any Financier?

On what terms hold you safe in this monstrous
engaged
~~arranged~~ & happened if support Govᵗ. Bill — Speculation?

if not, no concealment. Would frankly tell you

But Govᵗ. Bill. Irish members. "& Dublin Parlᵗ" inevitable

only bright spot & compensation in Bill

Parlᵗ. given. exclusion absolutely necessary

300 Irish members. Dublin — 100 in London

American Irish contribution. Perpetual Charitable

If League does not care about Foreign affairs, fund.

to rather command them — Let them stay in Ireland?

But a new plan. occasional presence in London.

To have a sort of intermittent Irish fever
in House of Commons. so astonishing & so
ludicrous — how many? Commons & Lords too?
how come & when? Special Boat. & Train?
excursion & return Tickets. which exchequer?
procession Westminster Hall. invade House

In my early days of public speaking I studiously acted on this advice, so far, at least, as the peroration was concerned, but I found that the sentences so carefully committed to memory were not infrequently used half-way through the speech to fill a gulf suddenly yawning at my feet when all ideas had momentarily forsaken the earnest but very nervous orator.

"Get your transitions clearly in your mind," was the late Lord Goschen's advice to me, "the bridges which lead from one subject to the next; for the language you can trust to the moment." This is good advice, but Lord Goschen certainly wrote out much of his speeches beforehand and was able on occasion, like Disraeli, to go through them with a reporter before the meeting. I recall one such instance in the case of a speech that I heard him deliver one evening in my school-days at Rugby when he was closeted with the representative of *The Times* for an hour in the course of the afternoon. Lord Goschen was very short-sighted and wrote a minute and very illegible hand, and this must have added to his difficulties in using notes. More than once, the present Lord Goschen tells me, his father would appeal to him: "I know I have something good here, but I can't read it. Can you make it out?"

Mr. Winston Churchill has not found any of his father's notes preserved among his papers, but here Lord Salisbury again comes to my help. "Lord Randolph," he writes, "once lent me the notes of a speech he was going to deliver, or had been going to deliver, to help me for a speech when I was an undergraduate. The notes were most elaborate—headings, sub-headings and sub-sub-headings. He told me at the time that he had used every method —learning by heart, elaborate notes, and impromptu in debate." I daresay that most of us have done the same.

There was one of many delightful week-end parties at Taplow Court in the early years of this century when guests wandering about the grounds on Sunday morning reported that they had found the late Lord Percy reciting his Monday's speech in one alley, Lord Hugh Cecil preparing himself in another, and Mr. Churchill practising his peroration in a third.

Of Mr. Asquith's notes I possess one example—those for the speech which he delivered in August 1920, on the proposal to place my father's statue in the lobby of the House of Commons, and which I begged of him at the time as a memorial of the tribute paid to my father's memory by a political adversary who has ever been as generously appreciative of the qualities of his opponents as staunchly loyal to his friends. These notes are very full, but the occasion was exceptional. " They are, of course," wrote Mr. Asquith in a letter giving me permission to reproduce a page of them, " more elaborated (as to language, etc.) than what I should normally use at a public meeting, or for a speech in the House." And he added that his practice as to extent of preparation varied so much and his habit of consigning his notes to immediate destruction was so inveterate, that he could not give me a more typical example. The last sheet of these notes is given on page 265.

Here there is certainly evidence of careful and even of verbal preparation ; but Mr. Asquith's style was natural to him and differed little in his prepared and unprepared speeches. In both there are the same clean-cut and faultless sentences, the same wide command of dignified and sonorous language, and the same secure and easy progress, through whatever parentheses he allows himself, to a conclusion that is not only intelligible but grammatical.

Far different was the case of the late Lord Balfour. I have been told by my father that, when he first entered the House, Mr. Balfour was a bad speaker, and he never acquired the easy flow and smooth delivery which do so much for the comfort of the audience. His preparation was generally slight and never verbal. His notes were few and little consulted by him when speaking; and I think I have observed that even when he affected to consult them, it was often only a gesture securing a moment for reflection. The right word did not always occur to him at once, and he was far too fastidious to use, as most of us do, the first word which presented itself, when it was not the best one. Thus he hesitated, and paused, and sometimes recast the sentence, and so, as I have found, occasionally disappointed those who heard him for the first time. But his mastery of the House of Commons was complete. "He plays on you all like an old fiddle," a friend whom I had introduced to the gallery once said to me after hearing Mr. Balfour wind up a debate, and, whatever the imperfections of his manner, he dominated us all, almost as much, perhaps, by his personal charm as by his intellectual pre-eminence. He had, besides, a rare gift for rising above the party squabbles which sometimes disfigure debate and placing the discussion on a higher plane. I recall, though only vaguely after the lapse of so many years, one such occasion. The House was discussing some untoward incident which had occurred in one of our West African Colonies, and the debate had degenerated into a wrangle between that strange type of Englishman who takes for granted that his countryman overseas is always in the wrong and those others who will admit no criticism of a man of their own race bearing great responsibilities and facing great difficulties among an alien people. It was the old problem of Governor Eyre in a new garb,

But let me add

There were accompl[ish]...

    feed
    stimulated
    inspired

unselfish ideals

   dauntless courage

  his several loy[alty] to colleagues & friends

  above all   fervid & dominant

    sense of [public] & [private] duty

his example   treasured memories

& it is fitting that his effigy
    take its place
   among famous figures
who in their long & honoured succession
impersonate & keep alive great
    traditions of this House

MR. ASQUITH'S NOTES

and happily with far less serious issues. Balfour rose from the front Opposition bench in an angry House where nearly every speech was adding fuel to the flames. In a few sentences he expressed his judgment on the particular incident and turned to consider the principles which should govern the relations of white men and black in these tropical dependencies. The House was lifted out of itself into a serener atmosphere and was grateful to the man who had wrought the miracle.

I have preserved the notes of two of his House of Commons speeches. Of these, the more interesting are those for the speech which he made on Mr. Chaplin's amendment to the second reading of the Budget of 1903, on the occasion of the abolition of the shilling duty on corn, for in that debate not only were Mr. Balfour's followers sharply divided among themselves, but the Opposition had fiercely attacked his personal conduct and denounced what they were pleased to consider his breach of constitutional practice. The notes are written, as was Mr. Balfour's habit, on long envelopes headed respectively " Preface I," " Self II," " Finis." He spoke at the opening of the second day's debate, and the notes show every sign of having been jotted down as the debate of the previous day proceeded. The first two contain about half a dozen notes apiece. The third is much fuller, though the matter covered by it occupied about the same time in delivery. The second envelope concludes with

> " Here should end the case !—
> But large question.
> Ministerial responsibility " ;

and on this follows the final sheet which is here reproduced.

Finis

Shall we deal with it quâ
  Personal defence. becoming Hear on   No leader more

"Impossible; humiliating; unfair to
      peace; to the Am: to the Conf;
      to the civilised world: & the world;
      to the whole of things. —

I profoundly dissent. —

To judge fairly they must adopt
            my point of view.

I do not belong to the happy band
    who think everything perfect.

| Treaties coming to an end. Tariff.
Colonial preference Prime Minister.

It cannot be denied new departures
Two courses open to a Gov^t.   possible.

      Silently make up your mind.
      Indicate doubts.   Peel
                              Gladstone

Incomparably more difficult than
      either. Corn Laws   or H. Rule.
            Foreign Countries. Colonies. H. populated
As regards Home population — it depends on the

The report of this portion of the speech fills about a column of *The Times* and would, I suppose, take about twenty minutes in delivery. These are by far the fullest notes that I have ever seen Lord Balfour use, and anyone who takes the trouble to look at the report will find that all, or nearly all, the notes find expression and development in what he actually said. But this with him was unusual, I remember on one occasion, when we were in opposition, being left in charge for some time during a Friday afternoon's debate. After a time Mr. Balfour joined me, and, with one ear on the debate, chatted delightfully on many subjects as they crossed our thoughts. After a time he said, " Well, if I am to wind up, I suppose it's time that I began to think what I am to say," and, pulling out half a dozen long envelopes from the rack on the table of the House, he wrote without hesitation a headline at the top of the first and a second headline half-way down; then did the same with a second and, I think, a third envelope; then more slowly jotted in a very few sub-headings and the work was done. I watched as he wrote, and was fascinated not only by the quick working of his mind but by observing how the speech at once presented itself to him as a whole. The framework appeared the moment he put pen to paper. Some details were added almost at once; more appeared only in the speech itself, occuring to him as he developed his argument or as suggested by the interruptions with which he met. But the first idea of the speech sprang from his brain as a whole, consecutive and complete, though he had certainly done no conscious preparation beforehand. I once begged of him another set of notes, now, unfortunately, mislaid or lost, the interest of which lay in the fact that after opening in the manner indicated by the first headline, he never again approached the " signposts " that he had jotted down, but followed a new train of thought apparently suggested as he spoke, by his own opening words, and I suspect that, in the case of Lord Balfour, notes, even when most complete, were never more than headlines and certainly they were never allowed to hamper his freedom of movement in action.

This, indeed, suggests one of the difficulties of preparation. If a practised speaker knows exactly what he is going to say, and has it somehow firmly fixed in his mind, he can say it and yet preserve a large power of variation in reply to interruptions or in response to the inspiration of the moment. If, at the other extreme, he has only the broadest outline of the speech before him, he is quite likely to be equally successful, and sometimes more so, just because he knows himself to be dependent upon, and trusts entirely to, the inspiration of the moment. But there must be many who, like myself, have found careful but imperfect preparation a fatal snare, for the knowledge that you have not only something particular to say, but that there was a particular way in which you meant to say it, is paralysing unless that way jumps to your mind when the critical moment arrives. It was the realization of this fact that caused me after a time to act upon my father's advice: " Don't take so much trouble with your speeches as I have been accustomed to do. I don't mean that yours will be better because you take less, but, now that so many speeches are called for, the burden is too great."

My father, indeed, took immense pains with his prepared speeches. Such a speech as that with which he opened his Tariff Reform campaign at Glasgow in 1903, or those in which he developed his " Unauthorized Programme " in 1885 meant not only months of study beforehand but days of actual work upon his notes. When he first spoke as a

young man in Birmingham he was not, I have been told
by relations who were his contemporaries, a ready or even
an easy speaker, and he himself said that in his early days
he could only deliver one speech a month because it took
him a fortnight to prepare it, and another fortnight to
recover from it. Of course, in his later days he often made
debating or impromptu speeches, and among them were
some of the most effective. But if he had time—and
especially for great meetings in the country or set occasions
in Parliament—he thought no pains too great to get his
argument into the best form and to secure that every
passage conduced directly to the particular result that he
desired to produce. For Parliamentary purposes the task
would be simplified because the question put from the
chair dictated both the subject and the scope of the speech,
but of speeches at public meetings he would say: "The
first great difficulty is to find your subject—to get your
line. After that the main task is to exclude everything
which, however good in itself, does not lead directly to the
particular conclusion that you wish to enforce." Is not
this exclusion of the irrelevant or the merely superfluous
the secret of all great art?

Given plenty of time—and to get it undisturbed he
habitually worked far into the night—his practice was to
make a first draft of the speech in writing. This would
cover four, or, more rarely, six or even eight, sides of
notepaper in a very small hand. From this draft he made
his speaking notes, and, in doing so, often discarded much
of what he had originally written and introduced fresh
matter. These notes, when finished, he would go over
at least once, more often two or even three times, until,
I think, they were clearly fixed in his mind. But even so,
when speaking he used his notes freely and never sought

to conceal them; but he could turn aside to demolish an interrupter or to answer an objection with no fear of losing the thread of his argument or forgetting the point which he had reached at the moment of the digression. This perfect ease and security on his part, coupled with his singularly clear voice, had much to do with the comfort and enjoyment of his audiences. And by the time I attended his meetings he seemed as easy a speaker, as free in his movements, and as completely master of his resources as any man could be, though even after that he still continued to develop his mastery of the technique of speaking until the last year or two of tremendous strain and lessening health. Few people, I think, who saw him just before a meeting when the work of preparation was done and he had resolutely banished all thoughts of speech and notes from his mind, or who listened to the delivery of the speech itself, so easy, so natural, apparently so spontaneous, without a sign of strain in voice or manner, could have guessed the immense and wearing labour that went to its preparation, but Mrs. Chamberlain, now Mrs. Carnegie, who could watch him at work in his library, has told me that few, if any, such set speeches in the country cost less than three days constant toil and that five was the more usual number. Again and again, I have known him shut himself up in his library from breakfast to lunch, from lunch to dinner, and again till the early hours of the morning, and emerge at last with nothing definite accomplished. "I cannot get my line," he would say, and he would admit at times that in despair he had taken refuge in a French novel. And then perhaps next evening he would say: "Well, whatever happens, I am going to make my speech before I go to bed to-night," and he would do it, though he had to work till three or four in the morning. When I think of the infinite trouble that he took, I am ashamed of such measure of facility as I have acquired by much practice and the all-too-ready acceptance of a lower standard.

But, although his preparation was so careful, my father would never do what some others of his day did habitually, that is, give to a representative of the Press the terms or even the substance of his speech before its delivery. To do this, he felt, would be to put himself under constraint to make the speech in that particular form and no other, and thus to subject himself to an intolerable strain at the moment of delivery. He used to relate that early in his parliamentary life—I think a couple of years or less after he entered the House—he took the chair at a public meeting in Birmingham at which Sir William Harcourt was the chief speaker. *The Times* reporter was closeted with Sir William for a couple of hours in the morning. Then he sought my father. " My editor," he said, " is prepared to place a column at your disposal if you will tell me what you are going to say." My father replied that he could not do it—he could not trust himself, the strain would be too great. " Then," said the reporter, " I am sorry, but there will be no report." " Well," rejoined my father, " I am much obliged for your offer, and I, too, am sorry that I cannot accept it, but I console myself with the thought that one of two things will happen. Either the public doesn't want to read me and then, though it is very kind of you to make the offer, it is useless to print my speeches, or they will want to know what I say, and in that case, sooner or later, you will have to report me."

But it is time to have done with both reminiscences and comment and to give an example of his notes. Here is a page of his notes for the Glasgow speech. (See next page.)

The speech was an unusually long one, occupying an hour

2. Realisation, ideal. Cement Union.
Consolidate race - meet clash, competition -
not only by isolated efforts - supported by forces,
now unfit growing states that speak common tongue.

How attain? Claim if so heeded in manner
worthy, dignity & magnitude - apart of
personal bitterness & even party controversy
Disclaim imputation, unworthy motives
Claim equal consideration
Recognise changes only successful if National
policy - not forced by great majority accepted as
consent by overwhelming proportion

Glasgow one, most prosperous. Why not let alone?
Venice

Not predict equal catastrophe for B. in decay
But signs, decay - cracks - foundations not
Am I wrong to warn? Strange that those who
indict for want of preparation, equally deliverance
for preparing for greater struggle - if defeated
disappear - meet with antiquated weapons & old
fashioned tactics

not well with B. in decay.
Last years great expansion. 1900 a record
Yet exports only increased 1890   20 millions
in U.S. a under Protection   110
Germany   56

in Free Trade Britain practically stagnant
Protected countries enormous progress

Character changed. Cobden's expectations
But Foreigners take less, our Manufr
& we take more of theirs

and forty minutes in delivery. It not only presented the general case for Tariff Reform, but developed a detailed programme and contained a number of figures. I think it is not too much to say that in form, construction and language, in clearness of presentation and cogency of argument, it is an almost perfect model of what such a speech should be, and contemporary accounts speak of the sustained power and ease of its delivery. It had cost him immense labour and his notes were certainly longer, and, I think, fuller than usual, but, subject to this qualification, they are typical of all that he used for set speeches. They cover eight sides of notepaper, divided into paragraphs by lines drawn half across the page, but with scarcely any special marks to draw the eye to particular points. He made a second speech at Greenock the next day, and for this also he had prepared notes before leaving home. Indeed, in the course of that campaign most of his meetings went in couples, and he found the strain of having a second speech on his mind, when delivering the first, so great, that he presently resolved not to think about the second till the first was over—either making such notes as he could on the morning of the second day, or, as at Newport, on the day after he had spoken at Cardiff, abandoning notes altogether and trusting to his complete possession of the subject and the stimulus and inspiration of the moment— a trust which was in this case brilliantly justified not only by the immediate approval of the audience but also by the judgment of his readers. *The Times* wrote two days later of this unprepared speech: " Nothing bears more eloquent witness, not merely to his physical energy, but to the mastery of the subject and the abundance of the resources on which he draws, than the way in which he is thus able, time after time, to follow up one remarkable utterance with another, perfectly new in character, and not less impressive"; and it compared these speeches of his Tariff Reform campaign to his series of addresses in South Africa, "preaching the message of reconciliation and unity."

With this account of my father's methods I have carried my theme as far as my knowledge goes. No set rule emerges from the examination that I have made. Each speaker has his own method—often more than one. One man makes elaborate notes; another makes none. One man writes his speeches; another never puts pen to paper. We may choose what system we like or have no system at all, and we can still find some model to justify our practice. But one conclusion, I think, stands out clearly; those who say to public men, "Oh! speaking is no trouble to *you*," have not seen them in the hours of preparation. Their wives and their private secretaries tell a different tale.

XXI

FROM A FAMILY POST-BAG

My grandmother Chamberlain was one of the eighteen children of Harry Harben, Wholesale Cheesemonger of Mile End, and his wife Mary Woodgate. Several of the children died in infancy or early youth, as was the way with the prodigious families of those days, but two of my great aunts were familiar figures in my childhood. A third was known to me only by name, for she lived first in Scotland and later joined her sons who had settled in New Zealand.

The others formed a remarkable family group, closely united to one another by ties of strong affection, mainly occupied by the care of their families and households, but widely read, interested in all the pleasures of the mind in which their modest means enabled them to indulge, staunch Unitarians, regular attendants at Chapel, and shrewd critics of the long sermons which formed a main feature of the services, and withal endowed with a pleasant sense of humour and a ready wit which on occasion showed itself in their letters.

Most of their letters were destroyed by them or their children as being too intimate for other eyes than their own, but one or two have been preserved as possessing a wider interest for their descendants.

Of my grandmother's writing I have only a few lines. In my father's desk after his death I found a little cardboard box wherein was a battered silver thimble with these words barely legible in the faded ink of nearly one hundred years ago :

" Here rests from her labours a faithful servant after seventeen years and a half of constant devoted usefulness to one mistress. This thimble was given to Caroline Harben by her grandmother, Mrs. Woodgate, and had she continued Caroline Harben might still have been in her service. But her little son Joey (more ruthless than Time) stamped upon its worn frame and finished what the Old Destroyer might have spared much longer.

" It was here laid to repose January 17, 1840, by its grateful friend and mistress.

" Caroline Chamberlain.
" Camberwell."

Charlotte, the next sister who survived childhood and was through life my grandmother's dearest friend, married Edward Bailey, an ironmonger of Holborn where they lived over his warehouse. I remember her in her widowhood, a stately old lady always dressed in black silk with a widow's cap, but as ready to share my childish games and interests as she had been to share and encourage those of my father in his boyhood. It was in the Bailey warehouse that my father and his cousins indulged that taste for amateur theatricals to which Balfour attributed some at least, of the characteristic quality of his speaking. For the most part my great-aunt's life was a very quiet one. Her letters are filled with the little details of daily life, her household cares, the daily doings of herself, her family and friends. Their interest has faded with the ink in which they were written, but one great event stands out—her visit to Windsor in 1842. She tells the tale to her sister in the following lively letter :

" 272 Holborn,
" *February 9th*, 1842.

" My dear Emily,

"As I promised your good husband that I would write you full particulars of the important event to-day, I sit down to do it though I have very little time to do it in, as I am engaged to dine with Caroline at two o'clock and it is now twelve. I have not been able to begin before. Well, so as not to lose any more time apologizing, so, to begin with the beginning, you know I believe that Bab was vaccinated last Monday week. Well, last Monday afternoon Mr. Fincham called and said he had come on a strange errand, but would I have any objection to the Prince of Wales being vacci from my child. Guess my surprise! I acceded, of course, provided always my expenses were paid and every precaution taken that my child should not take cold. Mr. Fincham said he would mention all those conditions to Sir James Clark who had enquired of him for a case. Well, Monday morning I had a note from Finchy to say that Sir J. C. would call to inspect mother and child in an hour or two. About half an hour after that came Sir J. C. and Dr. Gregory. They gave me a good stare and soon satisfied themselves that I was not a poor thin scraggy creature. Then Master Edward was brought in and they both exclaimed what a beautiful boy (in regard to health and size they meant) examined the arm which they said was a most perfect specimen of vacci and felt all about his glands, and then pronounced him perfect in every way as to health, system and free from all tendency to humour or disease. It was something to get their opinion even had I not the pleasure I had afterwards. Sir James then said that he would fetch me in his carriage at one o'clock. He said you may take a nurse if you wish it. I said, drawing myself up sky high, Oh Sir James I cannot possibly go if I may not. Oh well take a nurse certainly. Well then there was such a getting up a stairs, such a ringing at the bell, the servants were all half mad,

278

Mrs. Edward Bailey (Charlotte Augusta)
From a painting made when Mrs. Bailey was about thirty-two, by Watkins

Rebecca ready to jump out of her skin, Edward so fussy, whilst I walked about in all the quiet dignity of nonchalance. I had never bought baby a hood, so he had nothing to wear. That added to the fuss having to send out for that. I chose a little black velvet hat in the shape of a beefeater cap with a chenille tassel, he has a very pretty crimson cloak trimmed all round with handsome swansdown so he looked very nice quite a little Henry the Eighth. I wore my fur tippet (which I have had altered and looks very handsome) and cuffs and my velvet bonnet, and my (word illegible) dress which you may remember.

"Well Sir J.'s carriage came at one and took us to the station where he met us and we went by the railroad to Slough where one of the Queen's carriages met us and conveyed us to Windsor Castle. We drew up at the Queen's private entrance and were shown into a very handsome bedroom, where I suckled baby and presently Sir James came in and said: Now Mrs. Bailey bring up the child, but I did not take his hint of bringing it up myself, but told Rebecca to follow and we went up and up and up when a nurse dressed in white opened a door and he said no not in that room, and opened another door and said to my great surprise Your Majesty, Mrs. Bailey—and sure enough there was her little Majesty standing at the end of a small room and Prince Albert (that Adonis) at her side perched on a nursery fender which was before the fire and in the middle of the little room was a nurse holding his Royal Highness the Prince of Wales with his shoulder bare. Tho' I was taken by surprise I had sense enough to make my obeisance to the Majesty of England (Majesty forsooth!! I towered over the little lady). I then with a mother's pride drew the handkerchief from my dear little boy's face and they exclaimed, Yes, he is a fine little fellow, so I suppose Sir James had been praising him. The operation was then performed and my baby behaved admirably and the Queen and the Prince admired him much and said he was a sweet-tempered creature. The Prince said ' See how sweetly he smiles.' The P. of W. roared lustily, but then they pierced him in three places on each arm. The Queen seemed very much struck with the size of my baby and at last asked what day he was born, and when I said the 29th of September, said, ' Oh! then he is five weeks older than His Royal Highness.' She expressed a hope that my baby would not take cold. She then took up his hat and shewed it to the Prince Albert and talked in German about it and then said ' It's a nice little hat '—Then Prince Albert came across the room and making the most graceful of bows and with the sweetest of smiles and softest of voices said, ' I thank you madam for allowing our child to be vaccinated from yours.' I murmured obligation—honour— my side—Royal Highness—put my hand on my heart and sank at his feet (almost not quite) overpowered by the magic brightness of his blue eyes—The queen asked me many questions as to when, how, where he was vacci, how it rose and all about it and by whom—We then backed out of the royal presence and then went downstairs again when Sir James said there was lunch preparing for me but I declined it, for which I am now rather sorry as I should liked to have seen what they would give me, but however he made me take a glass of sherry and a biscuit which was served on a beautiful silver salver with most elegant glass with the royal arms on them a decanter of sherry and one of water. Then Sir James said something about the queen and I was to follow him up stairs, so we went into a small waiting room of the Prince's hung with blue silk and the Portrait of George III, Queen Charlotte and all their family when children. Sir James then said that Her Majesty had long wished to be revaccinated whenever a favourable opportunity occurred and this being such a very fine specimen would if I had no objection be so now. Of course I had none, and accordingly she and the prince were both done. We could not see them but could hear the Prince laugh and the Queen say, ' take care of my skin its very thin!' After that we went down again and then Sir James came and said: ' The Queen has directed me to give your nurse £5, you I shall see again, but I cannot stop now or you will lose the train,' and apologizing for not returning with me, he saw me into the carriage and we returned the same way as we went and I am happy to say baby is none the worse. Now what do you think of Fox of Bally o' Botherem!' Think of me, even me, having such good luck. But however I have seen no more of Sir James and if I do not hear of him to-day I shall write to-morrow and enquire after the young prince. The queen was dressed in French white watered silk made with a lace fichu and a gold chain with some large seals hanging on it at the waist a kind of gold cord suspended from the waist with some more gold seals and bracelets with more gold seals. I mean to ask Sir J. to explain, when I see him. The Prince had fawn-coloured Kerseymere trousers and Blk. Frock coat—the young prince a plainish handsome robe with long sleeves and a cap with blue ribbons and rosette lace and blue ribbons. He is a sweet little baby, more like the father than the mother. I have not time to say any more now but shall be happy to answer any questions you may honour me with. I am,

"Dear Emily,

"Yours affectionately,

"C. A. BAILEY."

This letter was intended only for her sister's eye. She drew up a more formal record for the baby, and had it attested by the nurse. To it she appended a note that, the baby having already been registered in the name of Edward after his father, she now had him christened Edward Albert in commemoration of this event. A few weeks later Sir James Clark wrote that he had " a little present from Her Majesty for Mrs. Bailey's little boy." It was a scarfpin with the Prince of Wales' feathers and motto in turquoises and rubies. The child died before its fourth birthday, and she could never bear to speak of the event again.

Another letter of hers gives a delightful glimpse of my grandparents' life at Highbury Place, Islington, whither they had moved from Camberwell when my father was about five years old. This letter was written to her daughter and describes the dinner given by my grandfather to welcome Dr. (then Mr.) Martineau, the great Unitarian divine, to London when he was called to the Essex Street Chapel.

" *Wednesday Morning, March* 30*th*, 1859,
" 271 HOLBORN, W.C.1.

" DEAR FANNY,

" While the remembrance of Caroline's elegant dinner and very pleasant evening, in fact entertainment altogether, are fresh in my mind, I will write of it, being alone, Emily having slept at Highbury, and having no urgent call on me this morning for any other duty.

" Well, I dressed myself in my Moiré and a fresh Widow's cap, and an enormous pair of plain net sleeves, by a quarter-past five, and presented myself before Emily, who pronounced the effect neat but not gaudy, then ordered a cab, in which I very soon found myself.

" I arrived at Highbury[1] about twenty-minutes to six, and was ushered into the drawing-room by a very quiet, pleasant-looking waiter. Caroline has had him several times, so doubtless Aunt Ellen knows him. There were Joseph, Caroline and Mary, all seated, looking rather stiff and uncomfortable and as if they were dreading an avalanche, but very nice ; Caroline, her pretty looks on, Joseph well, and Mary the very personification of a young lady and pretty withal ; she had on her black net, with a lace tucker, and with a black ribbon which was run through it, as is the fashion now—her shoulders looked beautifully white, and she had on her head an ornament made of beads, setting close on it all round like a wreath, and which was very becoming.

" The room also presented a large and pleasant aspect,

[1] Highbury Place, Islington.

the large round table was removed altogether, the mosaic one was in the bow, the vase in the corner by the door, and a card table with a cover on it in the centre, flowers in the centre of that. Then the garden looked so pleasant and fresh with the new grass and gravel.

" My going in relieved the stiffness a little, as we talked of indifferent matters and so took their thoughts off the fear of the overpowering intellect of the chief guest. Mr. Nettlefold presented himself next and then came Joseph's dreadful Incubus, and coming face to face with it in the broad daylight, all his imaginary fears vanished and ' Richard was himself again ' and the talk was cheerful and rather noisy for so small a party (young Joe[1] had joined us) till dinner was announced, which it very soon was. Mr. M. and Mrs. C., Mr. Blagdon and Mary, Mrs. N. and self, Joseph and Mrs. M. I sat next Mr. M. and Mrs. M. next Joseph of course. Two covers on the table. Asparagus soup—very good. Caroline thought it rather hot, I did not. That was helped all round and quickly removed— then the noble piece of salmon was displayed which Mr. M. would distribute, and helped it, as if to carve had been the study of his life, a little piece of thick, a little piece of thin and a smelt to everyone. There was a profusion of beautiful hot lobster sauce and cool cucumber—that was removed, and next to no time the table was covered again, boiled chickens at top, covered with white sauce and prettily ornamented with something green—a pretty little fore-quarter at bottom—tongue and stewed beef, asparagus, cauliflower, mushrooms and mashed brown potatoes. Mr. M. again displayed great skill in carving the chicks. Mr. Blagdon operated on the tongue. Champagne and Hock in course. Mr. M. enjoys a good dinner and never refuses the wine. Third course—Guinea Fowl, some kind of hot pudding, I daresay Caroline will tell you what, jellies, creams, and a peculiar dish—it looked like a sea or lake of custard surrounded by a range of snow-covered mountains, the peaks tinged by the rosy hues of the rising sun, some

[1] My father.

283

people might fancy it rather more crimson than rosy—
then cream and other cheese were handed round, then all
vanished, and the dessert made its appearance. Of course
there could not be much variety in that, this time of the
year. There were some noble-looking oranges. Everything that ought to have been so was smoking hot. I
never saw a dinner better served. Caroline determined
on a cook at last—but I daresay she will tell Ellen all about
her preparations and management.

" Mary was quite angry last night to think that I should
write before she would, but I told her that we should be
sure to tell of different parts of the affair. Even she and
Caroline were perfectly satisfied, but Caroline says she
suffered a martyrdom about it.

" As to the conversational parts of the entertainment, it
was very pleasant; there was not a single pause. The
two Josephs, Mr. Nettlefold and Mrs. Martineau were
busily engaged conversing together for some time. Mary
and Mr. Blagdon and Caroline and Mr. M. and self. I
took Mr. M. upon myself at the beginning of dinner for
I knew Caroline's mind would be a little preoccupied till
she saw how things were ' getting along,' and I plunged
boldly into Comte's philosophy, trusting to Mr. Martineau's
help for swimming safely ashore. Being discreet, and really
interested in it, I did not flounder. Very soon Caroline
was able to join in and Mr. Blagdon also and Mary turned
to Mr. M. and then I think we all talked—*who* listened
remains doubtful. We sat about half an hour when Caroline
bowed. Out we all went into the drawing-room; Dick
was the first evening guest. At about a quarter-past eight
the gentlemen made their appearance and we all had coffee,
then the evening company began to arrive in quick succession. Mr. and Mrs. Warren, Mr. and Mrs. Madge,
Mr. and Mrs. W. Sharpe—Sam ditto, Mr. Snider, Mrs.
Teschmaker, Mr. and Mrs. J. Preston, Charles and Emily,
Mr. and Mrs. Wainewright, and Annie Preston's hero and
comforter, Mr. Ireson.

" The dining-room had been cleared and thrown open

in a wonderfully short time and the rooms looked very pretty and well lighted. Everybody looked very nice. . . .

" Mrs. Warren had a magnificent black silk dress on, trimmed slightly with crepe. . . .

" I had a long conversation with old Sam Sharpe and made another plunge into dangerous regions but escaped again without slipping. I do not know how I should have escaped from *him* though, but Caroline thought I had had enough of him, so came to my relief. When I come to think of it, I had a good talk with everyone in the room, except that very unpleasant-looking man Mr Wainewright. Mrs. Madge and I sympathized in our feelings about him, and we agreed that a good rump steak and a jolly foaming pot of porter would do him a vast deal of good. As it is he is a cold, repulsive-looking man.

" Supper was served in the dining-room at a quarter-past ten. Towards the end of the evening Snider had an opportunity of delivering a little lecture to all who would listen, on his gun.[1] He had brought drawings with him. Mr. Cookson and Mr. and Mrs. Peter Martineau were there also. They were all gone by a quarter-past eleven; we—Charley, Snider and self—at twelve.

" There, my dear, is Maria with the lunch, and I have devoted nearly all my morning to you. Be grateful! It has turned cold and there is a sleety snow falling. ' Good Bording ' I will re-commence my journal this evening.

" Wednesday evening. It has been raining all the afternoon and I have not been able to leave the house. The roofs of the houses and all high places are thickly covered with snow, and it looks like Christmas as depicted in the *Illustrated News*. It has been raining this evening, so I do not expect to see any remains of it in the morning. . . .

. . . . . .

" Well, after they left I took up my book to divert my thoughts from diverging into painful channels—the second

[1] One of the earliest breech-loading rifles.

vol. of *Adam Bede*, a very prettily written book, hardly to be called a novel. I finished the vol. and fear the third cannot choose but be very sad; I almost dread to read it.

.　　.　　.　　.　　.

"Sunday to Carter Lane. Heard Mr. Ireson; found his sermon quite refreshing after John Scot Porter's. An awful small congregation, as all the world had gone to hear Mr. Madge's farewell sermon, as the stipendiary of Essex St. Chapel. . . .

"I see very little of Snider, he is so much absorbed by this gun affair. It is fearful to think of the result to him if it fails.

"This afternoon, if it continues fine, I shall call on Mr. Ireson. I should have done so yesterday only for the snow.

"I shall get the third vol. of *Adam Bede* for my evening entertainment, and shall live in the hope it will not be too sad. There, I must leave off as I shall have Caroline here.

"Caroline has been and gone—no particular news. She has nearly got over the fatigue of her party.

"I am going out directly, for, as the drawing-room is still 'in dishabille' (after the sweeps and cleaning), and it is five, some one is sure to call of our few visitors.

"Once more adieu, Your affectionate Mother,

"C. A. BAILEY."

I have said that my great-aunt was a staunch Unitarian. A glimpse of this side of her—and of her kindness of heart—is given in the following letter describing the gratitude of a young protégé, the son of an old Irish woman who made a precarious living by peddling combs and other nick-nacks at the corner of the street:

"271 HIGH HOLBORN,
"*September 23rd*, 1856.

"My grand excitement has been my young priest in embryo, young Gill. I enclose his letter. Please return it as George wants to see it. About a fortnight or rather more since, his mother called on me and sent up word that she wished to speak to me, but not to beg. It did not suit me to go down, so I did not see her, but the following Sunday going to the School I met her, stopped and spoke to her. She had called to say that her son had just returned from Douai and was going to Rome and that he wished to call and thank me for all my kindness to her and to him.

" I expressed my pleasure at hearing so pleasant an account of her son. In consequence of my speaking, I the next day or so received the accompanying letter which of course I acknowledged saying that I should be very happy to see him.

" He came on Saturday. I was pleased with him and much interested in him, and invited him to tea on the following Wednesday, not before as I thought that Em would like to see him.

" On Monday he called to say that he found he had to go into retreat at the Oratory at Brompton on Wednesday to prepare himself for receiving minor orders called the Tonsure on Saturday morning from the Cardinal, so I fixed for him to come Tuesday. He brought me two books to read—Cardinal Wiseman's Lectures on the Catholic and Protestant Faiths, and a controversy between a Protestant Society and Dr. Milner, a celebrated Catholic divine. The last book, he informed me, had converted a Mr. Bradshawe and, he hoped, would me. He should pray for me morning and night.

" He (Gill) came on Tuesday. Em (Emily Bailey) was pleased with him. Of course he has only two subjects of conversation—Douai and the glory and advantages of the Catholic Church. We were both very much struck at the complete state of subjection in which his thoughts and feelings—in fact all the powers of his mind—are. The Cardinal knows what he is about in making a protégé of him. He will have a most faithful, devoted working friend in him. He is very enthusiastic and at present genuine and would consider it a joy unspeakable to suffer martyrdom for Mother Church.

"When he first called, I had expressed very plainly my religious views, which I found he repeated to the Cardinal, who sent an intimation through him that if I liked to call and discuss the point with him, he would be very happy to see me.

"Of course, I declined. He left about ten and I engaged him to dine here on Sunday. He came with a round collar on (he had a stuck-up one before), and Mr. Solly also dined here. He (young Gill) came bent on my conversion, for the moment the cloth was removed and Mary out of the room he said, 'Mrs. Bailey, will you pardon me, if it be a liberty, but will you tell me who were the great apostles of the Unitarian creed before the fifteenth century?

"I expect the Cardinal put him up to that question. Of course, I referred him to Mr. Solly, which I could do with great confidence and pleasure, knowing from his truly Christian temper that no ill-feeling would arise from the discussion. I would not have allowed it with everyone, of course.

"The young man was not equal to cope with Mr. Solly, but Mr. Solly dealt so gently with him that his self-love was not hurt in any way. But he says on his return he shall be better prepared and will overpower him with his proof of the fallacy of our pretensions.

"He says Mr. Solly is the first Protestant clergyman he has ever met. He remained till about half-past ten, and went away rather discomfited, I fear, at not having made some impression. I hope he will not consider it was his fault and so have to do penance. He entreated me again to go to the Cardinal and not to trust to books. 'Go with me to-morrow,' he said, 'and I am sure the light of the truth will burst upon you.'

"I declined, but comforted him by promising that if ever any doubts crossed my mind, I would apply to him (the Cardinal). I told him I had read seven of the Cardinal's lectures and felt even more than I did before that I never could enter the Roman Catholic Church, at which he was rather astonished.

" He asked me if I would die for my faith.

" I told him that I was not prepared to say ' yes ' to that without some consideration.

" Oh," he said, " then I have some hope."

" But," I returned, " I am quite prepared to say that I would sooner die any death you may choose than become a member of your Church.

" At which he raised his eyes, clasped his hands, but said never a word.

" When he left he said, ' Well, Mrs. Bailey, if I do not see you again before I leave, I will write you from Rome and send you proofs of the truth, and receive my best thanks for all your kindness. I shall never forget you and when I am in Rome the remembrance of these visits will be very pleasant to me.' He says as long as he can remember he had such a strong desire to be a Priest. When he was a little ragged boy, as he walked along the streets, he used to pray to God to make him a Priest. When he was thirteen, he might have been apprenticed to a French cook, which for a boy in his situation would have been a fine thing; but he reflected that if he bound himself to the cook, he should never be able to be a Priest, so in spite of his mother's tears and the entreaties of his friends, he went home to comparative starvation. He had been with the cook a year, having capital living, so it was something for a boy to give up.

" Soon after an opportunity offered for him to obtain a situation in Cardinal Wiseman's household if he could have some decent clothes. I supplied him with a suit and he got the situation and very soon obtained the Cardinal's notice and was allowed to serve his Mass for him and was with the Cardinal a year when the Cardinal was called to Rome. Then he broke up his establishment and the poor boy was in despair, so in a fit of despair he asked the Cardinal to send him to college and told him all his hopes. The Cardinal told him he had been thinking about it and, seeing him so very earnest, he would; and a fortnight from that time he was at Douai, and he said all the time he was there he could hardly believe it was himself. He hopes to rise in the Church and do something to glorify her."

I conclude these extracts from a family post-bag with a letter from the youngest of my great-aunts, Mrs. Stanton Preston. It was written on the eve of my father's twenty-first birthday, but the opening sentences refer to another important event in the family, the cutting of her first tooth by her grand-niece, Penelope Lawrence, afterwards known to many generations of girls as the founder and first Principal of the famous Roedean School:

"DEAREST FAN,

"I write to congratulate you on Pen's first peg. I can fancy your inward rapture and the nurse's outward delight. How well I remember lecturing Sophy Lock on violent excitements—feeling myself every nerve quiver. What were the Pyramids to that enormous object of interest, which after all, by the by, was more felt than seen.

. . . . .

"I have bought Fergusson's *Handbook of Architecture*, two vols., for Joe, and have sent it this evening to be ready for the morrow. I wonder how Caroline will get on. I mean by this in her feelings of worry or confidence about the dinner. It is sure to be all perfect, but she has reason to be uneasy with two strangers as *chefs de cuisine*. It seems hard to have to think of cooking when I know her heart will be too full for speech. But the longer I live the more convinced I am of the horrible unreal state in which our conventionalities place us—there will be Caroline anxious about eels and entrées, when behind all that her mother's heart is welling up with love and thoughts too deep for words, full of hopes and aspirations for her first-born, and full too of the recollection of the day when that young man, now nearly fulfilling all a mother's heart could wish, laid by her side as a baby. I can fancy your Uncle Joseph offering best cuts and passing the Madeira, while a more costly liquid glitters behind his dimmed glasses. Such is life, and I lose my time in moralizing over its defects until I have done the best I can with it as it is. Here endeth the first chapter of priggism. I saw your cook to-day. Favour is deceitful and beauty is vain—so I have no doubt she is true and useful. I have a new cook on the twenty-fourth. She promises well—but blessed are ye who expect nothing."

XXII

MY COTTAGE GARDEN

I

My own cottage and garden in Sussex are, alas! mine no longer, though I am glad to know that they have passed to the possession of another garden lover who cherishes the little garden as I used to do. The cottage stands where two lanes meet. Its framework, if you could see it, is exactly like that of the farmer's great barn opposite—huge oak timbers such as went to the building of the old wooden navy, some straight or bent with age, some curved by the natural growth of the tree, but all hewed and squared with the axe and adze; no saw or plane has spoiled their beauty. Between the balks of timber the walls are wattle and daub, but one side has been clapboarded against the south-westerly storms and the opposite one, facing the lane, is half brick half-tile. The old tile roof sags and wavers with the yielding of the beams. Just to the right of the cottage and shadowing the north-west corner is a magnificent old yew. As we pass in through the little wicket gate and up the short brick path, you will see, in spring, hyacinths or polyanthus in the narrow borders on either side, to be followed later by some bedding-out plants—almost the only ones I allow myself, for the garden is to need as little labour as possible—out of which will rise in turn two healthy groups of scarlet martagon lilies and another group of the new hybrid martagons which tempted me at one of the Royal Horticultural Society's shows. Over the front of the house Ampelopsis and Wistaria creep, a Pyracantha breaks the line and Cotoneaster horizontalis, beloved of the bees, half hides an ugly water-spout; but what I pride myself upon is the narrow border, scarcely a foot wide, which runs along the house. Snowdrops (Elwesii) and winter aconite give me my first flowers here; then comes a clump or two of narcissus; but the moment to see it is when it is one mass of Anemone apennina with Primula cashmiriana thrusting up its purple globes among their blue stars.

Under the yew tree, by adding some good soil and plenty of old mortar rubble, I have flourishing colonies of Cyclamen coum for spring and Cyclamen europæum for autumn, when its scent carries me in fancy to Italian woods about Bologna where I have picked great bunches of them to brighten up the old Brun's hotel. Hepaticas, our own wild wood anemones and crocuses, help out the seasons. But come round to the southerly side of the cottage. Here against the clapboarding grows Wistaria again, but the nurseryman sent one so pale in hue that it scarcely shows against the white paint and reminds me that flowering plants should be selected when they are in flower. A good Pyrus japonica gives on the other hand a blaze of colour, and a purple Clematis, which I cut down nearly to within a foot of the ground, is covered with blossom twice in the summer. The yellow jasmine, J. nudiflorum, flowers in January with Iris unguicularis (stylosa) at its feet, and a white jasmine scents the rooms in mid summer. Here too I find room for Carpenteria californica and Choisya and the Californian fuchsia (Zauschneria).

The flagged terrace is supported by a low wall of loose stone not more than two to three feet high. Amidst the flags grow thyme and pinks (D. deltoides and graniticus), Campanula pusilla, Hypericum Coris; grape hyacinths and other things have found their way along the cracks from the narrow ribbon border that tops the low wall.

The border at the top of the wall is kept for low and early flowering plants. Here you will find Iris pumila in four or five shades, I. histrioides and reticulata and Tulipa Clusiana and linifolia with mossy Saxifrages to follow. There are just two bushes of Daphne Mezereum to break the low line, and a fine specimen of D. Cneorum, which later loads the air with its scent of honey, and a little bush of Plumbago Larpentae carry on the interest later in the year. The wall itself is kept mainly for Saxifrages of the pyramidalis type which did extraordinary well, but the male fern has seeded itself in the crevices and threatens to become a nuisance.

I know nothing more lovely among tulips for the rock garden than the two species which I have mentioned. The scarlet linifolia increased with me and I grew it from seed, but T. Clusiana had a sad tendency to " dwindgle," as a farm-hand I once knew used to say of his young turkeys. I retain, however, a warm affection for it, which is partly a tribute to its own delicate beauty and partly to my own vanity.

When I first went to Geneva, in early March 1925, to represent Great Britain on the Council of the League of Nations, I visited Dr. Correvon's famous Alpine garden. It was too early for flowers but a gardener loves to see plants growing only one degree less than to see them blossoming. Whilst walking round I happened to remark upon a group of T. Clusiana whose leaves were pushing up, though the buds were not yet showing. Later the same day an English lady went to see the garden and Dr.

Correvon mentioned my visit. "Ah!" said the lady, "you have had the Minister for Foreign Affairs here? It is a great honour for your garden."

"Minister of Foreign Affairs, pooh!" exclaimed the Doctor. "There is a Minister of Foreign Affairs in every country, but there is only one who can identify Tulipa Clusiana by its leaves."

The story spread (shall I confess? I helped to spread it) and my reputation was made. There was one subject at least of which I knew more than my colleagues!

A second terrace, grassed this time and supported by a rather higher wall, finds room in the border at the top for half a dozen species of Cistus. These lasted through several winters, but it is wise to take cuttings every year or two and nurse them through the winter in a frame lest a spell of specially hard weather destroy the established plants. Here I had a bit of luck. I thought this would be a good place to put a plant of Hypericum (Hookeri, I think) in my first autumn and found when I dug my hole that I was among roots which in my inexperience I did not recognize. They turned out to be a darkish orange Alstrœmeria and grew up through and around the Hypericum, making a colour combination on which I received many compliments.

The wall below this terrace was kept mainly for Aubrietia, Alyssum, Helianthemums and Erodiums, but some white foxgloves seeded themselves between the stones towards one end.

I am not going to show you my rose-garden in front of the oast-house, for it was not very successful, nor my border of flowering shrubs and trees, for though I dug the whole of it (and it lay on a belt of stiff clay) three times over with my own hands in one year, I could never rid it of the squitch, bindweed, ground elder and all the other poisonous weeds with brittle ramping roots which had taken hold of it in war time. I have only one word of advice to give to anyone so situated. Clear the border, summon all your patience, disregard appearances and plant potatoes on the ground till you have got it clean; and do this before, not after, your Cherries, Pyrus, Crabs, Lilacs, Berberis and the like have begun to grow and make shapely bushes or trees. Once that has happened, you will never have the heart to disturb them. By the thorough policy you will eradicate the weeds. Nor need we linger at the herbaceous border. Let us go straight to my rock garden, or, as I would have you call it, my Alpine garden, for my purpose was to grow the Alpine flowers, not merely to repeat the Aubrietias and Alyssums of the wall.

2

It must be nearly forty-five years ago that, one Sunday morning, when my father and I were visiting Kew Gardens, under the auspices of the late Sir W. Thistleton-Dyer, he took us into one of the enclosures where, he said, he had something new to show us. The novelty was an unheated greenhouse filled with pans of Alpine plants. I remember saying to my father as we drove back that if I ever had a garden of my own, I should not attempt to grow orchids but that I must have an Alpine house. Thirty or more years passed before I owned a garden; by then much more was known of Alpine plants and their cultivation, and I determined to have a rock, or as I prefer to call it, an Alpine garden instead of the house. A house would require daily care and watering, and I could visit my cottage only at week-ends.

Thus when I obtained my cottage the first thing to decide was where to place the Alpine garden. Below the terrace, the lawn, whose earlier use as an orchard was recalled by two old apple trees still standing in its midst, sloped down to a hedge in which a stile gave access to a small field. But the hedge was not parallel to the house, and the shrubbery border on one side of the lawn was not parallel to the yew hedge which divided it from the kitchen garden on the other, so that the lawn formed an ugly rhomboid. This was corrected at the sides by the re-alignment of the shrubbery border, giving room for a herbaceous border in front of the flowering trees and shrubs, and at the bottom by planting a yew hedge parallel to the terraces, in front of which we placed a herbaceous border, broken in the centre by a wide grass walk leading to the stile. Between the two hedges there was now an elongated triangle. To the right of the grass-walk my wife made a small sunk garden filled with polyantha roses; the left and larger section I chose for the site of the Alpine garden which would thus be hidden from the house by the yew hedge as soon as it had grown about four feet high.

There, then, was the site, not perfect but not a bad one. The next thing was to make the garden. My first attempt was a failure, though I put up with it for two or three years. I did not know what I wanted beyond the fact that I wanted a rock garden. I did not know what was necessary except rocks. I called in a local man and said, "Make me a rock garden and let me have rocks, not pebbles." He fulfilled my requirements with good-sized blocks of the local sandstone, and at first I was very pleased with the effect. I visited spring shows, pored over catalogues and planted enthusiastically and optimistically, but my plants did not grow. I could repeat the easier successes of the terraces, but the things which I most wanted to see succeed dragged out a miserable existence or died upon my hands. Only two things do I recall as making really fine specimens; these were a Lithospermum prostratum, heavenly blue, for which I chanced upon just the right position at the top of a big rock with a cool root-run down the back of the stone into deep earth. In two years or so it had covered the top and hung three feet or more down the rock face. The other success was provided by two plants of Anemone sulphurea which will appear again in this story. But of drainage and soil and how to place the rocks I had thought little and knew less. It was all to begin again. The experiment had cost something, but it had taught me much. I wrote some articles, was fortunate in finding favour with a generous editor and accumulated a sufficient sum to start afresh. This time I knew what I wanted and I found the right man to understand my ideas and supply my deficiencies.

The rules for an Alpine garden are:

1. See that the drainage is good.
2. See that the soil is suitable and that in different places you have the various kinds which you will require.
3. The rocks should be large. Like icebergs, only the smaller part of them should appear above the surface.
4. Let the soil be well rammed down around and between them so that no holes are left in which the roots as they grow fail to find sustenance. The builder knew all this as well as I did, and it was a pleasure to see him and his foreman handling and placing the great rocks. The largest weighed nearly 15 cwt.

I chose weather-worn limestone for the stone and I expressed my desiderata as follows:

1. I must have a cliff-face with northerly or cool exposure.
2. I wanted a peat-bog.

3. There must be a low Alpine meadow and

4. A high Alpine meadow.

5. There must be a moraine or scree.

6. The new garden must somehow be built around my beautiful Anemone sulphurea. They were doing too well to be disturbed.

I rejected the idea of a pool, for I felt there was not room for one, but I jumped at the suggestion of a Rhododendron forest. In the end the garden was all my fancy had painted; but here you must use your imagination. My Rhododendron forest consisted at first of two, later of three R. ferrugineum and three dwarf Himalayan hybrids. Daphne Blaygayana flourished among them. Give it a cool peaty root-run and throw a stone at it whenever you pass. It likes these rough love-makings and will reward you for them with its sweet waxy flowers in early spring. Androsace lanuginosa trailed over the rock in front.

I had not one but two cliffs, each some three feet high, and at the bottom a peat bed kept moist by drainage from the rocks and path. In the ledges and crannies of the cliffs I grew Primula marginata, Wilsonii, viscosa and some garden varieties, but Wilsonii never, I think, survived more than three winters. In the peat were P. rosea (this seeded itself freely and would grow in any damp shady spot in the path at the base of a rock), P. chionantha, involucrata and others, besides Orchis foliosa, Cypripedium calceolus and Pyrola rotundifolia, both collected by me in Switzerland, and Parochetus communis with a leaf like clover and a pea-shaped flower of the blue of G. verna. I name only enough flowers to give an idea of what I was striving for and the results obtained.

The low Alpine meadow, say twelve feet by eight, made a good place for Alpine crocuses and tulips and

Scilla autumnalis collected on the cliffs of Newquay and
Brittany. These were followed by Anemone fulgens,
and a marvellous magenta-coloured variety brought home
by Lady Chamberlain from Palestine. Later came A.
narcissiflora looking like apple blossom in bud, A. alpina
and sulphurea, and the yellow globe flower. The first
time I saw A. sulphurea it was a single plant in a pocket
of a great moss-grown limestone boulder beside a flooded
mountain stream in the Pyrenees and my heart leapt with
delight. The first time I saw A. alpina was when making
an excursion in the Jura with Dr. Correvon. It grew so
thick that in the distance I took it for a large patch of snow.
Then I added the great yellow gentian and other plants of
like size and similar habit. There was hardly one of these
which I had not collected myself, and the memory of the
places in which they were found added to one's delight in
seeing them grow and flourish.

The high Alpine meadows were on a smaller scale;
they were intended first and foremost for Gentiana verna,
but I always tried to get a succession of flowers if possible,
and I convinced myself by experience that except in the
case of those which live in some tight cranny of the rocks,
it is a mistake to plant one's precious things apart, as, in
his anxiety for their safety, the amateur is apt to do. Think
of the close short turf of the high Alpine meadow where
you find G. verna in masses. It is never alone; it has to
fight its way up and down through the turf itself and in
and out among Gentiana acaulis, Primula frondosa, Violas
and I know not what other small beauties. They grow
so thickly that you cannot put your foot down without
treading on several kinds, and they will be more likely to
succeed in your garden if you make them fight for existence
with plants of their own size as nature does. I planted

Narcissus minimus, Androsace carnea and Chamaejasme, Viola bicolor, Dianthus neglectus and such-like things with mine. But G. verna is notoriously contrariwise. After all, the best patch I ever saw in cultivation, two feet across each way and a sheet of blue like cloudless Italian sky on a summer day, grew within five miles of the centre of Birmingham. I asked the gardener how he managed it. "I grow them from seed," he said, "and prick them out." He did not appear to be aware that he had accomplished anything out of the ordinary. He had boxes of the seedlings in a frame. There is a variety of G. verna called angulata, which is a trifle larger in leaf, though otherwise indistinguishable to anyone but a botanist, which I found easier to grow.

There are few joys like a garden and in a small garden none which gives such constant interest and light occupation as an Alpine garden. In my own, every plant after the first twenty or so was planted and tended by me. It is the amateur's garden *par excellence*, for after this first making it requires no heavy spadework, whilst the plants have character and individuality and require constant attention and skilled treatment.

3

It is astonishing how much there is to say about a small Alpine garden. I have yet to deal with my screes, for in the end there were two of them, one less exposed to the full sunshine than the other. Both contained more chips than earth (indeed, I suppose the proportion was at least as ten to one) with limestone and granite mixed in varying proportions. Obviously the scree is the place for the Kabschia and Engleria saxifrages and many other treasures. Here, too, I grew Drabas, Hutchinsia alpina, Ranunculus

Seguieri, a lovely thing, Geranium Pylzowianum, to be watched closely lest it spread too far; its clear pink flowers prolong your flowering season. Papaver alpinum, orange and white, and Linaria alpina flourished in the scree and seeded regularly. Edrianthus pumilio with its grey leaves and lovely purple flowers sitting close down to the ground was another favourite, easily increased by cuttings. In the scree too I tried Omphalodes Luciliæ with its grey-blue leaves and feathery tufts of forget-me-not flowers of the palest porcelain blue shot with pink lights. The precise spot between two rocks had been specially made for it by an expert, but it slowly faded away. Then I found that admirable gardener, Mr. Hay of the Royal Parks, growing it as a bedding-out plant! He was kind enough to give me some plants and reveal the secret of his success—stiff loam and well-rotted cow-dung. Yet the plant comes from the hot limestone mountains of Greece and Asia Minor. To the four things which the compiler of the Book of Proverbs did not understand, he would, had he been a gardener, have added a fifth: the way of rock plants in cultivation. The best plant of Douglasia Vitaliana, a peat lover, which I ever had, grew into a fat cushion five or six inches across from a tiny slip which in ignorance or absent-mindedness I planted at the head of my limestone scree. Indeed I am disposed to say that whilst the scree is no place for any coarse thing, it is worth while to try in it any precious plant which has refused to do elsewhere.

It is a great advantage if you can water Alpines and especially the scree plants from below. In their native haunts, some sit in crevices on a steep rock-face where no rain lies and draw their moisture from the cool stones into which their roots penetrate deeply. Others sleep all winter under deep snow. They burst into life and blossom with amazing rapidity when the snows melt, but all through the hot summer their roots draw moisture from the water trickling just below the surface of the ground. In this country it is not possible to reproduce these conditions exactly; the raw damp days of February, when the air is cold and laden with moisture, are apt to be particularly deadly, especially to plants with hairy leaves. But something may be done to lessen their trials; a sheet of glass in winter is not a pretty object, but it is not at that time that you take your friends to admire your rock garden and the gardener in those months may well decide that safety first is his appropriate slogan whatever it may be for a political party. In any case let him try underground watering. If he has the conveniences or does not mind the cost, let him lay under his garden a leaden water-pipe with a few pin-prick holes in it. If, like me, he has not the convenience and is unwilling to face the expense, there is a simple alternative within everyone's means. Get a few two-inch agricultural drain-pipes; sink them vertically in the ground till their tops are only an inch or less above the surface, and hide them with a rock—the only one allowed to lie loose on the surface—or by a larger plant and, when watering, turn the hose or the spout of your watering-can down the pipe. A little care in the disposal of a few stones and some chips under the pipe will ensure the proper flow of the water and you can water at any time without danger of sunburn or of rotting out the crown of the plants. Incidentally, if you have not a convenient or sufficient rain-water tank and are dependent on the water company's mains, your water percolating through the soil will be more palatable to the plants.

Here you have the outstanding features of a rock garden

as I conceive it. It will of course need larger patches of colour to prevent it looking patchy. For these you can choose the dwarf Phloxes and Iris, the finer Aquilegias, the mossy Saxifrages, Anemones, Aubrietias, Helianthemums and the like. Once the garden is started, fill in gradually with other plants acquired from friends or growers (you need never pay more than a few pence except for special rarities) or, best of all, plants collected by yourself. In a short time you will be searching for space in which to bestow some newly acquired treasure and will be thinking which plant you will sacrifice to make room.

A word about collecting. In these days, if he can afford a trip to Switzerland, anyone can reach the Alpine plants, however poor a walker he is. I was past sixty before I saw the Alps in early summer and, coming straight from heavy office work, I was in no trim for climbing. Yet there were in my garden many plants which I had myself collected with Dr. Correvon or other friends in the week's holiday which I used to take after the sitting of the Council of the League of Nations in early June. Not an hour from Geneva I found a white Cyclamen europaeum which Dr. Correvon in all his rambles in the Alps and elsewhere had never lit upon. Another day he took me a drive along what is called the International Route (for it crosses the Franco-Swiss frontier more than once) and showed me a grassy slope where every outcrop of rock had its patches of Daphne cneorum. I had other glorious days with him in the Jura and yet others at Zermatt where the Professor of Botany at the University of Lausanne kindly made himself our guide. We went up to the top of the Görnergratch by train and before I could take my eyes from the glorious panorama of snow peaks and glaciers, he had found me a piece of Eritrichium nanum, the heart's desire of every Alpine grower. As we walked down, we passed through all the seasons from the places where the snow still lay in half-melted patches through which the earliest flowers were just peeping till we reached high summer in the meadows of the valley. That day I first saw Androsace glacialis and next day the Professor showed me a spot where the scarce Asplenium septentrionale was to be found.

Of course I had my disappointments. I lost my E. nanum by too much coddling when at home and neglect when I was absent. (I saw a capital piece only the other day growing in a stone trough in scree mixture in Sir Clive Wigram's garden at the foot of the Round Tower at Windsor Castle) but the Asplenium grew well in a crevice where it had Penstemon Davidsoni for neighbour, and the majority of my plants lived.

For collector's tools, a fern trowel with a long blade not more than one and a half inches wide, so firmly fixed *in* the handle that it will give you good leverage, and an Alpine ice-axe suffice. If any of the plants are short of fibrous root, plunge them in a bed of wet sand placed in the shade. It is amazing what root they will then make in a few weeks.

Reluctantly I end, for even to write of these bygone delights is itself a pleasure.

There are few joys like a garden and the Alpine garden is *par excellence* the garden for the amateur.

P.S. A cure for sleeplessness. If you find that after the worries and excitements of a busy day, say after winding up a debate in Parliament at midnight, you are too excited to sleep when you reach your bed, if then counting sheep passing through a gate proves, as with me, of no avail and you share my incapacity for thinking of nothing, visit your rock garden in imagination. I have put myself to sleep night after night in this way before my head had been five minutes on the pillow or I had covered six paces of my small garden.

XXIII

LIGHTENING OUR LABOURS

OFFICIAL files, tied up with the proverbial red tape, are usually forbidding-looking things. It takes a little time to know where to look and what to read among the mass of papers which accumulate about most subjects, and the minutes written upon them, able and instructive as they are, are generally strictly confined to a plain statement of the point involved and of the action recommended. But occasionally humour breaks out even in these discouraging surroundings. Mark Sykes once delighted his friends by illustrating the stock openings of Treasury letters: " My Lords are gratified to learn . . ." " My Lords are surprised to observe . . ." and so forth till the last " My Lords are at a loss to conceive . . ." represented by five little men in bed clasping their stomachs and obviously in great pain.

Fairfield at the Colonial Office occasionally illustrated his minutes in a like manner. He prepared a brief for my father's interview with the Bechuana Chiefs in the form of an imaginary conversation, " It was wholly admirable," said my father; " only the Chiefs did not give the answer he had expected, as, when, on my saying to Khama: ' You ask too much,' he replied: ' How can he ask too much to whom everything belongs?' Fairfield had not forseen that retort and had supplied no answer to it." The brief ended with instructions to the Chiefs as to their behaviour when presented to the Queen at Windsor. " This," added Fairfield, " is to prevent this kind of thing," and there followed a sketch of three little black men in the scantiest raiment turning back somersaults into the presence of a shocked and startled Sovereign. The Queen had indeed expressed a wish that they should appear in their native costume. My father had the task of explaining that it was unsuitable to the throne room.

Going in unannounced to see Lloyd George on one occasion when I lived next him in Downing Street, I found him chuckling over a file of papers. "What's the joke?" I asked. It was the first minute from Hilton Young, who had just become Financial Secretary of the Treasury, which had reached Lloyd George. An application had been made to the Prime Minister for a substantial grant for Antarctic exploration which the Exchequer was at that time in no position to afford. It had been referred in the ordinary course to the Financial Secretary who had minuted: "This may surely be refused. The South Pole is far away and, if Charity begins there, it will be a long time before she reaches home."

Lloyd George remarked that an amusing article might be written on official minutes and we began to recall some. There was Bright's famous minute written when he was President of the Board of Trade: "I have read Mr. Giffen's very able and interesting memorandum. I do not clearly apprehend whether he approves or disapproves the proposal which he discusses, but in any case I agree with him." Mr. Giffen, later Sir Robert Giffen, was, if I am not mistaken, at that time the principal statistical officer of the department and an acknowledged authority on his own subjects. It required a man as sure of himself and as grandly simple as John Bright thus to avow his own limitations while adopting the advice of one in whose judgment he placed trust.

Then there was the minute of a former Minister of Education, which is, I believe, still religiously guarded in the archives of that department. Marking some passage in a long memorandum with a pointing hand in the margin, the Minister had added, " This is the colonel of the whole question."

When I myself was made Secretary of the Treasury at the end of the year 1900, there was still in progress a correspondence with the Admiralty about the salary of one of the principal officers of a branch for which, as Civil Lord, I had been responsible. It was known at the Treasury that the Admiralty letters, though purporting to emanate from " My Lords " and signed by the Permanent Secretary, had in fact been written by me. So far they had been dealt with by my predecessor in my new post. In the natural course it would be to me that the last Admiralty letter would now come and it could not be separated from the file to which it belonged. It was an awkward dilemma ; many marginal notes and minutes were written in that file which had never been intended for my eye. I have always thought that Sir Francis Mowatt, then Permanent Secretary of the Treasury, acted with equal skill and candour when he placed the whole file before me, and remarking that obviously many things would have been differently expressed if my arrival at the Treasury had been foreseen and reminding me that I was now in the position of the poacher turned gamekeeper, added that I should here find what was to be said on the other side and undertook that if I would give fair consideration to the Treasury case, he would accept my decision whatever it might be without carrying the matter to the Chancellor. The Treasury objections failed to convince me, as Sir Francis had of course foreseen ; but I gained a respect for Treasury methods and for once I had the chance so rarely vouchsafed to us " to see ourselves as others see us." There was nothing in the marginal notes to feed my vanity. One of them ran simply: "This is silly." I think it fairly epitomized them all.

Of the men who have served with me in various offices, Sir George Murray, long since retired from office, but happily still with us, did most to lighten official labours. He was raciest in conversation as when, having failed to persuade me that something I proposed to do was inexpedient, he asked: "Well if you must do a silly thing like that, is it necessary that you should do it in such a d—— silly way?" and proceeded to indicate a much better method of carrying out my idea; or again, when he had at last wrung from me a confession that a Post Office appointment which I had suggested and he had opposed, was not wholly uninfluenced by parliamentary considerations, he cynically exclaimed: "Oh! if it's a job, why did you not say so at once? It's as good as done."

Asquith when Chancellor, told me that he had had before him a proposal for the construction of an underground passage from the War Office to the Horse Guards with cellars where papers might be stored and work carried on in case of aerial attack, upon which Murray had minuted: "This may be safely turned down. No sane enemy, acquainted with our institutions, would destroy the War Office."

Such flashes of humour in these dusty files are as rare as angels' visits, but my memory retains two other instances of Murray's caustic wit. When Postmaster General I had drawn up an elaborate brief for the use of Members of Parliament who were much troubled with Post Office " grievances " and did not know the answer. I had passed it to Murray with a request that he would examine it critically and make any alterations he thought desirable. He returned it to me with the following brief comment:

" Postmaster General.

" This is like the White Knight's story—very long, but very, *very* beautiful."

Later, when we were both at the Treasury, I asked Sir George to take the first opportunity of ascertaining verbally from Sir Anthony MacDonnell, then Under-Secretary in Ireland, what he meant by the " co-ordination " of the Irish Office, a subject on which both he and George Wyndham [1] were favouring us with a correspondence which was as obscure as it was voluminous. I had not long to wait for an answer: " I have seen Sir Anthony MacDonnell as you desired," Murray minuted to me. " As far as I can make out, what he means by co-ordination is the sub-ordination of everyone else to himself "—which is not a bad definition of what is usually meant by the blessed word co-ordination in the mouth of a masterful personality.

The Indian and Foreign Offices gave less scope for such sallies, though there was one Ambassador at least, whose dispatches were not only full of good sense and shrewd observation but were generally lit up by some flash of humour which made them doubly welcome, and memory dwells lovingly on a telegram reporting trouble at Mount Athos which, by an error in transmission, had been made to read, " The monks are violating their cows " instead of " their vows," on which Mr. Harold Nicolson had minuted: " This would seem to be a case for a papal bull." Dispatches from the Government of India and even the Viceroy's letters were uniformly grave and strictly confined to the

[1] Chief Secretary for Ireland.

business in hand, but one occasionally got a startling flash-
light on happenings that seemed to belong to another age
as they certainly belonged to another civilization.

I remember once asking Balfour during the Great War
whether the papers I sent him about Afghanistan gave him
the kind of information that he wanted. He replied that
what he wanted to know was what the Amir was really
thinking and doing. The attitude of Afghanistan was of
course of great importance to us at that time when India's
military resources, like our own, were strained to the uttermost. The Amir Habibullah was a strong ruler, and a really
remarkable man, who steered his course with great skill and
shrewdness through those difficult years, and kept the peace
in spite of the incitements of German agents and the desires
of the more restless and fanatical of his own people that he
should declare " jehad "; but we had then no Minister at the
Afghan Court and were dependent for direct information on
a weekly newsletter from an India agent, so I sent Balfour
the last newsletter which we had received from him. The
writer stated that he had accompanied the Amir to Candahar
where His Majesty was greatly interested in laying out the
palace gardens. " Often have I seen His Majesty," the letter
continued, " surrounded by the high Officers of State,
directing the laying out of the flower beds "—an idyllic
scene amidst the war which was then raging in three
continents. But there followed abruptly a passage describing a scene of a different kind. It ran pretty much
as follows : " Yesterday in the presence of a vast concourse
of people on a hill outside the town, a woman, being the
last of her clan and having refused blood-money in satisfaction for the murder of her husband, solemnly and in
accordance with the Holy Law, cut the throat of the
murderer."

But this is too grim a note to close upon. Let me end these random recollections with a lighter tale.

When I was at the Admiralty in the closing years of the last century, the name of a certain officer was put forward for a Good Service Pension. He had an unblemished record but for one incident which had occurred when he was a sub-lieutenant at Greenwich Naval College, when his papers showed that " My Lords' severe displeasure " had been expressed " for an improper answer returned to the examiners," and a footnote solemnly set out the offence as follows:

Question: " Describe a Daniell's Cell." [1]

Answer: " Not much is known about Daniel's cell. It was probably about thirty feet long by twenty feet wide and full of lions. But the lions are dead and so is Daniel. *Sic transit gloria mundi!* "

He got his pension.

[1] A type of electric battery.

INDEX

315

318